THE NOUGHTIES

2000 2001 2002 2003 2004

2005 2006 2007 2008 2009

From GLITZ To GLOOM

BRENDA POWER

The Collins Press

FIRST PUBLISHED IN 2010 BY
The Collins Press
West Link Park
Doughcloyne
Wilton
Cork

British Library Cataloguing in Publication Data
Power, Brenda.
        The noughties : from glitz to gloom.
        1. Ireland--Social conditions--1973-
        I. Title
        941.7'0824–dc22

ISBN-13: 9781848890268

Typesetting by The Collins Press
Typeset in Bembo, 11 pt
Printed in Great Britain by J F Print Ltd

Front cover image: Brenda Power
Back cover images: Same-sex couple ©iStockphoto.com/MotoEd
Construction site ©iStockphoto.com/ilbusca; Beautiful eye
©iStockphoto.com/Vlingva; Mobile phone ©iStockphoto.com/bezov; Four
Courts, Dublin ©iStockphoto.com/audioworm; Drinking buddies
©iStockphoto.com/sjlocke

Contents

THE NOUGHTIES

CONTENTS

Introduction

IN THE DEEP recesses of a kitchen drawer recently, buried among the used batteries and blunt pencils and mysterious Allen keys, I found our Millennium Candle. In the final days of the last century these stumpy little gold-scripted candles were a gift to every home in the country, as a nod towards an Irish Christmas custom that was, even then, dying out in the glare of imported neon and fairy lights: on Christmas Eve, older generations lit a candle in the kitchen window to light a passage for the Virgin Mary and her baby, in case they found themselves lost in the dark of an Irish boreen and in need of a bed.

We didn't much bother with candles back then, apart from keeping them handy for fancy dinner parties and power cuts. This was long before we discovered that a candle could balance your chakra, scent your home with lemongrass and mandarin, and cost €90 from a designer perfumer, so the gift had a poignant simplicity at a time of fevered celebration and far-fetched fears – the little candle was meant to light our passage into the new era in a time-honoured way.

From the look of my little candle it was lit just once and then chucked in the drawer to wait for the next millennium or an ESB strike, whichever came first, and, if I remember correctly, there was some fairly predictable carping about the cost of such a pointless and gawky gesture. But in hindsight it was a most prescient gift. Because if ever there was a nation that was stumbling blindly into the unknown and in urgent need of guidance and illumination, it was definitely us back then. At the time, there was little warning of the great changes the new decade would bring and, apart from the fear of the non-existent Y2K bug – which was going to crash computers and cause planes to fall out of the sky on the stroke of midnight – and the difficulty of getting a babysitter for New Year's Eve, the future looked pretty bright in the early days of the Noughties.

Reading back over my newspaper and radio columns from those days, I was surprised to discover that the sense of affluence and prosperity was already well established by 2000. Our romance with designer brands and conspicuous luxury was in full spate and the hottest label of the year was the 00-reg plate on your shiny new car. Even though the economists now tell us that the boom had, at that time, just a year to run before it began to falter, we raced blithely on without it, a bit like Wile E. Coyote in those cartoon scenes where the elusive Road Runner leads him a dance off the edge of a cliff and he sprints on for yards and yards before plummeting with a shriek and a whistle and a big billow of dust: we didn't start to fall until we chanced to look down, after Lehman Brothers went bang, and realised we'd long since run out of road ourselves. And as for the 'soft landing' we'd been promised, well, they don't happen even in the Looney Tunes.

I had two young schoolchildren and a ten-month-old baby when we rang in the New Year in 2000. My fourth baby was born a couple of weeks before the September 11th attacks in 2001 and he sat on my lap, sucking on a long-drained bottle, as we watched the second plane hit and the towers collapse, live on television. And he was first among us to feel the ripples of what would be the most life-altering, globally-experienced disaster to date – he'd been due surgery for a stomach problem the following Friday but it was cancelled because of the national day of mourning.

I remember seeing candles, this time signalling sympathy, flickering red in stars and stripes holders on the reception desk of the hospital when we went to schedule another appointment, and marvelling at how an incident so far away, however barbaric, could touch us here. Since then, of course, we've become wearily accustomed to the realisation that every fresh terror initiative will make corresponding and immediate inroads into our liberties, our comforts, our certainties and our peace of mind. At the time of writing, a would-be terrorist has just ratcheted up the threat a notch by stuffing his underpants with explosives and attempting to ignite them with a plastic syringe full of flammable liquid on a US-bound aircraft at 30,000 feet. That must have been quite a tense journey for him, all the way from Amsterdam to Detroit but, apart from the fact that this ingenuity is going to make for interesting encounters with airport security staff in future, we've got to acknowledge that anyone determined enough to inject his own crotch with combustibles for the sake of his cause is not going to be easily discouraged – a stunt like that takes, well, balls. Which means we've got to live with the ramped-up security measures at airports, not a prospect that would have troubled us unduly before the huge growth of budget air travel of the last decade but now, even in a downturn, is a routine headache for just about everyone.

And my last baby arrived in the height of the good times and the middle of the scorching summer of 2003. I recall trying to organise her baptism, later that year, and getting a hard time from a parish priest who wasn't sure he could fit us into his packed dance-card. I doubt somehow, after Ferns and Ryan and Murphy, that he'd be quite so cavalier about a new recruit today. But those were the days when the sunny, prosperous years seemed to roll out ahead of all of us as far as the eye could see, when people thought nothing of giving little baby girls gifts of diamond bracelets and Dior dresses and exquisite designer hand-knits and cashmere. Fortunately, I had the pessimistic foresight to hide them away so as to show them to her in a leaner future, when she might not believe such bounty was possible.

I have to say she's still as underwhelmed as she was six

years ago, and I sort of hope she stays that way. Maybe the only ones who were truly dazzled by the bling of the boom years, after all, were those of us for whom wealth, prosperity and beautiful things were novel and unfamiliar. And maybe that was why we spent like lunatics, and laughed like drains when the price of property here outstripped the real estate values of Beverly Hills, because we knew it wouldn't last.

The younger folk, for all the good fortune they've come to take for granted, will probably find it easier to adjust to our new circumstances than we imagine. At the height of the boom, after all, the twenty-somethings of the day were the first generation in our history to have lesser expectations than their parents did at their age: they couldn't look forward to better jobs, because we had full employment; or better homes, because property was prohibitively expensive; or better lifestyles, because commuting and childcare costs ate into their disposable incomes and their quality time. Now, once the cartoon mushroom-cloud of dust settles on our collapse, at least there's the opportunity to learn from our mistakes and bank the experience of our blind, acquisitive, reckless folly. At least they can't blame us for a shortage of material.

Funnily enough, they didn't give us candles to light our way into this new decade. There would have been uproar at the waste, of course, but it would have been an even more resonant gesture this past New Year's Eve than on the one ten years earlier. As an echo of the old Christmas tradition of offering shelter and welcome to an impoverished family, it would have symbolised the simplicity of our most basic needs and duties. And, on a less sentimental note, it would have been a useful reminder that, for all the bling and glitz and razzle-dazzle that illuminated our footsteps into the uncharted territory of the Noughties, we've got to find our way back out again in the gloom of a much humbler light.

2000–2002

December 2000

Robin Hood in reverse

IMAGINE IT IS Budget Day, 2002. Since generous tax breaks over the previous two years have meant that house prices continued to rise, the biggest crisis facing the new Minister for Finance today is homelessness. Even a small one-bed apartment in an old local authority block will set you back almost three hundred grand, and so the thousands of people squeezed out by spiralling rents and crushing mortgages are sleeping on the streets. Now money is no object, since the economy is still thriving, but opinion is divided on the best way to tackle the issue. So the Minister listens carefully to all the advice and then, on Budget Day, unveils his bold and extravagant new strategy. He will invest a generous £330 million in making life easier for the homeless, and here's what he's going to do: a waterproof, goose-down, top-of-the-range sleeping bag will be issued to every citizen in the land, along with a high-quality thermos and an all-weather primus stove. Thus, the Minister explains, everyone will be furnished with the minimum necessary to avoid hardship, and to ensure equality and certainty across the social spectrum. And, he goes on to announce, this is just the beginning of a £1 billion investment in the homelessness problem – in next year's Budget all citizens will additionally receive a battery-operated reading light and heated blanket combo, as well as a stout umbrella. This inventive new measure is broadly welcomed, although with the predictable cavilling from the usual bleeding-heart suspects. Middle-income earners are pleased – the extra sleeping bag will come in handy for the kids' sleepovers. The comfortably-off are particularly charmed – they'll stow the flasks and stove in the picnic compartment of the Lexus estate and maybe even use the sleeping bags to camp out for a night or two in Provence next summer. And as for the really needy, well, it won't solve their problems, of course, but it's a lot better than what they had.

Far-fetched, right? Except it is a pretty fair analogy for the way in which our current Finance Minister approached the childcare crisis when he drafted last Wednesday's Budget. Instead of targeting his £330 million expenditure on those most in need of assistance with their childcare costs, the Minister handed out thousands of pounds in extra child benefit to every family in the country, regardless of whether they needed or sought it. And the net result is that in almost every case, this money has been misspent, and unless his strategy changes before the next Budget, then the planned total spend of £1 billion will be similarly squandered.

Take, for example, your unemployed couple with three children on the bottom rung of the income ladder. He can't find work and, because childcare costs so much, she can't even begin to think about taking up the training course that might equip her to enter the labour force. The increase in child benefit announced last Wednesday brings them an additional £20 a week, which would not pay for a single day's childcare for their three kids. Add on their £8 apiece social welfare increases and then come next June, when the increases kick in, they'll be £36 a week better off. Which is just about enough to keep pace with inflation, help pay off the moneylenders who financed Christmas 2000 and maybe even fund a small weekly treat for the kids. But it won't lift them out of the poverty trap, and it won't go anywhere towards meeting their childcare needs, and it certainly won't put much of a dent in the child poverty statistics which indicate that one in five Irish kids goes to bed hungry a couple of nights a week.

Next let's take the working couple with three children, earning £20,000 apiece. The revised tax and PAYE conditions will net them an extra £72 a month, and their child benefit will bring in an extra £80 a month. Yet the cost of keeping three children in full-time childcare works out at between £800 and £1,000 a month. The extra cash will be a help, but it won't make childcare any better, more flexible or easier to find. Given inflationary pressures, they're facing pretty much the same financial juggling act in 2001.

Now your stay-at-home mother of three, whose husband earns £50,000 a year, is in a much happier position after Wednesday. She resisted last year's individualisation lure to return to work because childcare costs, along with all the additional expenditure of going out to work – clothes, dry-cleaning bills, lunches out, car expenses – would have fairly cancelled any financial benefit. She also factored in the un-quantifiable cost to her children of the loss of her care and the upset of spending ten-hour days in busy crèches, and figured they'd be all better off if she stayed home to mind them, at least while they're small. From next June she'll be getting an extra £80 a month in child benefit which, according to the Minister, is intended to help with the costs of the daily childcare that she doesn't need. Instead, it may go towards paying a babysitter for a few extra nights out a month, or straight into a bank account to fund the kids' college education when they leave school. And even if she wanted to work a few days a week, when the children are older, there's nothing in the Government's childcare strategy to make that likely because it's next to impossible to find after-school care for those few hours before she'd get home.

In the last two instances, then, the child benefit is arguably going to people for whom it does not address a particular need, and in the first case it is getting to the right family, but it isn't enough. And yet the very substantial sum of £330 million, the extra cost of the childcare measures announced last Wednesday, could have gone a long way towards really tackling the issue if it had been more imaginatively spent. If the Minister really wanted to give both parents the option of returning to work, as well as a suitable acknowledgement of the efforts of those who choose to stay working the home, then indiscriminately throwing money around just wasn't the answer. And that's because there is no single answer – instead, we need a range of measures to focus on the specific circumstances of each of the parents in the above examples.

The stay-at-home mother with the well-paid husband does not need the extra £80 a month – that's a nice little treat, some extra spending money paid out of the taxpayers' pockets. But for a woman in her position, the Homework Club idea that works so well in Britain could offer the possibility of returning to the workplace in the future. Researchers in Britain identified those two or three hours, between the end of the school day and the end of the average working day, as the culprits responsible for keeping many women in the home when they'd prefer to work outside. After all, while it is undeniably a wrench to leave a small, lonely, uncomprehending baby in full-day care five days a week, schoolgoing children are a different matter. They've got to spend five or six hours in school anyway, and they've got their own social lives, their own interests and their own friends to occupy their spare time. The Homework Clubs, where they can get their work done, gossip, swap Pokemon cards or play with Gameboys in a free classroom under the supervision of a State-employed adult, have proved a big success. It has the added advantage of sparing exhausted parents the stress of facing into hours of homework when they return from work each evening. There are rumblings from the Government about the possibility of keeping schools open after hours for just such purposes, and so perhaps this is one area in which parents themselves need to take the initiative.

For the middle-income couple who both work and

maintain their kids in full-time care, tax breaks are one possible solution. The childcare that allows them to work ought to be deductible as a legitimate expense, just like motoring costs to a commercial traveller. In many instances such people are employing a childminder on the black economy but, if it was worth everybody's while, then the carer in turn might be able to reap the benefits of individualisation by declaring her income. One of the most frequent objections to the notion of tax-deductible childcare, though, is that such a scheme would be of little benefit to long-term unemployed families such as in the first case above – if they wanted to avail of training courses, for example, they'd have to pay for childcare. And yet it is surely not beyond the Government's ingenuity or means to provide crèche facilities or fund childminding services in tandem with every FÁS course, for example, thus providing extra employment in the black-spot areas most in need of it.

And the child benefit expenditure could arguably be better targeted on the needy as well. Although groups such as CORI object to the demeaning connotations of means testing, a much fairer result could surely be achieved by paying a minimum level of child benefit to every family and then simply beefing up such payments to those families who are in receipt of social welfare, including income support. It is difficult to see how working parents, who after all enjoy the individualisation and tax relief benefits denied to unemployed households, could reasonably object to a more dignified and more just division of the budgetary surplus, which would direct the bulk of the money to the families who need it most.

May 2000

The 99p trick

ONE OF THE smartest retail strategies ever used in this country has to be the famous Dunnes Stores 99p price tag. They were the first to exploit this psychological sleight of hand – by just shaving a penny off a round sum, they enticed shoppers to suspend logic for as long as it took to get to the checkout, and to believe that £2.99 was a lot cheaper than £3.

Being clever businessfolk, Ben Dunne and his siblings must have done their sums and figured that they'd be handsomely compensated for all those pennies they handed back in loose change. Now this same Ben Dunne, who helped build an empire by calculating the return on a penny, expects us to believe that he handed over millions of pounds to Charlie Haughey without even noticing and without expecting anything back. Well, sorry Ben, you might have caught me once or twice with the old 99p trick, but there's a limit to everybody's gullibility. Rich businessmen like Ben Dunne and P. V. Doyle and Dermot Desmond don't get to be rich unless they can tell a good investment when they see one, and Charlie Haughey was clearly a very good investment. We don't know yet how exactly that investment paid dividends but I have a small clue, from personal experience, as to how the whole thing might have worked, and how it ticked along so smoothly for all concerned.

Back in the early 1980s I was a young freelance journalist with *The Irish Press*, writing features and news reports, when I was asked to interview a small-time businessman about a clever new firewall system he had developed.

He had not come to the paper looking for publicity, instead we went to him after hearing of his invention, and that is a significant point. Because in the course of our chat, I asked if he'd approached the relevant Government department with his invention, since it was designed to stop fire spreading through terraced homes of the sort the local authorities like so much.

Funny you should ask that, he said – he had actually made enquiries and in reply he got a message back – he named the messenger – saying that if he gave £40,000 to Charles Haughey, his invention would get the official nod and he could make a lot of money. He didn't pay it, he said, because he didn't have it – forty grand would have bought you a nice big house in Ballsbridge in 1984 – but he appeared to accept that this was the way things worked.

I thought it was a bit unlikely that a big millionaire like Haughey would bother skimming a trifling sum like £40,000 – it must have been a party donation that was being sought but even still, my friend seemed genuine and it stank of blackmail, so I thought I'd check it out. My editor at the *Press* advised me to put in a query to Haughey's press man, P. J. Mara, but even to a naive young reporter that didn't seem like a very promising lead. And then, just by chance, that evening I was sent on another story and who should turn up but the man himself, Mr Haughey. This seemed to me to be an excellent opportunity to check out my story, and he was more than gracious when I asked if I could have a word in private. But when he heard my question, his mood changed just a tad. He went ballistic, demanded my name, rank and serial number, thundered, 'How dare you?' and threatened, 'I'll see about you.'

By the time I made my way back to the *Press*, a little shell-shocked but thoroughly convinced that I'd hit a nerve, P. J. Mara had phoned the editor to complain. I was taken aside and told that this was not the way that reporters, especially when they are tender of years and very tenuous of employment status, ought to approach the Taoiseach of the day, particularly if they fancied a future in the Press Group.

That, I am sorry to say, was the beginning and the end of my career as an investigative journalist. I've never been able to track down that businessman again, so I don't know if he told me the truth. I don't know if any lives might have been saved by his firewall, had he been able to cross Mr Haughey's palm with £40,000.

All I know for sure is that my question rattled Haughey, and he and his henchman tried to make trouble for me with my employers as a result. And I know that when I hear Haughey's contemporaries now express their shock at the extent of his ill-gotten gains, and when I hear Ben Dunne insist that no favours were given in return for two million pounds, I am much inclined to be sceptical.

P.S. The businessman contacted me after this article appeared and subsequently supplied a written deposition to the Moriarty Tribunal.

December 2000

Appeasing the money god

THEY BEGAN APPEARING at the end of November. First the trees, all silvered branches and improbable girths, strung with this season's lights and colours in the bay windows of the million-pound houses along the avenues of Dublin 4. Then came the flickering candelabra displays (electric, of course) in the upstairs windows, then the glowing fun silhouettes of Santas and snowmen in the children's bedrooms. Next the wreaths, the light-up, musical, fake-pine-scented wreaths with spray-on snow. And then, in the last few weeks before Christmas, the outdoor lights began to appear, gaudy baubles desecrating stately old oaks or tarting up spindly shrubs, snaking up banisters and circling doorways, until, eventually, whole stretches of the world's most expensive residential real estate began to look like a Macy's Parade float. Every now and then you might have glimpsed the outline of a crib, but then it was usually perched up in a fanlight, where it might just impress passers-by, but from where its gloomy echoes of poverty and want and spirituality didn't have to put a damper on the glittering decorations inside the house.

This year, more noticeably than ever before, the original meanings of all our festive decorations, those with both Christian and pagan roots, have been discarded with even-handed alacrity so that we could pay undiluted homage to the one true God of the Christmas season – Money. In the same way that the ancient Europeans brought an evergreen into the house as a symbolic salvaging of the old year's gifts as the solstice heralded a new beginning, we now strive to appease the Money-God with ever more lavish displays of our gratitude for his bounty and benisons.

Lighting up a Christmas tree in a window – even if those lights ought to be tiny candles and not Habitat bulbs – is an old, old practice that pre-dates Christianity's appropriation of the Winter Solstice to celebrate Christ's birth. Stringing all-weather baubles along a tree in the garden, however, has origins that are much more recent and relevant. It's a fad we've imported from the land that makes no secret of deifying wealth and success, which is why it is entirely appropriate that flashy, showy American customs should supersede our traditionally more understated celebrations. It is particularly fitting that the citizens of the most exclusive neighbourhoods should make their houses and gardens high-voltage and breathtaking shrines to their own conspicuous wealth – these gardens where no unsuspecting tree has escaped gaudy decoration are a fitting metaphor for the year just gone, when no chance to flaunt wealth, no occasion of showy spending, no scope for noisy indulgence was missed, whatever the cost to taste or traditional values.

It was certainly the year in which we set about battering any residual guilt, reservations or unease about our new-found wealth into quivering submission. And even if you couldn't afford it, that was all the more reason to join the battle. And so determined house buyers landed themselves with the sort of mortgages that, just a few years ago, would have bought you a respectable Boulder Canyon villa straight out of *Lifestyles of the Rich and Famous* and now just about covers the cost of an average suburban Dublin semi.

But a mortgage is like a tightrope across the Niagara Falls – once you embark, it doesn't do to start looking down and thinking about the size of the drop, and you've got to keep going for the other side at all costs. It certainly doesn't do to remember that a mortgage is a whopping great debt to be paid off with colossal interest, or else you lose your home. And so the thousands and thousands of housebuyers, who borrowed almost £20 billion in the space of a year, have fixed their eyes on the far shore, that land of milk and honey where they'll own a substantial equity in a des. res. that has tripled in value, and keep marching resolutely towards it. And, unless a great gust of wind comes to knock you off kilter, maintaining a steady course in an overheated economy is indeed a taut balancing act where perception is reality – as long as we can still con ourselves into believing we're on solid ground, then it's a *trompe l'oeil* that might just work on foreign markets and banks and investors as well. Which goes some way towards explaining why putting on the Ritz, flashing our cash and spending like there's no tomorrow has come to be seen as our best insurance policy against a rude awakening on a chilly, hungry dawn.

And so 2000 became the year of spending conspicuously. It was the year when the city streets were suddenly awash with open-topped convertibles, even up to late November. A record number of soft-tops were sold in Ireland this year, in blithe disregard for the fact that we don't exactly boast the climate for tootling along bougainvillea-scented boulevards with the warm wind in your hair. It was the year when wealthy parents chose to advertise their wealth by presenting their teenage children with 'fun' cars, the yellow BMW convertible coupé aimed to make it annoyingly clear to other motorists – as they sat in their sensible saloons and prayed for a downpour – that this was no family car borrowed by the son and heir for the day, but his own little runaround for trips to the tennis club. It was the year when making the neighbours jealous, rubbing the noses of the less-well-off in your unimaginable wealth, became a perfectly legitimate aspiration. It's hardly a coincidence, for example, that the biggest fashion trend of the year – and one that was greedily seized upon by the social savants on the Irish scene – was the craze for all-over logo prints. This year it wasn't enough to have a Prada or Chanel or Gucci label stitched discreetly to the inside collar of your shirt, it had to be printed all over in an in-your-face pattern that neatly captured the Noughties mood with fashion's chic cynicism. Louis Vuitton, purveyors of, amongst other things, the £1,300 make-up box, opened an outlet in Brown Thomas to cater to a growing taste for all things obviously flashy and achingly, patently expensive. The extraordinary proliferation of 00-reg cars on the roads this year – all of which, remember, will be sadly passé by this time tomorrow – bore witness to a more modest version of the label trend. For the past 12 months it was simply the coolest, the most fashionable, the most cutting-edge badge to display on your motor, far hipper, say, than the leaping cat on a second-hand Jag because, by buying new instead of sensible second hand, you were telling the world you could afford to discount the few grand you'd paid for the privilege of driving your shiny new vehicle off the garage forecourt ... which was all the more vital if, in fact, you couldn't.

It was the year of the million-pound estate house, when the first tranche of custom-built homes in an exclusive estate were snapped up almost as soon as they went on sale. Previously, the million mark had only been surpassed by period homes with original features, but new money put a greater premium on state-of-the-art kitchens and Danish flooring and landscaped Astroturf.

It was the year when the seriously wealthy finally

abandoned any pretence that they were more concerned for the charities they patronised than the glory that conspicious giving drew upon themselves. Businessmen queued up to bid more than a million pounds to play golf with Tiger Woods, in perhaps the year's most vulgar and stomach-churning glimpse into the self-regarding insularity of the world of the well-rewarded. Charity balls and functions with £500-a-skull ticket prices were heaving at the seams and the clever chaps behind *VIP* magazine packed 'em in to make their glossy magazine even more unmissable to the pampered and vain. Now you may reason that anybody who can afford to spend £500 on a charity dinner could just as easily afford to donate that £500 to charity and buy his own dinner, but it doesn't work like that. These folks won't give unless they get something in return and, this past year, the most delicious return of all was the chance to be pictured, in Armani tux or Maria Grachvogel gown, sipping Cristal and talking to some hire-a-celeb at an unassailably worthy function.

It was the year when the poor were tossed an additional £8 a week in social welfare – that's £2 less than the price of a single glass of flat champagne in the Morrison Hotel – and expected to make do, while wealthy parents scored the cost of an extra round of cocktails on an across-the-board child benefit hike. It was the year when everyone wanted to be a millionaire – from the Eircom shareholders to the dot.com prodigies – but with a minimum of effort. And so the Millionaire gameshow, after all the hype, attracted only the humblest minds, the wariest contestants, the losers who needed a lifeline to get them up to a grand and eventually scurried home with less than they would have earned on a good night at the bingo. In Britain the show attracts the top drawer, like Camilla Parker Bowles' cousin who turned out to be the first million-pound winner, and the professional quiz competitors. Here, though, it draws the weakest link, the type of folk who hitched their wagons to the Celtic Snail, mere sneering fodder for the Tiger Cubs for whom one million pounds really isn't such a lot of money any more. After all, it won't buy you a decent house, or a decent lifestyle, or a few decent sets of wheels for your children, or even a round of golf with Tiger Woods. And, anyway, winning it on a tacky game show in front of an audience of a quarter of a million gaping viewers doesn't come anywhere near to being sufficiently conspicuous for the current generation of consumers.

December 2000

From Dunkirk to El Paso

'AND AFTER THIS,' the stout US cameraman turned to his chums on the podium outside Government Buildings, 'we're heading off to Dunkirk, right?' Close, but no cigar. Still, you can hardly blame the pampered hacks of the White House press corps if they were a mite disorientated – they'd been flown in on Air Force Two at the Godforsaken hour of 8.30 that morning, whisked by speeding bus and Garda outrider escort from the airport to the Phoenix Park to Merrion Street and then, after some rather lavish hospitality courtesy of Guinness, they were due to brave a turbulent frontier with nothing but the free whiskey from their press packs for comfort. Dunkirk, Dundalk, where they fight them on the beaches – you can see how the confusion might arise. The elite White House pack had even colonised a room in Dublin Castle all to themselves, and us ordinary domestic reporters were shooed from the door when we tried to peep inside – waiting for Bill inside Government Buildings, we were even ticked off for straying into the White House press folks' private coffee room and nibbling on their cherry muffins.

For these crews and reporters, who track the President

through national and global incidents and engagements, the big story was the unfolding denouement of the race for his successor, and they were far more concerned to get his opinion on the US Supreme Court ruling on the Florida recounts rather than the colour range of fishermen's sweaters down at Blarney Woollen Mills. The *Washington Post* and *New York Times* reports of his visit next day carried rather patronising guff about adoring crowds and flag-waving urchins along with Ladybird book outlines of the North's political stand-off. And so, even if the television crews eventually managed to distinguish Dundalk from Dunkirk and capture footage of the 60,000-strong crowd in the town's main square, it seems unlikely that the full warmth and excitement and gratitude and genuine enthusiasm of Bill Clinton's welcome here last week could have been adequately relayed to the voters who are about to replace him with a shallow product of political nepotism whose eyes are too close together. Which means that the nation which elected George W. Bush as its leader is even less likely to grasp just why Bill Clinton is held in such regard here, and how crucial was the role he played in the last few years' dramas.

Viewed from the comfort of the White House press bus, the cheering crowds must have looked a lot like starstruck peasants, frenzied by the celebrity and charisma of a leader they themselves know from daily familiarity to be human and flawed, and whose place in the American history books will be headlined with his impeachment and his philandering. Their general take on his last Irish visit has been superficially cynical – he wanted to leave the American people, and especially the 70 million who claim some Irish connection, with memorable images of his greatest political triumph and lots of moving sub-Yeatsian eloquence ringing in their ears. Why else, after all, would he have quoted a linen teatowel ($10 in the airport shops) in Dundalk to sign off with hackneyed blarney about the wind at your back and the road rising before you and God holding you in the hollow of his hand? Dundalk had been flagged as the politically sensitive venue for his keynote address, which turned out to be less hard-hitting than sentimental, persuasive and impassioned. But Bill Clinton, perhaps more than the commentators waiting for some hard copy, has a deft feel for imagery and symbolism, and it was to this the crowds responded in Dublin and Dundalk and Belfast. With 60,000 people thronging the streets of Dundalk, waiting in the icy rain for four and five hours and drawn from all around the Border, there was little need for the anticipated strong political statement from the President to put pressure on the violent dissidents – by turning out in such numbers in such discouraging conditions, it was the people of old El Paso who made the most eloquent statement of all.

Watching Bill Clinton working a crowd or delivering a speech in a voice breaking with emotion, or wiping away a tear, as he seemed to do during Bertie Ahern's address in Dublin earlier on Tuesday, you can't help wondering if this guy's for real. In his book *Primary Colours*, former Clinton aide Joe Klein seemed to suggest that the President was pretty handy at switching on the surge of emotion when requred, and in the film John Travolta played him as a consummate showman with a particular gift for absorbing the sentiment of a moment and reflecting it back with a turbo charge. Last week, too, we saw plenty of evidence of what Klein described as 'the power handshake', the full body manoeuvre where he grips the hand, massages the shoulder, strokes the upper arm and cups the elbow while fixing the victim with an unwavering gaze – Clinton, apparently, will never glance over your shoulder to see if somebody more important has entered the room but then, if you're President of America, that's probably an unlikely prospect in any gathering. And so he worked The Handshake on an endless stream of dignitaries and politicians in the Guinness Storehouse last Tuesday and managed to despatch them all from his grip – including Jackie Healy Rae, whose head gleamed with so much hair oil that he looked as though he'd been French polished for the occasion

– wearing dazed and silly grins. At close range he is not a particularly handsome man – his face is too ruddy and boneless and, from fatigue and jet lag last Tuesday morning, his eyes were narrow puffy slits in a rather blotched face. And yet, far from flagging like an ordinary mortal as the day wore on, he seemed to draw vigour from the hectic sequence of events and the applause of the crowds that gathered all along his route throughout the afternoon. Outside the Storehouse a crowd of a few hundred people had assembled to wait for hours in the rain for a fleeting glimpse of his armoured limo – through the darkened bulletproof windows he was just about visible as a dim grey silhouette, but the waiting women still shrieked at the vague figure and pronounced that he was 'gorgeous' on the basis of very little first-hand evidence. The eye of the beholder, though, is notoriously partisan, and requited passion confers classical qualities on the most homely specimens, and so by the time he had finished his Dundalk speech and was swaying along to 'Danny Boy' with his wife and daughter clasped in his arms, Bill Clinton was gorgeous. If he hadn't been sincere, then he'd faked it so well he fooled even himself that night, because it certainly felt real. Part of the reason he appeals so mightily to women, like the ladies who had abandoned their Thomas Street stalls to wait at the Storehouse wearing a lipstick shade they reckoned was 'Monica Lewinsky Red', is that he has a reckless streak. Only a real chancer would court a besotted intern in the corridor outside the Oval Office, and it took the same recklessness to challenge the so-called 'special relationship' with Britain that had, as he said, for so long 'paralysed' American policy towards Northern Ireland, and to set in motion the sequence of risky events that brought the ceasefire into being. When he spoke so bluntly and undiplomatically of the Northern leaders as 'drunks in a bar' last year, Bill Clinton revealed some of the depth of his feelings about the issue and revealed a glimpse of the passion, spontaneous, impulsive and sometimes ill-advised, that has defined his Presidency. He's a man who takes gambles for passion, which is probably why he generated so much passion in response last week. Which is hardly something the toughened souls of the White House press corps, who are even now glancing over Bill's shoulder as George W. makes his entrance, could ever really appreciate.

January 2001

Sport, Booze and Shopping – the new holy trinity

WHEN HE LANDED in Bangalore yesterday at the start of his first ever official visit to India, the Taoiseach was greeted with a religious ritual which is reserved, according to reports, for important guests AND visiting deities.

It being India, apparently, you never know who might pitch up in the first-class arrivals lounge of the airport – maybe a pale-skinned foreign premier trying to drum up some business, a former Big Brother housemate, or a stray god with half a day to kill. The Indians are prepared for all such eventualities, so yesterday they were more than able for Bertie and his gaggle of senior Ministers.

The greeting ritual involves draping a garland of sandalwood flowers around the neck of the god or Taoiseach – delete as appropriate – and placing a third eye, called a tika, in the centre of the forehead. The tika has an especially honourable significance – ordinary mortals do not acquire the eye of wisdom until they learn to conquer their desires, but superior beings, and Fianna Fáil leaders in particular, are well known to have mastered that.

Now the sight of Bertie all decked out in these ancient symbols of Indian faith and custom set me thinking of the welcome the Indian prime minister could expect if he were to visit us. We also have an ancient faith, religious traditions and unique customs – so imagine he landed here at the beginning of Lent, a time of special religious observance for generations. Would he be draped with brown scapulars, given a bottle of holy water in the shape of a glow-in-the-dark Virgin from Knock, told that meat and alcohol were off the menu, and have HIS forehead anointed with a smear of ash?

Despite the fact that these are the traditional expressions of the religion the majority of us still profess to hold, the PC brigade would be up in arms at the very thought. How offensive, how backward, how oppressive, how insulting to the man's own religious beliefs any such gesture would be. Instead, he'd be given a tour of the Dundrum Town Centre, escorted to Fagans for a pint of Bass, and photographed looking baffled in a Dublin football jersey. Sport, booze and shopping are the holy trinity of our new religion, after all, but nobody seems to find their veneration the least bit offensive.

Funny, then, how we don't consider the Indian people backward or ignorant when they express their faith. And, although the Catholic Church teaches that the worship of false gods is a mortaller, Bertie, clad in the symbols of a religion that acknowledges many deities, didn't look offended. Embarrassed, maybe, but not offended. Nor was there any great outrage from church leaders here at the spectacle of the Mass-going Taoiseach sheepishly sporting his third eye. That, of course, is because we pride ourselves on our tolerance. We are so tolerant, in fact, that we eagerly tolerate the intolerance of other faiths and races, so as to make ourselves look all the more tolerant by contrast.

Last year, for instance, a council chamber in Cork was being refurbished and it was decided, without much consultation, to get rid of the crucifix that had hung on the chamber wall for more than 30 years. Because it was deemed potentially offensive to any Muslims or Swedenborgians who might stray into the council chamber, the cross was removed. And thrown in a skip. So, as a demonstration of religious tolerance and sensitivity, a crucifix was dumped in a bin. I'm still trying to work that one out.

I suspect that most foreign nationals who come here to live and work have figured out that this is a largely Catholic country – they may even know that immigration is a relatively recent trend here. I reckon they have braced themselves for the shocking sight of a crucifix every now and then – there's a huge unmissable one in the middle of Phoenix Park – and they can handle the sight of a Christmas crib in a hospital foyer. At a push, I'd say, some could even withstand hearing a middle-aged politician use the old saying 'work like blacks', since it is part of the vernacular, conveys honest admiration and, like it or not, is historically accurate.

Proud as we are of our own tolerance, then, we don't seem to be able to credit our new neighbours with any at all. On the contrary, we act as though they are all narrowminded, prejudiced, dogmatic and hysterical, ready to take offence at the slightest accidental slip. We expect that they'll settle for nothing less than the complete sanitisation of our language and the dishonouring of our own faith. This does everybody a disservice. If you can't respect your own creed and customs, then your grand gestures towards those of others are worth nothing at all.

No doubt that picture of Bertie with his tika and his sandalwood will be used to great hilarity in satirical magazines and quiz shows for some time to come. But it ought to remind us that great nations do not discard their culture and beliefs in pursuit of vanilla-flavoured modernity.

And I thought Bertie looked quite fetching with his third eye, even if, as leader of a very tetchy coalition government, he'd probably have preferred if they'd put it in the back of his head.

February 2001

Drumcree: marching into the history books

LIKE EVERY OTHER Southern reporter who has covered the Drumcree story over the years, I've done my share of arguing with Garvaghy Road residents about the wisdom of continuing to block the annual Orange March. Viewed from down here, after all, it seems a petty reason to crank up the tension and jeopardise the peace and even risk lives at a volatile time in the Northern calendar. So why not seize the high moral ground on a Himalayan scale and let them march? Let them off in their fancy dress, their funny hats and robes, if that's what they want to do, have a carnival, have a laugh or even have a day at the beach and leave them to it. It seems fairly clear that the Orangemen's enthusiasm for the project is directly proportional to the residents' opposition, so it stands to reason that an attitude of amused generosity from the locals would take all the fun out of Drumcree for Johnny Adair and his mates. But you've got to understand Portadown, the nationalists would argue back, to realise that this was not just a simple skirmish to be won or lost in the no-man's-land of PR and spin. Portadown is a place where the main shopping centre has a Catholic entrance and a Protestant entrance. Portadown is a place where a young Catholic man could be kicked to death within 15 feet of an armoured car containing four armed RUC members, just because he didn't make it across the few yards of ground that would have taken him to the safety of a 'Catholic' street. It's difficult for an outsider to grasp the solidity of the invisible boundaries that mark out the Unionist and Nationalist territories. Portadown is a place, as a caller to *Liveline* reported this week, where the staff of a Christian bookshop will turn away a customer with a Dublin accent because 'we don't need Paddy's pence here'. Portadown is all about territory. Being a Nationalist in Portadown means never feeling at ease outside of your own designated safe area, and being an Orangeman in Portadown means never having to say you're sorry for marching wherever you like. And that has always been the core of the problem. Most of the moderate nationalists in Portadown will tell you that the Drumcree issue could be solved tomorrow if only the Orangemen would talk to the local residents. The Orangemen say they'll never talk to Breandáin MacCionnaith, but he was nowhere in sight back in 1986 when the Garvaghy folk first began writing to the Orange Order about the march, and he was not the reason why those letters went unanswered. And he's hardly the reason why the Orangemen won't even enter talks through a South African mediator. They insist the march is part of their tradition, and they're right, and a crucial part of that heritage was never having to seek permission to bang a Lambeg drum outside a Catholic home.

But it may be time, now, for the Nationalists in Portadown to make that grand gesture of allowing the march, if only to administer the *coup de grâce* to the imploding Orange Order. The past week has seen the Order and its supporters beset by unsustainable contradictions – they've blocked all the Queen's highways to protest at the closure of one road, they'll petrol bomb the RUC but they won't let Peter Mandelson even tweak the badge on their caps, they won't talk to terrorists but they'll welcome Johnny Adair's support, they want a peaceful march and they won't condemn violence if that's what it takes to get it. These internal conflicts prove it really is all over, bar the shouting and even the shouting is beginning to fade. The final irony would be if the Nationalists on Garvaghy now gave them permission to walk the road, and they took it. They'd be walking on her Majesty's highway, but on the grace and favour of the Nationalists. They'd be walking through a new Northern Ireland, where tradition was respected but intimidating rituals had dwindled to the status of archaic curiosity, down the Garvaghy Road and straight into the history books.

May 2001

In defence of domestic slobbery

HOURS AND HOURS of painstaking work went into recon-
structing Francis Bacon's art studio at the Hugh Lane Gallery
in Dublin, after his estate decided that the honour of housing
Bacon's place of inspiration should go to his native country.
Now television footage of the completed studio would not
immediately suggest that hours and hours of painstaking work
went into tidying up Francis Bacon's studio, even though some
friends who have seen the end result say that a disgraceful
amount of artistic licence has been taken with the display, and
it is actually much neater now than when the great man
himself laboured there.

There were times, they say, when it was waist-deep in
discarded painting rags and empty linseed oil bottles and torn-
up magazines and other assorted inspirational or incidental
material, and to have edited all these worthwhile gems out of
the finished product meant an unconscionable interference
with a true representation of Bacon's working environment.

Still, we get the picture – Bacon was not, it is fair to say,
the sort of chap who worried endlessly about the bacterial
propriety of his worktops and did not add much to the Lever
Brothers share price with his tireless consumption of citrus-
scented wipes and deodorant room-sprays and antiseptic
cleaning products. Personally, I was quite pleased to see the
Hugh Lane Gallery get his studio, since I now realise that I've
actually got his kitchen, and probably one of his bathrooms as
well. It is clear that teams of art historians have been sneaking
in under cover of darkness, over the past few years, and
meticuously recreating Bacon's domestic living space in the
amusingly ironic surroundings of a suburban semi-d. It would

certainly explain how work surfaces that were perfectly neat before supper are strangely buried under layers of displaced utensils and tea cloths and spilled drinks and stray Rice Krispies by the following breakfast time. Still, I don't seem to be alone in acquiring a life-sized relic of the painter's disordered life – if last year's experience is anything to go by then, by the time 200 trader travelling families are ejected from the scenic site they currently occupy alongside the River Dodder, South Dublin County Council will have his garden.

The careful, precious reproduction of the Bacon studio – which looks, to the untrained eye, like those photos the Simon Community and Alone sometimes release of the squalor in which they find poor, elderly people existing – tends to reinforce an intellectual conceit that a concern for cleanliness is a poncy, empty-headed, middle-class obsession, and that truly free spirits have more on their minds than the e-coli bugs on their chopping boards and stubborn stains on their furniture.

You'll always find that biographies of the most successful, beautiful, admirable, high-achieving women through history approvingly record their disdain for mundane domestic skills – I'll bet Emily Pankhurst's kitchen was no sight for the unwary, it's hard to picture Margaret Thatcher or Cherie Blair setting about the toilet bowl in rubber gloves, and I've just read an account of the life of the war reporter Martha Gellhorn who had, apparently, profound contempt for what she called 'the kitchen of life', the dull, necessary tasks of everyday comfort best left to dull, necessary housewives. And Nigella Lawson didn't get to be a domestic goddess because of the precision with which she scrubs her pots after use – instead, she looks as though she might well lick them clean, slowly and sensuously and with beads of chocolate sauce clinging to her nose, a notion which sends every red-blooded man into a sticky sweat.

There is much, of course, to recommend the view that a fastidiousness about domestic hygiene is, indeed, the product of an empty mind, and that people who have real lives don't have time to trawl the supermarket cleaning product aisles in search of new delights for the cupboard under the sink.

Every television commercial break lately seems to bring glad tidings of yet another turbo-charged antiseptic, anti-bacterial, Scandinavian pine forest-scented, e-coli-resistant, foot-and-mouth repellent, deodorising grout cleaner for the kitchen tiles, all of it pitched at a particular breed of middle-class mother of 2.7 perfect sprogs. The underlying message beneath the marketing of all this tattle is that the homemaker who neglects to stock up on wipes and disposable dusters and freshening sprays and antibacterial gels and mousses and creams is putting her family at an unconscionable risk of slow, certain death from virulent, lurking bugs. It makes you wonder why Saddam Hussein feels he has to bother spending a fortune on the development of germ warfare, when simply disrupting the supply of antibacterial cleaning gunk and gadgets and sprays and fluids to the United States would obviously lay the population low in a matter of days.

None of this is much of a laughing matter from an environmental point of view – we are, apparently, the last generation that will escape the destructive effects of our outrages against the globe's natural resources and defences – and the packaging of most of these products will still be poisoning the environment long after the Chernobyl site is blooming with fresh spring flowers. Last week, Darina Allen weighed in to suggest that this cleaning frenzy is dangerous as well, since these products kill off 'good' bacteria as well as the uglies, weaken our immune systems and make us more vulnerable to illness and infection.

I'm absolutely 100 per cent behind all these arguments, solidly defensive of domestic slobbery as a statement of personal liberty, convinced that women with real lives wouldn't know one end of a squeegee mop from another and that a true domestic goddess leaves the washing-up until tomorrow. But where the supercilious scorn for neat homes and manicured lawns becomes a little hard to stomach is when it's used to belittle the concerns of householders and local authorities about the huge summer influxes of traveller families to urban areas and the disgraceful messes they leave behind.

Last summer the same huge group of travellers currently installed on the Dodder banks – most of them driving brand new vehicles and on a working vacation from their homes elsewhere – left behind 200 tons of rubble. They moved on, said Mick Fagan of South Dublin County Council, only when they'd made the place uninhabitable for themselves. Which is probably quite an achievement. Travellers and their spokespeople doggedly refuse to see that they'd be far more welcome, on their return trips, if they left their temporary sites looking a little less like a scaled-up version of Francis Bacon's studio, instead of smugly relying on the intellectual snobbery of media allies to sneer at concerned residents and their middle-class, antiseptic, antibacterial, deodorising, citrus-scented obsessions.

July 2002

Neutered ships and dancing grandads

YOU MIGHT HAVE missed this, but during the week that venerable shipping newspaper, *Lloyds' List*, announced that it will no longer use the feminine form to describe seafaring vessels. Bowing to the march of political correctness, the paper is to turn its back on the centuries old maritime tradition and, from now on, will refer to a ship as 'it' and not as 'she'. This decision will leave the *Eithne*s and the *Deirdre*s and the *Niamh*s of our own naval service sounding like ocean-going drag queens, while the old *Queen Mary* herself will reign supreme as the Danny La Rue of the high seas. But, in a most unsisterly act, the news has been greeted warmly by many female commentators, who appear to have been labouring under intolerable oppression caused by this tendency to define certain inanimate objects, like planes, trains and automobiles, in feminine terms. Now, personally, I can't detect any strong sense of blissful liberation from the discovery that ships have been neutered – indeed, and I know this makes me a witless backbencher in the fraught world of gender politics, but I always felt vaguely flattered by the allocation of a female personality to creatures that are so graceful, so beautiful, so efficient, and so imperiously and unapologetically demanding of expensive high maintenance. This just seems to me another of those small, incremental curtailments of personal liberty that are presented to us as victories for equality, justice and freedom of expression. Today, it's just a matter of personal choice whether or not to describe a ship as female – tomorrow, whose to say it won't be a criminal offence, punishable by a fine or imprisonment or both, to say, 'God bless her and all who sail in her'? It doesn't seem that long ago since the *Evening Press*, in its innocence, ran a spoof April Fool's Day story suggesting that smoking was to be banned on buses. Well, the uproar that one caused. But now, some liberated and enlightened years on, Dublin Bus has put spies on its buses to seek out those few hardy souls who continue to light up on the public transport, so that they may be brought to justice and distract our eminent judges from the far more important business of dispensing suspended sentences to rapists. I'm not a smoker, though if I wanted to smoke I'd prefer to buy the fags myself rather than inhale somebody else's second-hand nicotine, but I reckon it's probably punishment enough to have to suffer foul breath, yellow teeth, and lungs that have more tar on them than your average County Leitrim byroad, without living in fear of entrapment on the top deck of the 16A to boot. I don't have a mobile phone, either – I prefer to adopt the attitude of the rural shopkeeper who reportedly said of the euro that she'd be ignoring them because they were just a fad and they wouldn't last. But it does seem rather draconian to propose, as the new legislation apparently does, that drivers might be stopped and searched to see if they are carrying such an offensive weapon. And locating a well-hidden mobile phone could well involve the sort of body searches folks of Middle Eastern origin might now expect at Kennedy Airport – they have become increasingly, modishly tiny, bearing out the old line that mobile phones are the only possessions that men compare to see who has the smallest. New research, it seems, suggests that mobile phones are at least as big a threat to a driver's concentration as several large whiskeys, but common sense suggests that the famous penalty points system – which this Government has entirely failed to implement in the course of its term in office, could well have covered their misuse in a moving vehicle without all the bells and whistles attached to this new law.

As well as not smoking or carrying mobile phones, and being a positive temple of virtue, I don't hang out in trendy young people's night spots, either, unlike the 72-year-old who recently made a fruitless attempt to gain entry to the Q Bar in Dublin. He took his case to the Equality Authority, which decreed that he had been barred on ageist grounds, and awarded him €1,000 compensation. So there, folks, is just this past week's tally of fresh impositions on your personal liberty – you can't call a ship 'she', you can't be sure the next passenger on Dublin Bus isn't an undercover agent, you can't make a mobile phone call from your car, and you can't go for a quiet Tequila Slammer in a noisy club without the risk of meeting your grandfather on the pull.

May 2002

A sacrifice to drunkenness

UNDER THE 1908 Summary Jurisdiction (Ireland) Act, it is a criminal offence in this country to be found drunk while in charge of a donkey. The maturity of the donkey in question, whether or not said donkey has reached the age of majority or whether he is still in his salad days, doesn't seem to count. It is still a crime.

Being drunk in charge of a child, though, that is a different matter. If the child is under seven years of age, then the drunken parent or guardian IS guilty of a crime, which is punishable, under the same 1908 Act that prohibits giving bad example to donkeys, by a fine of £2, or €2 and 54 cents.

Once the child is over seven, though, then, unlike a donkey, he is entirely at the mercy of a drunken minder. He can be left at risk from liquor-fuelled rage or incompetence, or – as an Equality Authority ruling established earlier this year – he can be sent outside to wait in the rain while his parents exercise their God-given right to drink themselves stupid in a pub, and woe betide the barman who intervenes.

Just before Christmas, a drunken father abandoned a toddler by the side of a busy motorway in Dublin. The man was found by Gardaí walking along the road, beer can in hand but, when taken into custody, he forgot to mention that the baby was still out there. It was hours before the little fellow was found, frozen and traumatised and cowering under a hedge for shelter from an icy winter's night. The child was taken into care, but so far, no criminal charges have been brought against his father. If he does end up in court, though, he can now plead sane automatism (an unconscious, involuntary act of which the defendant has no memory, and in which an excess of alcohol might just have played a part) and most likely, walk free.

Our general attitude towards children who get caught up in drunken adult situations seems to be that it is just their tough luck. They are collateral damage, an acceptable level of casualty, now and then the inevitable victims of a society that celebrates and indulges insane alcoholic excess. Baby Oisín Reilly, 18 months old when he was knifed to death after the adults who were supposedly caring for him drank themselves insensible on cider and poitín, is the latest sacrifice to our veneration of drunkenness.

The man who guzzled illegal liquor, lost his reason and stabbed Baby Oisín nine times with an army knife is free today after the judge decided that jailing him would serve no purpose. Now we have been assured that this was a unique case, the killing motiveless and uncharacteristic, and the judicial reasoning and the legal argument quite beyond the layman's comprehension. Sane automatism sounds like a very serious defence, right enough, but nobody can say for sure if the jury actually bought it.

Since jurors are prohibited from giving their reasons for a verdict, all we know for certain is that they did not find John Reilly had the high level of premeditation and intent required to ground a murder conviction, and so they found him guilty of manslaughter. He did not set out to stab the baby, any more than a drunken driver intentionally kills a hapless cyclist. But, no less than a drunken driver, he was responsible for getting himself drunk. And he got himself drunk, just like a driver, while in charge of a deadly weapon – in his case, not a speeding car but a lethal knife.

The judge accepted that Reilly's response to the cocktail of liquor was inexplicable, but, legal geniuses out there, riddle me this: if nobody knows why John Reilly savagely butchered a baby with drink on him this time, how on earth can a judge or a psychiatrist or a character witness be so sure he won't do it again?

I know Judge Paul Carney is an honourable and compassionate man, but I am shocked by this sentence. In a country with an appalling rate of child murders, nobody who takes the life of a baby, other than in a tragic and unavoidable accident, ought to go free. The only restrictions the court placed on Reilly's liberty was that he keep the peace for five years and cease to carry his lethal army knife. But surely he might also have been required to give up alcohol for the rest of his days, or else serve his full sentence? Even in a country that elevates drunkenness to the level of a national sport, that would not have been too great a price to pay for killing a baby.

May 2002

Finessing the ghosts of Fianna Fáil Past

PUT YOURSELF, FOR one moment, in Bertie Ahern's gleaming hand-tooled slip-ons. There you are, doing a walkabout in Castlebar, trying to break the land-speed record for high-velocity flesh pressing, keeping a watchful eye out for young women wielding cream dainties in an offensive or threatening manner, when suddenly you spot it: a great big human custard pie, in the form of one Pee Flynn, hurtling straight for you. He is grinning a grin so cheesy that, with a crumbly biscuit base and a dash of Bailey's seasoning, it'd keep the Bunratty banqueting tourists in dessert for a whole year. There is no time to duck or dodge, no amount of fancy footwork will get you out of the trajectory of the seat-seeking missile that is this proud, campaigning Daddy, and you can't exactly cut and run. In the millisecond before impact, your practiced brain reviews your options as they might appear in the following day's newspapers – Bertie fleeing down a Castlebar backstreet, pursued by stout party with right hand extended. Or Bertie taking it full on the chin, clasping an old comrade warmly to his bosom in statesmanlike manner, regal in his contempt for the pettifoggers and the cavillers who would nitpick about straying party donations and bogus non-resident accounts. Query to self: what would Nelson Mandela do?

Once Pee had presented himself to be greeted, before the avid eyes of the country's media, there was little Bertie could do but greet, and be damned. And that, to judge by the outraged calls to *Liveline* all week, is pretty much what happened. Listeners queued up to condemn Bertie for failing to shun Pee Flynn on the hustings in Mayo, for shaking his hand and telling him he was looking well and enquiring whether he was getting in any golf lately. Which hardly, let's face it, amounts to a ringing absolution of all of which Pee stands accused, but folk were indignant just the same. Bertie made a quick decision as to which option – to shun or to shake – would leave him with the least amount of egg on his face, and the casual, friendly greeting won by a mile. The mystery here is not so much why Bertie enveloped Pee in such a chummy embrace, but how he allowed himself to end up in a position where it was the lesser of two political peccadillos in the first place.

Before the campaign started in earnest, Sean Haughey pronounced himself 'incandescent with rage' – a unique mental image which we will just stop here to contemplate for a moment – at Bertie's apparent preference for his constituency running mate and rival for the last Fianna Fáil seat, Deirdre Heney. Now Sean doesn't come across as a paranoid hysteric, so when he says he reckons there's a dastardly plot to erase the Haughey name from the Fianna Fáil roll call, he may just be on to something. Whatever the reasoning, Bertie has so far dodged the prospect of a campaign photo-call that might just include Sean's Da – so how come he couldn't avoid encountering Beverly's old fella?

It may well be that the party machine was a tad taken aback by the ire of the normally mild-mannered Sean Haughey, and feared incurring the same anger from Beverly, who has all the look of a woman you wouldn't cross lightly. Bad enough to have Sean Haughey muttering about a campaign to oust him because of his family history, but if Bev joined in the chorus then Bertie might just begin to look like Niccòlo Machiavelli's mean older brother — what was that phrase again, the most cunning, the most devious of them all?

And abandoning an old political ally when he is in trouble, however much he might have brought that trouble upon himself, is not a course of action that plays too well with the broader Fianna Fáil constituency. Take Terry Keane and the Charvet shirts, the Coq Hardi and the Big Fella's cheque and, all together, they still won't outweigh Charlie's shafting of Brian Lenihan, back in 1990, in the balance of his transgressions in the eyes of the most staunch FFers. Had Bertie sidestepped Pee in Castlebar, as well as irking many local supporters, he would have offered clear proof that he was embarrassed by the history of the administration just ending, and he'd have been loudly reminded that he couldn't distance himself from the era quite as easily as he could distance himself from the man. Had Pee stayed at home, he'd have been conceding that he was a source of shame — not a positive message for the high-profile father of a candidate to put about. And it's been suggested in the past week that Pee should have been 'finessed' off the scene before Bertie and the cameras arrived, although one suspects that if Pee was a likely subject for 'finessing', it would have been done long before now. Pee Flynn may well be part of the past that Fianna Fáil claims to have left behind, but Beverly — deprived of the whip and yet, says Bertie, a strong supporter of the party — is a living reminder that those legacies are not always so easy to disavow.

Like Sean Haughey, she has strong constituency support, much of it inspired by local contempt for 'Dublin meeja' diktat and, like him, she is determined that her family name will not be written out of the party's history without a fight. Oh, and if she's elected then there's the minor consideration that she'll be an extra bum on a Fianna Fáil bench, and one that Bertie may well need if he's to return triumphant to Leinster House on June the 6th.

And so, when the ghosts of Fianna Fáil past and Fianna Fáil present pitched up in full and glorious technicolour on a street in Castlebar last Monday, the ghost of Fianna Fáil yet-to-come had little option but to stand his ground.

June 2002

No such thing as living beyond your means

THERE IS A commercial running on television at the moment which always holds me spellbound with the same grim compulsion as a particularly messy car crash. It shows Mr and Mrs Average relaxing over the Sunday newspapers at their kitchen table in a scene of domestic bliss. There are no wailing children tugging at their sleeves to demand another bowl of Coco-Pops, no slopped coffee stains seeping through the pages of the property section, no tell-tale glasses of Solpadine gently fizzing beside the congealed remains of last night's vindaloo takeaway. Yes, this pair seem to have it made. Then Mr A pipes up to read, to his beloved, a little snippet that's caught his eye. No, it's not the latest news on the doings of John McEnroe or Ken Livingston, not a sports result or a death notice or an update on the Middle Eastern crisis, no, not even the revised wording of the Nice Referendum. It is an advertisement.

Now, it is only in the fevered imagination of advertising executives that couples actually read advertisements out to each other – ads for bargain weekends away, ads for cut-price reading glasses – and receive a hugely enthusiastic response from the other party. So in this one, Mr Average's contribution goes a bit like this – Oh, look, pet, I see here that we can amalgamate all our loans into one big loan and reduce our repayments. On cue, Mrs Average turns cheerfully from the knitting patterns and says, that's great, dear, does it mean we'll be able to afford a new kitchen?

And then, on screen, we are given a breakdown of this couple's financial situation. And this is where the car crash analogy kicks in – this pair have debts that would make John Ruznak of AllFirst fame look like George Redmond, a prudent and frugal economist. They have a large mortgage, a car loan, holiday borrowings, miscellaneous squanderings and now all they're concerned with is cooking the books so they can wade further and deeper into debt over some shaker-style units and gleaming granite worktops. You already owe for your house, your car, your week in Marbella, your top-of-the-range plasma screen television and your sit-and-ride lawnmower – so why not have a new kitchen? In fact, have two.

This is not a cautionary advert, like the ones for seat belts or safe driving, not a warning against assuming a lifetime of repayments that will have the wolves and the bailiffs still sniffing around the doors of the Sunnyside Old Folks Home in forty years' time. Instead, the notion of assuming still more debts, while you are already up to your neck in borrowings, is presented not as a doomsday scenario but as a rather smart lifestyle choice. And so it seems to me there is just no such thing, any more, as living beyond your means.

Because you will always find a financial institution to repackage, reschedule and amalgamate your borrowings with the same sleight of hand that David Copperfield uses to make an elephant disappear – common sense tells you the jumbo hasn't really vanished into thin air, but the eye is more complicit in its own deception, especially if you are willing to be convinced.

A few generations back, when the country was a poorer place, people feared debt even more than bereavement, because of the stigma it carried, and only the most destitute bought goods or groceries on credit. Now, we are all actively encouraged to make merry with money we don't actually have, whether to travel to Japan for the World Cup or to buy a new car, because the success of all this financial fiction depends entirely on the mutual consent of Peter and Paul to be robbed and paid with the same coin, in turn. If they both get nervous and start looking for their money up front, that's when the whole lot comes crashing down.

This week the financial markets were rocked by the discovery that a huge Wall Street player called WorldCom Inc. was pretending to have billions of dollars, writing all those zeros into its accountancy figures, when the money didn't actually exist. And as long as the markets remained convinced that there was no jumbo-sized debt on WorldCom's books, everyone was happy. They were trading with money they didn't have, in the hope of sustaining the pretence long enough to conjure it up. Which doesn't, when you think about it, make them a whole lot different from legions of merry borrowers on a far more modest scale.

It's just a shame that WorldCom's chairman didn't read that Sunday paper advertisement, like cute Mr and Mrs Average, and amalgamate all his borrowings. Then, as well as being elected President of the New York stock exchange for his financial wizardry, he could probably have had a new kitchen as well.

June 2002

Yes, it must be love

WELL, I'M STILL not the better of last Tuesday's excitement. What a great day for the country, how proud we felt, how chuffed at all that international attention. Not for the football match, now, but the big celebrity wedding up in Monaghan.

Isn't it great that these wonderful, beautiful, rich, famous people can stoop to mingling with the likes of us – even if it is through a tight cordon of imported security goons and Gardaí funded by our taxes?

Aren't we blessed to be considered civilised enough to host a knees-up like this, even if the famous guests do speed past the gawping local peasants in their bullet-proofed, smoked-glass limousines? And how grateful we are for the crumbs of a photocall, when Sir Paul and his intended appeared at the gates of the castle so we could gaze upon them for free – yes, without having to pay for next week's exclusive picture spread in *Hello!* magazine. Is there no end to the bounty that has been heaped upon us by these gilded beings?

When it was suggested to Heather Mills, now Lady McCartney Mark Two, that she might have been marrying her wrinkly rocker for his money, she scoffed at the very thought. If that was her intention, she reasoned, she'd have married someone much wealthier. Sir Paul McCartney has a fortune in excess of £715 million sterling. Now if she was really after a life of luxury and fame, Heather would have set her cap at someone better-known, better-looking and better-off, the sort of chaps you find loitering on every street corner. Well, you can understand how an extra million or two would make all the difference between living in comfort and just muddling through. Yes, it must be love.

Still, even though the McCartneys are just about making ends meet, they did turn down a million-pound offer from *Hello!* for those photographs. Instead, they decided to provide a single picture from the wedding day to the media, in return for a donation to Heather's landmine charity.

I guess celebrities have to party too, and if you have the money, why not fly in pink peonies from the Far East and hire a private castle and stage a midnight fireworks display and honeymoon in the Hamptons. But I do wish they would stop trying to annex some charitable purpose in order to justify their self-indulgent excesses. If Paul and Heather really wanted to aid the landmine charity, they could just write a fairly substantial cheque – £715 million sterling would go a long way towards excavating the minefields and supplying the impoverished victims with plastic legs. Whatever happened to giving until it hurts – especially when we know she'd still need him, and she'd still feed him, if he had only £64 million.

We have become such docile observers of rich celebrities and their very public charities that we'll applaud the most ludicrous displays of greed and vanity masquerading as good works. Before the World Cup the Beckhams hosted a fund raising party for their famous friends. They allowed the television cameras in to film a scene of such preening, extravagant gluttony as to make the last days of the Roman Empire look like a temperance outing. They raised some £400,000 for charity, a figure that was announced and then solemnly applauded by guests, like Mohammed al Fayed and Richard Branson, who were probably carrying that much in loose change. Arrange these words in the proper order – camel, heaven, rich man, eye of needle. Jemima Khan, wealthy girl about town, is much praised for her fund-raising efforts to combat third-world malaria. And how much does she need to raise? A million pounds, or the annual wardrobe budget of any one of her pampered mates.

And there is no shortage, in this country, of celebrities and socialites to ponce around at fund-raising parties, wearing clothes and jewels worth more than they'd ever dream of donating. I could name them, but they'd probably sue me, and hand over the money to a charity with great fanfare.

One of the few famous people in the world who is genuinely using his influence towards a cause that could not be eased by personal generosity is Bono – his drop-the-debt campaign really has the capacity to improve the most desperate lives.

As for some others, they'd lend their names to any passing concern, so long as it offered a glittering celebrity ball and a chance to pose in a new designer rig-out. Do us all a favour, rich folks, spare us your bleeding hearts, your humanitarian campaigns, your cherished causes, your vegetarian curry – just write the cheque, and party in private.

July 2002

A precious life lost or a PR victory gained?

THE LITTLE BABY girl was carefully swaddled in her pastel blankets, her eyes closed and her lips slightly parted as though she was lost in the deepest and most peaceful sleep. And she was, of course, lost to the deepest sleep of all, because she had been tucked up safely in her humble cot when an Israeli missile strike crushed her home and killed her beneath the masonry last Monday. Her two-month-old body was paraded through Gaza City streets, last week, as Palestinians grieved for the many children killed as they slept during the attack that also killed the military commander of Hamas.

Only the bloodless little arms betrayed the fact that the child was dead, her head and face were unmarked by the fatal blow. She was a healthy and well-fed little girl, with soft plump cheeks and thick black curls, somebody had invested much hope and love and care into the eight weeks of that child's life. She was perfect, a perfect symbol of the heedless cruelty of men's wars, a perfect reproach to Ariel Sharon's triumphant claims for the success of the missile strike, a perfect totem for the Palestinians to wield before the world's press. An aunt of the little girl, one of the few family members who survived the bombing, was quoted in the papers last week as saying that it will only be in revenge, in further death and the bereavement of other families, that she will find any comfort. Which, more than anything that the politicians say about the difficulties of resolving the Middle Eastern crisis, speaks volumes for the unimaginable depths of hatred that keep it alive.

Anger is, of course, a most natural reaction to a sudden, deliberate death; a wish to visit the same pain on those who inflicted it upon you is a predictable instinct and one as old as the Biblical prescription of an eye for an eye. But it is when this desire assumes the status of a legitimate military response that all hopes of peace begin to look very desolate indeed.

To go to war, to wage a battle that will involve the loss of innocent civilian lives necessarily involves dehumanising the enemy. It requires the combatants to detach themselves from any human empathy with the other side. It demands that they be able to look upon images of their crushed homes, their shattered lives, their dead babies without flinching or regretting a single act. Connect, even for a second, on a fundamental personal level with the person whose life or whose family you have decided are worth sacrificing, and you are lost.

Looking at that little baby's body being hawked through the streets of Gaza last week, I couldn't help wondering what she really symbolised for either side. For the Israelis, of course, she was an embarrassment. It is far better to reduce your enemy and his children to unrecognisable blobs of carbonised matter – as was done with the target of Monday's strike – than to have them lying about looking intact and picturesque in death. But for the Palestinians, what was she? One precious, irreplaceable little life lost, or one precious public relations victory gained?

The military commander of Hamas, a group that has sent suicide bombers out to claim the lives of babies and children no more guilty of any crime against them than that little girl was to the Israelis, was staying in a residential area. He must, of course, sleep some place at night but, in the heat and fury of so bitter and dirty a war, it just doesn't make sense that such a high-profile and obvious target as the military commander of Hamas should be surrounding himself with his wife and his children, not to mention several unwitting families who were unaware that he was staying in the middle of their poor neighbourhood. Perhaps he thought it was a good place to hide – clearly he was wrong. Or perhaps the kind of people who consider suicide bombing a legitimate military manoeuvre feel that their personal safety is a poor second to the chance of a tactical 'spectacular'. If you are an advocate of the suicide strike as a means of causing maximum civilian casualty and outrage, then this was a win–win situation: if the Israelis held fire for fear of the international consequences of taking out a human shield made up of sleeping children, then all to the good. If they did not, and lots of poor children huddled on pitiful little mattresses in impoverished little homes were lost in the process, then at least you had an excellent photo opportunity. It is not always the enemies' children who are coldly sacrificed for a particular end, because when warring men lose the ability to feel the grief of a bereaved parent, it is gone and it doesn't really matter which side that parent is on.

Last week, the Northern Assembly Minister Nigel Dodds, went to the home of the Catholic family whose son was murdered in a random, drive-by, sectarian hit in Belfast a few days earlier. As a hard-line, anti-Agreement Unionist, he wanted to assure the family that their son's death furthered no cause he believed in, and to tell them that their loss gladdened no hearts amongst the ordinary decent Protestant people he represented. But as a father, on a level much deeper than the political divide could plumb, he wanted to tell them that he knew how they felt. He lost his nine-year-old son to spina bifida some time ago and standing there, in Gerard Lawlor's Catholic family home beside a young body in a coffin, beside the remains of another child's life into which another set of parents had invested such love and care and hope, he cried with them. His own child had died of natural causes; this was no occasion for a comparison of man-made outrage, just a sharing of parental desolation at the breach of the most cherished natural law.

There will be other children to bury in the North before Nigel Dodds' political career is much older, other families to grieve with, other funerals to attend in the future. Weeping and crying and expressing regret won't bring the dead back, as so many grudging geniuses brilliantly observed in the wake of the IRA apology. But when the hardliners from one community can lament and freely weep for the loss of a child from the other side, then it is not a future without hope. There was much wailing for that little dead Palestinian girl, hauled through the streets in her baby blankets, but very few genuine tears from the people whose regret might make a difference.

June 2002

Keeping up with the baby Joneses

IN A RECENT fit of spring-cleaning zeal, I burrowed under the stairs to dig out contributions for the Corpo's annual household junk collection. In there, hidden under broken lampshades and orphaned wellies, was the very first baby buggy I ever bought. When the lever on its side wore out – so that it tended to collapse at inconvenient times and deposit its wailing contents onto the pavement – the buggy was stowed, rather than dumped, with the vague hope of a repair job that never happened. And there it lay, taking up space that could have been used to store equally useless and redundant rubbish, because I didn't have the heart to throw it out. Grubby and tattered as it was, I could still recall how it looked when it was new and, long after the whiffs of mould and puke and fossilised Liga crumbs stamped their authority all over it, I could still remember how it smelled. It was the best and one of the most expensive buggies in the shop, coming with all manner of sunshades and rainhoods and panniers for nappies and bottles and creams and wipes, and with an endless variety of positions for baby to enjoy – sitting, lying, facing front or back or, when the lever snapped, sliding onto the wet ground. As cute childhood mementoes go, though, it was a tad bulkier than a pair of baby's first shoes, and so off it went in the household junk lorry last month. And the blow of parting with so symbolic an item as our first baby carriage was softened, somewhat, by the realisation that, if I do feel like coming over all dewy-eyed over a set of infant wheels, I've still got six other buggies to choose from.

That's right, at last count I discovered I had bought no less than seven different tot transporters in the course of producing four children, not counting carrycots and car seats. These included a double buggy, assorted umbrella buggies that were stolen, worn out or left behind on holidays, a three-wheel all-terrain buggy for negotiating the harsh tundra of Dublin 6, and a marvellous French wheeled contraption that folds into a backpack with a sunshade, a rain cover and an on-board satellite navigation system. Well, nearly. All of these were absolutely indispensable at the time of purchase, all of them neatly filling a gap in the fleet that had been unidentified until the new item was spotted in some catalogue, some shop window or some *Hello!* picture of Posh and Becks toting their sprog.

I am mildly relieved, though, to see that I am not alone and that, according to a new *Which?* consumer study of baby goods, your average doting couple spends around £3,500 sterling on nursery products for their newborn infant in the child's first two years. And I have to admit it is hardly news to me, either, to discover that most of it is unnecessary, overpriced and market-driven consumerism that has far less to do with making baby cosier than with making other parents jealous.

The authors of the *Which?* Guide to Baby Products blame the media and the retailers for manipulating the anxieties of vulnerable new parents by promoting and highlighting the designer wares of famous parents and trendy babies. These parents, say the *Which?* folks, are ripe for exploitation because of their understandable wish 'to give their babies the best start in life'. And so the nasty media and the cunning shopkeepers are contriving to convince these trusting souls that Junior will harbour a lifetime of resentment if he doesn't leave the maternity hospital snug in a Bill Amberg leather baby sling like the one Madonna bought for Rocco. Oh, come off it. Since when does 'the best start in life' inevitably involve the most expensive and the trendiest infant accessories? Most of us, including me with my seven different buggies, spent our own babyhood in a giant, old-fashioned pram, usually with a gaggle of siblings heaped at the other end. Not only did the same pram do an entire family, it probably went on to further glorious service in another household, before being stripped down, reconditioned and reincarnated as a go-cart. They were very comfortable, those old prams – they might not have folded flat to fit into the boot of a people carrier, or collapsed to the size of a golf umbrella or converted, at the flick of a lever, into a convenient wheelie rucksack device, but then small babies don't seem to set a lot of store by these refinements.

Changing lifestyles, of course, make for different requirements, and old-fashioned prams were bulky and impractical – but so also, according to *Which?*, are the most expensive of the three-wheelers, and they make shopping next to impossible. And yet the action of parents who pay out up to €1,000 for a titanium-framed, Land Rover-engineered jogging buggy that won't fit in the door of the local newsagents is blamed squarely on the media and the retailers, and not on the consumers who are daft enough to put image and style before common sense and economy.

You'd think that the *Which?* people, consumer experts that they are, would have figured out by now that a new baby offers an unequalled opportunity to make the most brash, the most visible and the most extravagant style statement without fear of reproach – you're not just showing off if you buy a €1,200 sheepskin-lined pushchair just like Jamie Oliver's, dear me, no, why, you're only trying to give your baby the best start in life, of course. A spokesman for Mothercare, reacting to the allegations of undue retail pressure on new parents, announced, 'Customers are not skimping at the economy end of products, because they realise each baby is so important ...' So there you are – 'skimp at the economy end' with a €99 pushchair, or – Heaven forbid – buy a perfectly serviceable second-hand buggy, and you are advertising your selfish negligence to the whole wide world.

The manufacturers and retailers certainly pander to the notion of the new, costly, state-of-the-art nursery gadget as a public expression of parental commitment, but then they would, wouldn't they – anything to shift a few more pastel-painted doodahs. But it is the parents themselves who fuel the whole fantasy with gusto. It is parents, with too much money to spend, who have demanded designer ranges of products that ought to be boring and practical and long-lasting: fashion and hard-wearing practicality are mutually incompatible qualities, so these things are designed to fall apart after a couple of years. That's the only reason I've gone through seven, honestly. With smaller families and greater affluence, there's just no demand for a pram that lasts two generations. At least, not unless Posh Spice has one.

June 2002

Romance with alcohol

NOW, LET'S SEE if I've got this straight. A while back, the Equality Authority ruled that publicans can't refuse to serve drinkers, whatever the day or the hour, on the grounds that they have children with them. Cue great outrage from publicans, and from most normal people who reckoned that this ruling was a godsend to the sort of negligent parents and guardians who can find the money for a night's drinking but somehow can't afford to pay a babysitter.

No, no, no, wailed the Equality Authority, that was not it at all, that was not what we meant at all. It doesn't mean that a publican can't REFUSE a drinker who has children with him – it means that a publican can't refuse a drinker who has CHILDREN with him. Clear on that? It was just a restatement of the existing law, a minor clarification really, nothing to get excited about. Publicans were still at liberty, of course, to refuse a drunken person on legitimate grounds – indeed they are, on pain of legal consequences, obliged to stop serving somebody who's had too much.

But no, of course the ruling didn't mean that a person who'd been refused because he'd had too much booze could then just go home, drag a toddler out of his cot, return to the pub toting said sleepy infant, and demand drinks on the house or else. Oh, and a small mineral and a bag of crisps for the child, and look lively about it.

But if it didn't mean any of the above – that drunks could use kids to blackmail publicans into continuing service, that stingy parents could use a smoky pub as a crèche with impunity – then why on earth does the new Justice Minister, Michael McDowell, feel it necessary to engage the parliamentary draughtsmen to compose a new law to rectify a situation that had simply been clarified? And if the law hadn't been changed by the Equality Authority ruling, how can it be changed back?

What is required here, of course, is for some sort of review or appeal procedure which would allow somebody, somewhere to declare that the equality ruling in question was an intensely stupid decision and that its consequences are the inevitable result of the most pointlessly distorting PC acrobatics, the bending-over-backwards of a legal position in order to validate a particular 'cultural' imperative by whatever means possible.

The man who took the action that gave rise to this finding – that a publican could not refuse service to a customer on the basis that he was accompanied by a child, whatever the hour of night – was a Traveller. He claimed he had been refused service because he was a Traveller. He also claimed that he had been refused because he had a child with him. In all logic, the Equality Authority couldn't find that his Travellerness was an issue, since he'd been served in the same pub many times before, including that day. But the facts remained that (a) he was a Traveller and (b) he had been refused service in a pub and so (a) plus (b) inevitably equalled (c), which was that somebody had to pay him compensation. And so he was awarded €1,000 because, in a bid to get the man to stop drinking and go home, a barman had pointed out that he was drinking in the company of a 13-year-old boy. When this was first drawn to his attention, the claimant had sent the boy outside to stand in the rain while he kept drinking. After the unfortunate child returned, that was when the dastardly, and costly, refusal of service was offered.

And just how costly it may yet turn out to be, not just to the publican but to innocent third parties, we don't yet know. Even Michael McDowell's impressive legal expertise is likely to be pushed to the limit in the framing of legislation which will reaffirm the publican's right to exercise control over the age, condition and conduct of clientele, without strengthening it unduly. Bars and restaurants in this country are not particularly child-friendly as things stand. A lot of eating-houses will grudgingly offer you a 'Kiddie's Menu', and charge you €7 or €8 for a small plate of chips and a couple of sausages, and €2.50 for the soft drink to go with it, but they won't have a high chair for your toddler. So you're condemned to a swift, expensive and stressful meal, holding a wriggling infant whilst trying to stop the others dunking reconstituted chicken nuggets in their coke, because the last thing these places want is for you and your noisy, sugar-crazed, high-carb'ed brood to get too comfortable and take up tables that could be better occupied by more lucrative clients.

If the Government really had to legislate for this daft Equality ruling, there was an opportunity to oblige licensed premises to facilitate family groups, perhaps to set aside areas for people with children in the same way as they can allocate space to folks with nicotine addictions. At the moment, and regardless of that Equality ruling, people with young kids are not heartily welcomed into pubs, and only the most hardened, most single-minded of drinkers would dream of bringing them for regular or lengthy periods. The irony is that these are precisely the sort of families that the Equality Authority was striving to facilitate with this ruling – the ones who least need encouragement.

But if publicans were compelled, by new legislation, to be more family friendly, to provide baby-changing facilities and suitable seating and family-designated areas with televisions that showed something other than 24-hour Sky Sports, then perhaps pubs might just become places where entire families could go to socialise with ease, rather than emporia for the determined and exclusive consumption of large quantities of strong drink. And if, in time, a new generation came to see alcohol as a normal, enjoyable but comparatively minor ingredient of a pleasant leisure time, rather than an end in itself, then we might start to breed a little normality into our deeply screwed-up national relationship with drink.

Instead, the end result of this entire farrago will be to make pubs and alcohol even more potently redolent of forbidden fruit for youngsters who may, under the new laws, be legally prohibited from entering licensed premises for the first time until they pass 15 – just the right impressionable age to embark on a routinely dysfunctional lifelong romance with alcohol. And all of this arises from an Equality Authority ruling that changed absolutely nothing. Just clarified a few points. And so we are all clear now, right?

September 2002

Enda's stand-up act

IT IS DIFFICULT to figure out what exactly Enda Kenny was thinking of, when he used the word 'nigger' in an anecdote told to a group of journalists earlier this month. What rush of blood to the head, you've got to wonder, convinced him that this would be a good career move? Was he pitching for laddish camaraderie, was he trying to debunk his rather prissy and buttoned-up image with a daringly risqué act?

If so, he has certainly emerged with all the smouldering menace and hip credibility of Tony Blair's holiday denim rig-out — look at me, I'm wearing sandals without socks, I said a naughty word in company, amn't I the wild one, all the same? Just because Kylie Minogue succeeded in reinventing a sweet, wholesome girl-next-door as a raunchy, pouting, edgy sex symbol doesn't mean the same thing will necessarily work for a nice, mild-mannered, cherubic Fine Gaeler — take off for a lost weekend with Ozzy Osbourne, Enda, and after the customs officials have uncovered a pair of fur-trimmed handcuffs in your carry-on baggage, then we'll be impressed.

More baffling, though, than Enda's motives in the first place, was the horrified and indignant reaction of those journalists who lived to tell the tale, not to mention the various spokespeople for the various causes who were wheeled out — once they had been brought round with smelling salts, obviously — to call for Enda's instant and ignominious resignation. It is not entirely clear what, precisely, are the implications of his crime that are so profound as to disqualify him from continuing in the role of a potential Taoiseach. With what, exactly, has he been charged?

He does, of course, stand accused of telling a joke that wasn't particularly funny to a group of people who have far more pressing calls upon their sense of humour. I have been in the company of male journalists who have sniggered, obligingly, at the most crude and offensive jokes recounted by persons in, and very, very close to, High Office. I have often heard gleefully relayed tales of vulgar, sexist and deeply misogynistic quips and antics by senior politicians and their hangers-on, though, oddly enough, these rarely made the front pages of the newspapers, even though they were at least as unfunny as Enda's stand-up turn.

Now, woman is the nigger of the world, to quote John Lennon's memorable phrase, and yet demeaning, viciously anti-women jokes and swear words are rarely seen as little more than valuable male-bonding material. When Roy Keane allegedly used the 'c' word to Mick McCarthy, which was then helpfully, if scantily, asterisked in the newspapers just in case anyone was at all confused about what he said, there followed much hilarity about Roy's evident ignorance of basic anatomy. Mind you, he had also advised the Ireland manager to stick something or other up his bollox, which did compound the case for Roy being no loss to the Chair of the Royal College of Physicians. But somehow swear words that offend and belittle women are perfectly freely employed as common currency, while terms that are seen to belittle other specified groups are fiercely and primly resisted. The context, of course, is relevant – the 'c' word is always nasty because it reduces women to a single biological function, whereas some black people claim a proprietorial immunity that allows them to use the word 'nigger' about each other. The newsreaders who quoted Enda Kenny last weekend weren't deemed offensive, so much depends on an objectionable context.

All of which brings us back to the puzzle of how, exactly, Enda Kenny transgressed in repeating what was, in the context, somebody else's use of the word nigger to a group of journalists in a setting that he imagined was private. Is the allegation abroad that he is, as a consequence of that ill-advised foray into comedy, a racist? If so, that accusation is clearly unfair and unfounded. You need slightly stronger evidence than an ill-advised joke to convict someone of an odious crime against humanity, and there is nothing in Enda Kenny's perfectly decent and respectable career path to date to substantiate such a charge.

Whatever it is that he has done wrong, it is evidently so serious that he has had to spend the week apologising for it – he phoned several relevant organisations over the past few days to assure them of his complete contrition.

But if the charge against him is not racism, then what is it? Sloppy and careless use of language by the leader of a major political party? Hardly, since we saw Bertie Ahern, at the September 11 commemorations last week, speak movingly about how the anniversary left him with an 'uneerie' feeling, and there was no national outcry at that particular linguistic atrocity. Mind you, Bertie would never be so dumb as to make a slip-up like Enda's in the company of such sensitive flowers as a bunch of political correspondents – he even managed to stymie their gloating over the Bertie Bowl climbdown by announcing the end of the project on the eve of the Twin Towers anniversary, thus relegating it to page two headlines next morning – even a year on, clearly September 11 is still a good day to bury bad news.

No, the real charge against Enda Kenny is not racism, not latent fascist anti-immigrant leanings, not secret membership of the National Front. He has been found guilty of having absolutely no media cop-on. Zero, none, zilch. He has shown no respect for the relentless integrity of the media corps, (who will fearlessly punish any, well most, PC lapses), not to mention a pitiful grasp of the rules of engagement between the press pack and the political spinners.

Because for all the media whingeing and lamenting about the unconscionable expense of the Government's army of special advisers and aides and shadowy consultants, woe betide any politician who dares open his mouth without conferring with at least a half a dozen highly-paid sages in advance –

especially on the matter of a spontaneous gag.

Bertie Ahern has more advisers than Tony Blair, a costly state of affairs but one, nonetheless, that surely militates against him ever finding himself in the company of journalists on an occasion when a dodgy quip about coloured folk might seem sidesplitting fare. In reality, Enda Kenny's unwise joke revealed nothing more sinister than a cheesy side, when we have developed a taste for political Easi-Singles – uniformly turned-out, rigorously inoffensive and bland, processed, packaged, and refined (whatever happened to Brian Cowen's accent?) so as to expunge any individual flavour. And, Enda – note to self – if you'd told that same quip with the 'c' word in the punchline, then you'd be a man, my son.

October 2002

How did we get to here, from there?

LAST WEEKEND, A young lad was stabbed to death in Dublin. He'd just been to the cinema with his girlfriend, they'd been going out together for three months. He was almost 17. A few days ago, a young fellow was brought before the Children's Court to face a charge of manslaughter. He's 15. The other day a man, who was sleeping rough in a shop doorway in Dublin city centre, was set on fire. The act was clearly premeditated – the arsonists had to go and get their hands on petrol or paraffin to burn him – and the culprits are believed to have been youths. They were, apparently, mirroring an incident in the film *A Clockwork Orange*, which was shown on television very recently. And in the Children's Court this week, a judge felt it necessary to tell the parents of three youngsters, who are facing very serious charges, that they would have to take a keen interest in their children.

How did we get to here?

Tucked into the pages of the *Irish Independent* today, sitting rather incongruously amid the stories of clerical child abuse and heroin dealers and Northern Troubles, is a relic of a very different time. The magazine *Ireland's Own* is 100 years old this year, and the free centenary edition marks that fairly impressive achievement.

It is ages since I've seen a copy of *Ireland's Own*, and opening its pages again is a bit like turning the handle on the door of a childhood bedroom, where everything stayed pretty much as you left it, old mementoes and pictures and forgotten trinkets all still in place, as if those innocent, abandoned treasures knew something you didn't – that you'd want to come back, some day, and find it unchanged.

Kitty the Hare, not looking a day older than she did thirty years ago, is back with another spine tingling tale of a rural haunting, faith and begannies she is, God between us and all harm, as sure as I'm telling you my story.

The feature on Irish family names and crests is there, along with the obligatory GAA item and, one of my particular favourites, the lyrics of popular ballads. People used to write to *Ireland's Own* – perhaps they still do – requesting other readers to supply them with the words of songs which they'd obviously intended to make their party pieces. Some of their mangled efforts to identify the desired song left you envying the audience who would eventually get to applaud them – I'd love to have heard a recital, for example, by the woman who wrote in seeking the lyrics to a song called, 'I Met Him on a Sunday and They Do Run, Run'. The pen-pals page was always worth a look, where new friendships required nothing more than a shared age group and a couple of hobbies in common – now, I believe, the page is popular with death row prisoners in the States, who get second-hand *Ireland's Own* from homesick Irish priests and nuns.

And at the back of the magazine, as always, there's the children's club. It has a small picture to colour by numbers, a crossword *as Gaeilge*, and a page of jokes: Man – can I put this wallpaper on myself? Shop Assistant: Certainly sir, but it'd probably look better on a wall. What's black and white and red all over? A sunburnt penguin. And if you want to join the children's club, it'll cost you just €7. I remember, as a kid, having a path worn to the village for postal orders to send off to these magazine clubs, and some of them send secret passwords and invisible ink and plastic wallets in brown paper packages that felt like Christmas morning.

From *Ireland's Own* you'll get a badge, a set of markers, a writing pad and your very own membership number, and you'll get a birthday greeting every year until you reach 16.

So in the Ireland still glimpsed through the pages of this 100-year-old magazine, teenagers read ghost stories, learn old ballads by heart and join a club to get a packet of markers and a scribble pad. When did that change? When did kids start to need mobile phones and computer games and designer runners just to keep up with their friends, when did the words of the songs they sing become crude and vulgar and even less tuneful than 'They Do Run, Run'? When did kids, still young enough to qualify for the birthday club in *Ireland's Own*, start carrying knives and weapons as a matter of routine? When did *A Clockwork Orange* replace Kitty the Hare as suitable entertainment for young minds, when did parents stop reading to their children and when did they start needing judges to tell them to keep an eye on their kids? When did children begin stealing and fighting and killing other kids who might, in the world that *Ireland's Own* once reflected, have been their pen pals?

How did we get to here, from there?

October 2002

Twisting the rule of thumb

THE PHRASE, 'A rule of thumb' is such a commonplace term that few ever stop to wonder where it originated. But in its time, the practice it defined was just as commonplace a part of everyday life as the phrase itself is today.

The 'rule of thumb' was coined by one Judge Butler, exactly 230 years ago. He was considering the circumstances in which a man might beat his wife, and the means which he might use. And so he decreed that beatings were perfectly permissible, so long as the husband did not use a rod which was thicker than his own thumb. And that was the rule of thumb, and that, too, was the official mindset which determined legal and social attitudes to domestic violence until relatively recently.

Up to nine years ago, for example, a man could not commit the criminal offence of raping his own wife. Rape, according to the statute books, could only be inflicted on a woman by a man other than her husband. Which was a lingering legacy of the view that a woman, once married, effectively became the property of her husband. The notion that this proprietary claim included an entitlement – indeed, perhaps even an obligation – to beat an obstinate woman was grudgingly reviewed over the generations since Judge Butler helpfully defined his rule of thumb, but the notion of a woman as her husband's sexual property was far more reluctantly relinquished.

Now any time statistics about domestic violence are discussed, you can fairly predict a reasonable intervention from those groups that support battered husbands, pointing out that women, also, physically abuse their spouses, that it is not simply a male offence. And this is true, just as there are women who murder their children, just as there are children who murder other children, just as there are sons and daughters who terrorise and abuse their parents.

And any time there is a review of the law, or a clawback of an accepted position, that appears to weaken the defence of female victims of domestic violence, you can fairly predict a chorus of lamentation from women's groups, warning of increased suffering and brutality and powerlessness as a result.

Just such a cacophony of outcry greeted last week's Supreme Court decision on the matter of ex parte barring orders. The court held that it was not just unconstitutional, but an affront to all the premises of natural law, to have an individual barred from home on the word of a hostile spouse, without a chance to enter a word of a defence or without even notice of the proceedings. Various women's groups responded by arguing that the vacuum which this ruling creates — apparently all ex parte interim barring orders may have been retrospectively voided – will leave women's lives at risk. Men's groups, on the other hand, welcomed the change in the law, citing many grievous injustices brought about by the impugned provision. The fact that both views have undeniable right on their side serves to underline society's dysfunctional attitude to a crime complicated by tribal memories of a historical imprimatur, on one side, and by the righteous indignation of the wronged on the other.

Certainly there are women who beat up their husbands. But international statistics suggest that they are rather in the minority — just 5 per cent, in fact, of domestic abusers are women. So a fairly convincing majority of spousal battery is carried out by men. And not just working-class men, or alcoholic men, or traveller men. Women's Aid concedes that most women who use their shelters are working class or travellers, for the simple reasons that they are the ones with less money and fewer options when they have to flee for their lives in the middle of the night. But from their experience, through the Women's Aid domestic helpline which takes some

8,000 calls a year, the group acknowledges that wife-beating is not specific to any class, or any creed, or any skin colour, or any socio-economic stratum. Nor is it always the work of drunken men, although incidences of wife-beating increase on occasions when more drink is consumed, like Christmas or, as recent statistics indicated, during the World Cup. So perfectly sober, perfectly respectable, perfectly professional men are just as likely to beat their wives, and their children too, as the drunken, unemployed, loutish stereotypes of popular fiction.

And all of the statistics you will find, from global studies on the subject of male domestic violence, tend to point in the same direction – that it is much more common than anybody suspects, that most of us are acquainted with a battered wife, whether or not we are aware of that fact, that women are frequently killed by violent male partners, and that most women who die in this way will have reported episodes of domestic violence in the past. In civilised Sweden, for example, one woman is killed every ten days by a man known to her. In a 1995 survey on domestic abuse carried out by Women's Aid, entitled 'Making the Links', it was discovered that 18 per cent of adult women in this country reported experiencing domestic violence of some degree. According to Garda statistics, a quarter of all the violent crime annually reported to them involves women making an allegation against male partners – husbands, boyfriends, sons.

So here's what we know, for sure: men beat up the women they profess to love, the women they married, the women they live with. And they do it quite frequently, and they do it for reasons that might be as trivial as the fact that they had a bad day at work and the dinner wasn't ready when they came home. And here's something else we know for sure: sometimes these battered women end up dead.

So against the backdrop of these facts, there is little doubt that extreme, emergency provisions are essential for the sake of these women's health, sanity and even their lives. And Section

4(3) of the Domestic Violence Act of 1996, specifically struck down by the Supreme Court last Wednesday, was designed to be just such a provision. It was drafted and intended for the most urgent and exceptional circumstances, and it permitted a legal pass that even the original draughtsmen acknowledged, in the surrounding caveats, was extraordinarily harsh.

In cases where there was an immediate and serious risk to the health and welfare of the spouse and any children involved, this section permitted such a spouse to go to the District Court and, without notice to the other spouse, to have him summarily barred from the family home. Without having a chance to defend himself, without even a clue of what was going on, such a spouse could return from work of an evening and find that he had committed a criminal offence by simply entering his family home.

Which is, indeed, draconian stuff, as the Chief Justice termed it last week – after all, the entitlement to know what you are accused of, the need for criminal laws to be clear and open so that citizens may abide by them, the opportunity to speak in your own defence before life-altering judgements are given against you, all of these are guaranteed under both Constitutional and ancient natural law principles.

So how come this piece of legislation slipped through all the built-in Constitutional safeguards, past even a President who was a Constitutional law expert, to be passed as recently as 1996? If it was so clearly, obviously, fatally flawed, how on earth did it survive until now?

The answer to that is probably an uncomfortable one for both the women's support groups, and the family courts, to consider. Because this is, arguably, a perfectly legitimate piece of legislation that has been rendered grotesque by sheer abuse – by women, by their lawyers, by the judges. A powerful piece of legislation clearly designed to be used sparingly and in the rarest circumstances has been rendered unjust and unworkable because those employing it never accorded it the respect it deserved, never exercised the restraint it required, and used it as a weapon instead of a shield of last resort.

The Supreme Court pointed out that the legislation should have had a specified and prompt return date – perhaps seven days, perhaps just 24 hours, perhaps the duration of a court sitting – by which time the other spouse would have to be notified and given an opportunity to make his case in court. It had no such time limits, but then, it ought to have been clear as day to the lawyers applying for it, and to the District Justices granting it, that the shortest possible time limit was implicit in its design. Instead, ex parte interim barring orders were granted, matters could be wilfully dragged out, and months could pass before the husband got a chance to come before the courts to argue his case.

And it seems to have been an especially easy weapon to abuse. Last year, more than 1,000 interim ex parte barring orders were granted – that's one thousand people, almost exclusively men, summarily evicted from their homes and separated from their children without a hearing, without a defence, without even notice of the proceedings.

That seems to have been the standard level of use of this provision and yet, according to statistics compiled by Women's Aid, that figure represents just one third of all the applications for interim ex parte barring orders. Which means more than three thousand spouses went to court claiming they were at serious, immediate risk of significant harm. But when those cases went to full hearing, if they ever did, only around 600 were found to be entitled to a barring order, once the other side got a hearing. Which would seem to suggest that, in thousands of cases last year alone, these contentious provisions were wielded unjustly and irresponsibly, argued for by lawyers, pleaded for by clients, entertained by District Justices.

So here's what we know for sure: most domestic abuse is perpetrated by men. Most battered spouses are women. Where women are the victims of violent attacks, even murders, these crimes are most often carried out by men they know. Wife abuse was socially and legally tolerated until relatively recently.

And women and their lawyers have abused legislation designed to redress and make amends for this situation and, as a result, have inflicted unconscionable suffering on thousands of innocent men and, perhaps, deprived genuinely needy women of an essential recourse. Physical violence is not the only form of marital cruelty, attrition and abuse.

December 2002

Bob McCartney's Christmas cake recipe

EARLIER THIS YEAR I was on the panel of the BBC's *Let's Talk* programme in Belfast – their version of our *Questions and Answers* – and among the other guests that night was Robert McCartney, QC, the leader of the UK Unionist Party. Now it would be fair enough to say that he is not a man with whom I would expect to share much common ground, political or otherwise – I suspect I know where he stands on the National Question, and it certainly would not be shoulder to shoulder with me. So even though I had never met Mr McCartney before, I just knew I wouldn't like him at all, at all.

I really liked him. He turned out to be one of the most gracious, warm, entertaining and humorous men I've come across in quite a while. We might indeed differ on the matter of the fourth green field, but when it came to Christmas cake recipes, we discovered, we were twin souls. Over a few glasses of wine in hospitality afterwards, it emerged that Bob, as I call him myself, bakes an assortment of festive confections to distribute to those friends on his Christmas gift list who are the hardest to buy for – the sort of wealthy chaps you'd expect a well-heeled QC to knock about with, the men who have everything. Apparently they lap up Bob's Christmas cakes like they were mother's milk, and think warm thoughts about him for the rest of the year.

As it happens, I also bake Christmas cakes for selected friends who have everything, including, fortunately, the robust digestive system of an empty garbage truck. If you soak the fruit in a mixture of tinned strawberry juice and rum for a full week until the sultanas swell to the size of marbles, I find, you will have a dark moist cake that will last months and months, you will have to dodge Garda checkpoints after a single slice, and any left over wedge will serve as a sturdy door stop come the following November.

After we had discussed the relative merits of marzipan icing, and resolved the old 'Ginger – Fresh or Dried?' Debate, Bob expressed polite interest in my strawberry-juice-and-rum method, but decided he would stick with his Bushmills and grated nutmeg.

Watching him stalk out of Parliament Buildings in Stormont last night, as a protest over the contents of that juicy, wayward briefing document, I wondered if he had his Christmas cakes made. Were they sitting in fragrant tins, giving off that wonderful Christmas cake scent of cinnamon and wood smoke and incense and warm whiskey, waiting to go to deserving homes? Was he tempted to throw in a tin of Chivers strawberries, juice and all, and dowse the fruit for a week? And was he perhaps wondering how he was going to find the time to finish the icing, when that unexpected gift from some careless civil servant brought all proceedings at Stormont to a premature end and let him home early?

The journalists who found the document, helpfully marked with the word 'Secret' just in case they had managed to overlook it in the press room in Farmleigh last Wednesday, must have felt that all their Christmases had come together. For the Anti-Agreement Unionists, though, the offering of this sensitive manuscript really was the gift for the men who had everything. The Anti-Agreement lobby don't need provocation to declare the whole business dead in the water – but evidence that the Irish Government suspects the IRA is still primed for action was a positive embarrassment of riches. The fact that the document also concluded that the Provos are no threat to the process was easy to ignore, since that probably counts with the Anti-Agreement types as still further proof of the IRA's perverse malice. In reality, the observations about the ceasefire probably angered David Trimble far less than the description of his party as 'dysfunctional', a comment he chose to disprove by running away with the ball and sulking. But perhaps a spell of seasonal cheer might mellow the mood of the Unionist leaders, and they may indeed return from the eastern horizons, come early January, as three wiser men.

And anyway, maybe David Trimble had Christmas cakes of his own to ice – he does enjoy cooking and he is a devoted family man. In his home, and in Bob McCartney's, and in mine, and in yours, I hope, all the cares and concerns of the working life will be suspended, for the next few days, while families set about rituals that change little across creeds and continents. Whether your job is lofty or humble, whether you are a brain surgeon or a bin technician, for the next week or so you'll be a Christmas tree lights repair person, a turkey collector, a Brussels sprout peeler, a drinks pourer, a guest greeter, a ham slicer, a dishwasher. Nothing, for a day, will be quite as important as making the spuds crispy on the outside, and no professional or political setback quite as disappointing as cutting the cake and finding that the fruit has sunk because some idiot told you to throw in a tin of strawberries.

There is no better time of year to dwell on all that we share, regardless of beliefs, and to put our differences in perspective. I hope all of Bob McCartney's festive baking turns out a treat, even if he budged not an inch on the marzipan question. Christmas cakes are a bit like people, you see – no matter how crucial one ingredient might seem in the mix, the basic recipe is much the same, slice them and in their hearts they'll look alike, and when they mellow a little, well, then it's hard to tell them apart.

2003–2005

January 2003

Grown-up pester power

EVERY YEAR, WHEN the first batch of Christmas toy adverts hit our screens around mid-September, the cry goes up – 'Ban them, ban all advertisements aimed at children, remove this source of pressure on overstretched parents to satisfy their kids demands for the latest gimmick/electronic game/baby doll.' The value of so-called 'pester power' to the retailers and the manufacturers of plastic rubbish is annually lamented though, arguably, overstated. What the moaners are slow to concede is that small children are actually quite easily distracted from their hearts' desires by a determined parental campaign, come Christmas morning they are just as likely to be pleased by a surprise substitution as they would have been by the coveted and more costly alternative, and, if all else fails, they are basically powerless in the face of the word 'no' used early and often.

The same, however, cannot be said of the children whose turbo-charged pester power is currently being engaged by an advertising campaign currently running on television. These adverts press all the same buttons as the slickest of Christmas marketing, contriving to manipulate all the same pressure points of parental guilt and obligation while planting in the fertile ground of young minds the suggestion that a prize is certainly within reach if it is conceivably within their parents' means.

The advertisements, for an EBS 'product' which facilitates the re-mortgaging of family homes so that the departing fledglings might raise the deposit for their own fresh nests, shows an elderly father and a twenty-something son seated at the kitchen table of a modest home. It has the feel of a dramatic scene in which the most grievous of family news is being revealed and, in a way, that sense is appropriate: the older man looks troubled and anxious, the son a tad defiant but also on edge, and the father is indeed being told of a scenario that will change and diminish the quality of his life. He is being asked to re-mortgage the home to raise €20,000 for his son's new house, and he looks just as trapped and troubled by the suggestion as you might reasonably expect.

As advertising campaigns go, the EBS strategy is about as cynical, calculated and grasping as it is possible to imagine, and makes the most high-octane Christmas toy ads look like mild endorsements on a parish newsletter. Small kids who set their hearts on expensive gewgaws at Christmas time can at least be deflected with promises that Santa Claus will certainly do his best – the same line probably wouldn't wash with a 25-year-old with a booking deposit burning a hole in his pocket, a fiancée in tow and a glowing prospectus for a new townhouse clutched in his sweaty paw. And the ad makes it sound so easy, so painless all round: after all, runs the unspoken suggestion, what do the old pair need all that lovely equity for, anyway, look at the cut of that old codger, one foot in the grave, would it kill him to find €80 a week to pay off a miserly little mortgage, it's not as if he's going to need it for mobile top-ups and Smirnoff Ices down the Spy Bar? His house cost him less than the price of a foreign holiday when he bought it back in the early 1970s, what would he know about trying to find a quarter of a million yo-yos for a flimsy terraced two-bed with no parking space and scaled-down furniture in the showhouse? You need help, he can deliver and, for the EBS, paydirt – two shiny new mortgages where previously there was none.

The ad operates on the number of different assumptions, some of them unhealthy and even corrosive, positively designed to generate resentment and ill-will in the sterling cause of generating extra revenue for a lending institution. This current generation of teens and twenty-somethings is probably the first, in as many decades as you care to review, that does not automatically have the expectation of doing better than their parents. Adults in their mid-fifties, perhaps married for 30 years, lived through the hungry 1980s and were well poised to benefit from the boom years of the Celtic Tiger. Surviving hardships and lay-offs they most likely had their mortgages paid off, they had a chance to educate their children to a level that was, for a change, constrained only by academic and not financial potential, unlike the obstacles their own parents had to face. And, for the last eight to ten years, as their youngsters grew beyond the need for babysitters and endless ferrying to football games and ballet classes, they've had a little freedom and the means to enjoy it. Perhaps they bought their first ever brand new car in the millennium year, like so many others, maybe they've added a conservatory or a hot tub or a small beachfront mobile home in Wicklow to their inventory of luxuries, and they have the time and the spare cash for the odd sunshine holiday. They may not have had it easy as young marrieds, but at least they could buy a home and run a car without too much peer pressure to ensure it was spanking new, they didn't have the expense of mobile phones or DVDs or alcopops, and, crucially, they were on the right side of the economic incline, looking forward to better times instead of looking back at them.

In their forties, financially more comfortable and emerging from house-purchase debt, they could consider returning to education, doing some computer training, re-skilling for a labour market that was beginning to boom.

Their children, by contrast, won't have it quite so good. They have no real expectation of securing jobs that are significantly better than those their parents held, they cannot expect a bigger car, a nicer house, better holidays, a rosier future in a more peaceful world. Their outlook on all fronts, in fact, is pretty grim, which makes them all the more susceptible to subliminal marketing urges to make the old folks cough up some compensation.

Which rationale derives directly from another assumption that the EBS's objectionable little campaign is making – that parental obligation never ends. That it is the parents' duty to do all within their power to ensure that their child does, in fact, better himself and improve on his parents' own lot, and that this obligation supersedes any claim those parents might ever have to some comfort or peace of mind themselves. So you're just coming up to retirement, you've a few bob to spare after raising and clothing and feeding and educating your children through twenty-odd years of damned hard work and worry, and you had some vague intention of getting a life, and actually enjoying it with your spouse for as long as you've got your health? All of a sudden, that prospect has been recast as selfish, thoughtless and downright negligent, and older people made prey to emotional blackmail from adult children and ruthless extortion from opportunistic financial institutions.

The son in the current advertisement looks to be in his mid-20s. That means he was probably working – if his parents haven't already forked out to equip him with a professional qualification –through the last five boom years. That means he had a chance to make a fairly decent income, thank you very much, and every opportunity to put aside, say, five grand a year – that'd be £100 a week, or less than the cost of a mobile top-up and a decent night out. But he didn't, perhaps because the vested interests that now want him to put the squeeze on his parents are the very same ones who once encouraged him to splash his cash on swanky cars and exotic holidays (using, of course, their bespoke tailored financial packages). Life is tough, kids, and not likely to get any easier, get used to it. And for parents who find themselves being invited to small urgent family conferences by pestering kids, like that poor old fellow

in the EBS advert, here's a way out – tell them to write to
Santa Claus.

February 2003

She was with her father ...
of course she was safe

LITTLE DEIRDRE CROWLEY'S eyes were difficult to meet, as
she beamed eagerly from the front pages last week alongside
the inquest reports of her obscene death. Those bright eyes
caught mine, many times before from many other newspaper
pages and television images, during the months she was
missing. Alive with merriment and the childish certainty of
being loved, that enchanting little face was just about the only
reason the story of her abduction registered at all, however
briefly and inadequately.

I remember seeing that photograph, when she was still
alive and missing, I recall briefly checking for an update on
the story, and then rapidly losing interest, even feeling a little
impatient that an instinctive concern for a child in danger had
been engaged without real cause. She was with her father, for
Heaven's sake, it was simply a domestic dispute, awful for those
involved, of course, heartbreaking for her mother who was
missing out on those irreplaceable early months of a child's
journey into life, but still. She was with her father, not like
those other abducted children whose images become familiar
during the few fraught weeks of fruitless hope for their safety,
before their bodies are found. She was with her father, it wasn't
as if she was in any danger and, knowing how the secretive
family courts work in this country, who could guess at the
rights and wrongs of the custody matter?

So her disappearance never seemed quite as serious as the

plight of children abducted by strangers, and so I doubt that I was alone in failing to make a mental 'snapshot' of Deirdre's face and keeping an idle eye out for her in crowded places. Suspected sightings of missing English children are frequently reported here, even when those unfortunate kids have travelled no further than a deserted wood close to where they vanished, because we so much want to help. We keep our eyes peeled in the hope of saving another child from the fate of James Bulger, who was spotted by no less than 38 adults on his way to his death, and of easing the parental anguish it is all too easy to imagine. But Deirdre Crowley moved amongst us like a little ghost, up and down the country in the company of her father, for a year and a half.

You might have seen her on a train or a bus, I might have stood beside them in a line for a McDonalds Happy Meal, or a supermarket checkout or a cinema queue, we might have walked by the pair of them on any street of any country town, and we never noticed. Because she was with her father, at the very least she was safe, and who really wanted to get involved in a row between parents?

The details of the double shooting that killed Deirdre and her father, as they emerged in evidence to the inquest last week, were haunting and harrowing. It appears she died instantly from a sawn-off shotgun blast at close range, but that he did not. He almost missed, in fact, and died more slowly from shock and haemorrhage. It is disturbing and pointless to contemplate what demons drove a father to put a gun to the face of his little daughter, the child whose summer sandals he'd strapped on that morning and whose toys and food he'd bought and whose crayon drawings he had admired, and to pull the trigger. What despair, or spite, compelled him to take her with him once he had resolved to kill himself, who knows? But it is almost as distressing to dwell on what might have happened had Christopher Crowley survived.

Ten months ago, a man walked free from a court after he was convicted of the manslaughter of an 18-month-old baby by stabbing him nine times in the neck with an army knife. The jury did not set him free – manslaughter is the second most serious offence against the person on our criminal statute books – but the judge suspended a five year sentence, in the 'unique' circumstances where the man had claimed 'sane automatism' to account for an evidently purposeless and uncharacteristic attack. He was very drunk on a cocktail of cider, beer and poitín at the time, and had no recollection of killing the baby. Who is to say that the toddler didn't wake up when he was moved from his makeshift bed to make room for his drunken uncle at 5 a.m. – babies have a very flexible idea of what constitutes getting-up time – and cry until he was silenced? Parents with no criminal record are regularly before the courts for injuring and sometimes killing crying children in fits of drunken or stressed-out frustration. They are not always treated as leniently as John Reilly was, although the same assumption – that they could not truly have wished to injure their child – often goes a long way towards their absolution.

Almost one child a month was murdered in this country over the past two years, most of them by close family members. Police in the North, at the moment, are conducting DNA tests to locate the mother of a newborn baby girl found stabbed and bludgeoned in County Down last March. She is being asked to come forward voluntarily and is promised compassion – she must be very 'confused', the police say. But somebody was sufficiently composed to stab and batter and dump that baby.

Christopher Crowley must have been very confused, too, but he was also composed enough to acquire a shotgun, saw it down and keep it with him, on all of his travels with his little girl, in anticipation of the day he would use it to deprive her mother of ever looking into her charming little face again. He had no record of criminal behaviour, the killing of his child was so unforeseeable and out of character that, had he survived, he might well have been able to put up a convincing defence of temporary insanity, diminished responsibility, sane automatism.

Where children die violently in this country – through deliberate or negligent action – the adults to whose care their safety was entrusted are overwhelmingly likely to be to blame. And yet our judicial system treats them more leniently, not less, in spite of so monumental a betrayal of their children's trust. Because they must have been confused, because they were genuinely remorseful after the event, because they had relinquished control, through excess alcohol, over their motiveless actions, our prosecutors and courts are more forgiving of them, and not less.

But perhaps if there was more candour about the risk which some parents and relatives pose to their children, more honesty about the reality of that threat and how it is far more to be feared than the random malevolence of strangers, and perhaps if it was more harshly punished and not treated as a baffling and rare aberration, then we might all have looked out for Deirdre Crowley a little more carefully.

March 2003

War Babies

ON THE FRONT of the Trócaire box, distributed for this year's Lenten collection, there's a picture of two grubby little Guatemalan kids. The girl, whose wary, hopeful smile shows a mouthful of weak and crooked teeth, is ten years old and, on her back she's carrying her little brother, a toddler swaddled in a bundle of gaudy rags. Now, nothing quite catches a child's attention like the gaze of another youngster, and so my own kids are fascinated by the little Guatemalans, and intrigued by the notion of their need.

One day we discussed what they might buy, this girl and her baby brother, when they get all those coins unearthed from sofa cushions and donated from piggy banks and left over from shopping trips. It's hard to impress on an Irish child that there are some their age in the world who might actually want a pair of shoes or a warm sweater or medicine or food that wasn't sweet and sticky. So they listened politely to my suggestions for what Maria and Miguel might buy when they get their Trócaire money, and then they added their own: a Harry Potter video, a pogo-stick, an Easter egg, a Game Boy cartridge. These, to my children, are the limits of material desire, and they simply cannot put themselves inside the skin of these hungry, shabby, poor little creatures who will never enjoy a book or a toy or a childhood, never see a television or a Disney film or a classroom, never know what it's like to have a solid home or a carefree day or a full belly.

When news of the bombing of Iraq came through in the early hours of yesterday morning, for some reason it was the faces of Maria and Miguel, the waifs on the Trócaire box and half a world away in Guatemala, that came to my mind. I have seen so many pitiful, ragged, grubby Iraqi children smiling those same puzzled, timid smiles at Western cameras this past while, that they have all fused into a composite image of doomed, bewildered innocence. The little girl with her baby brother on her back, and a responsibility beyond her years on her shoulders, she trudges through every war zone, every famished landscape, every freezing refugee camp. She is there amongst the street children of Brazil, the child soldiers of Sierra Leone, the African Aids orphans, the ghosts of Sarajevo. She always wears the same odd uniform of home-made hand-me-downs, in dirt-dimmed jewel colours, mixed with the tattered remnants of Western cast-offs – all cartoon characters and sassy slogans – salvaged from charity hampers. She is curious and trusting when strangers come to her village or her encampment – she has yet to learn contempt for well-dressed Western visitors with their cameras and their consciences because she is a child, after all, with a child's resilient expectation of love and protection. Statistically, she is unlikely to live long enough to discover that she is wrong.

No more than my own kids can imagine the deprivation of these countless hungry, needy children, I cannot put myself in their mothers' shoes. I know how it feels to watch a baby show the first signs of a common illness – a chest infection or a stomach bug. Sleepless nights, you think, a lot more laundry to be done, a run on the disposable nappies, doctors' visits to be arranged, cranky infants to be comforted. But to live with the knowledge that such trivial ailments could bring death, all for want of a few cents' worth of everyday drugs – that, I just can't contemplate. And that has been the daily reality for Iraqi families for the past 12 years. UN sanctions meant hundreds of thousands of tots died from the simplest complaints, but the same privations did not stop Saddam Hussein amassing a multi-billion dollar fortune to become one of the world's richest men.

The hospitals of Iraq are quiet places, lacking the frantic bustle of normal emergency wards because there's no call for urgency when you don't have the drugs or the tools to save lives. But on the fifty new and lavish palaces that Saddam Hussein built himself since 1990, work went on unhindered.

I envy the certainty of those who know that this war is right, or that it is wrong, who are convinced that it was avoidable or inevitable, who have no doubt that it is a necessary humanitarian evil, or an exercise of greedy belligerence. I know I wish the allied forces hadn't gone to war, but now I hope to God they win. I know I'd rather they didn't have to use Shannon Airport to get to the Gulf, but I don't want their forces hindered by vain and foolish political posturing here. And this, I know for sure . . .

The little girl with her baby brother on her back, she will die many times over during the course of this war. She'll be trapped in bombed-out shelters, poisoned by tainted water, starved, frozen, gassed, burnt. And when it's all over, she'll still be there, foraging in the smouldering ruins, searching for dead parents, queueing for protein biscuits, hunting down a clean drink for her little brother, and smiling her hopeful smile for Western cameras amid a landscape scarred with broken houses, broken lives, broken promises.

May 2003

'Tipping is not a city in China'

THERE'S A LITTLE café down the road from where I live, all skinny lattes and panini wraps, very popular with local arty types, but not exactly designed for women with baby buggies. From time to time, though, I have braved the obstacle course of chrome stools and granite counters and pitying looks to eat there. For breakfast they do a bagel and cream cheese, the famous snack food of New York Jewish origin, close your eyes and you might even think you were in Manhattan. So long as you have never actually been in Manhattan, of course. As I recall, the menu describes a hot toasted bagel 'smothered' with cool cream cheese. In reality you get tepid bun and a mean little sachet of Philadelphia, and you have to do the 'smothering' yourself. At which point you discover that there's scarcely enough cheese to cover the bagel's modesty, let alone to suffocate it in creamy ecstasy.

For this treat, you pay just under €4 – not exactly fast food restaurant prices, even though they operate the McDonald's principle of clearing your table before you've finished chewing so you don't get too cosy. When I went to pay for this overpriced food and underwhelming service last time, I noticed the following little sign on the cash register. 'Tipping', it said, 'is not a city in China'. So. As well as paying over the odds for a pre-packed cheese portion and a bla, as they say in Waterford, with ideas above its station, I was expected to cough up even more for the privilege of being sold short and hustled out.

Which, I realised as I dutifully rummaged for some spare change, these business folk are perfectly entitled to expect. Of course we will pay handsomely for shoddy quality and off-hand service, after all, we have Form. We've done it before, we do it all the time, we are fools with our money as we are fools with our votes, easily parted from both by the most insulting and transparent of promises. Lashings of cream cheese on your bagel, an end to hospital waiting lists, good educational facilities for your kids, real chocolate on your €3 cappuccino – yes, we'll have some of that, thanks very much, just show us where to pay and here's a little something for yourself.

So Health Minister Martin has just realised, to his wide-eyed astonishment, that people are still waiting for hospital treatment, more than 20,000 of them, with no sign of the lists abating, more than a year after he promised they'd be whittled to nothing.

And Education Minister Dempsey has just realised, to his gobsmacked amazement, that teenagers from disadvantaged homes are still not making it to university in healthy numbers. His solution is to stigmatise those students who do take up third-level places as the pampered offspring of fat-cat spongers who must be penalised for the inequalities in our education system because they must be to blame. He is targeting, he says, the sort of people who enjoy two foreign holidays a year – well, if you can stretch to a second package trip to Majorca in 12 months there must be something fishy about your finances, right enough – and so he is proposing to end 'free' education for the middle classes.

This idea that education is 'free' will probably come as news to the same middle classes, who have for years been labouring under the illusion that they've been paying for it out of their taxes.

But it seems to me that our State agencies have a curious snobbery about the notion of 'free' anything. If you don't pay extra for your health care, your transport, your kids' education, if, instead of going private you expect the state to fund these services in a climate of crippling direct and indirect taxation, then you are not just claiming what is your due – instead you are a charity case, a supplicant, a cheapskate, a person who thinks Tipping is a city in China, and you deserve all the brusque, off-hand, condescending service and the shoddy quality that they feel like dishing up.

You will wait in line for your hernia operation and like it, you'll send your children to rat-infested schools and be grateful for the chance, you'll stand in the rain waiting for the 16A without a murmur because, in the words of that 1980s pop song, only losers take the bus. After you've paid up, first in tax on your income and then in VAT on just about everything else you need to survive, you will be moved along so the next customer can be fleeced. If the education Minister was honest about why so few poor kids go on to university, he'd admit it has nothing to do with the middle classes shirking their fees, and everything to do with the rip-off mentality that pervades this state.

They don't go to university because they fell through the net long beforehand, when they left primary school unable to read and write, because they were among the 10 per cent of Irish school kids who are functionally illiterate in sixth class, because they are hustled out to make way for the next batch without anyone bothering to check if their needs have been met. So our state services have much in common with our rip-off restaurants – they'll serve you when it suits them, they'll charge you what they like, they'll dish up any old muck, you'll swallow it and pay for it and nobody cares if you leave hungry or unsatisfied . . . oh, but don't forget to tip.

November 2003

Someone else's war

NOTE TO WOULD-BE dictators everywhere – please think twice before putting a giant statue of yourself in the capital city of the country which you intend to oppress. You are just asking to have it toppled and danced upon by thankless peasants and invading forces, and it all makes for a very unseemly photo opportunity indeed.

The sight of Iraqis whacking Saddam Hussein's fallen bronze face with the soles of their shoes – a devastating Arab insult, it seems – and of his statue teetering and crashing amid a cheering crowd had to be one of the most satisfying sights of the year. And it was also one of the images of this high-visibility war that needed the least explanation. Since the conflict began, three weeks ago, the problem of mediating the visions of war that landed in our living rooms seemed to be a major concern for many parents. How to explain the bombing and bloodshed to their children, how to protect kids from adult anxieties and tensions about a major world conflict – these questions filled many thousands of column inches over the past few weeks.

At one point, it seemed to me that I was the only female journalist in the country whose pre-school kids had not piped up, in their charming little lisps, to ask profound and searching questions about the war in Iraq and I was growing weary of all these agonised opinion pieces about how the war coverage might traumatise our pampered Western children – what a luxury, when you think of it, to have to worry only about the images of cruelty and suffering, and not the realities.

Which is not to say that children don't register memorable images of all kinds, and ask questions that are sometimes difficult to answer – they are often far better at cutting to the chase than adults. So the footage of Saddam taking a fall in central Baghdad on Wednesday was wonderfully simple to explain – more challenging, though, were the pictures of two innocent children whose destruction was equally, sadly, all too clear.

The first was 12-year-old Ali, the little Baghdad boy who lost his parents, and both his arms, to an American bomb. Poor little Ali was a heartbreaking sight as he lay with his bandaged stumps on a grubby bed in a dingy hospital, weeping with the pain of his burns and his loss. The kind nurse mopping his face was a pitiful reminder of all that's been stolen from him by other people's battles – he has no parent to dry his eyes, no hands of his own to make that most simple and affecting of childish gestures, to wipe a little fist across a snotty, tearstained face.

His was precisely the kind of war story that had the concerned parents in a flap – should we let our children see Ali, would they be frightened and upset, would they worry for their own safety? And yet there was no such agonising over the tale of the second child who made smaller headlines here this week – perhaps because she was a bit too close to home.

Katelyn Ryan is standing before a Christmas tree, wearing a blue tracksuit she probably inherited from an older sister – you can just about see her little fists below the ribbed cuffs. She is a face from a family snapshot of a happier time, a little out of focus, a little dazzled by all the festive gaiety. Unlike Ali's case, the cameras did not visit her hospital bed, though her grandmother's description conjured images of injuries no less horrific than those of the small Iraqi boy. Katelyn's face had been charred beyond recognition in a petrol bomb attack on her home, her eyes ruined, her little hands burned off. She, like her baby sister and her mother, were the innocent victims of someone else's battle. Some coward, some thug threw a petrol bomb into the small terraced house where she was sleeping on Sunday morning. After two days in agony, little Katelyn died on Tuesday afternoon.

Two children, thousands of miles apart, both sleeping peacefully in their beds when someone else's war burst into their homes and destroyed their lives. So why is it that Ali is the only one whose image seems to trouble us, why do we worry about what to tell our children of him, and not of Katelyn?

I was able to explain to my children what happened to Ali, upsetting though the story was. I could say his country was ruled by an evil man who tortured and murdered and starved his people, that other men had come to drive him out, that they used big deadly bombs to crush his palaces, and that they didn't take enough care to protect little Ali and his family.

I couldn't tell them what happened to Katelyn, because I don't know. Who are they, these cowards and thugs who treat infants as collateral damage in their schoolyard squabbles? For what stupid, petty, trivial, inbred little spat did Katelyn die? Where do they get these weapons, their guns and their petrol bombs and their hunting knives, and how do they manage to wield them with such licence? What sort of communities shield and tolerate these murderous savages? Is it too unfashionable, too illiberal to demand that secure places be funded and built to lock them up for a lengthy spell? How do we shield our children from dangers that are real and immediate in a society that permits people like this to walk the streets, and exonerates them with bleeding heart excuses, about their low self esteem, their social isolation, their attention deficiencies? These are tough questions – no wonder we'd prefer to dwell on sorrowful images from distant Iraq.

February 2004

Conspicuous Compassion and covering your exposed ass

FORGET ABOUT YOUR conspicuous consumption, darlings, that's so nineties now. The new trend for Cheap Chic – wherein the truly affluent and savvy shop in High Street stores for designer knock-offs because they've really nothing to prove – has made flaunting it the sole preserve of the bling-bling Beckhams and all those sad souls who try too hard. No, thrift is the new retail therapy and the hippest way to allay your status anxiety these days is through Conspicuous Compassion. A new British study has concluded that the trend of supporting high-profile causes, wearing coloured ribbons and John Rocha-designed brooches to proclaim your concern about breast cancer/racism/animal rights/third world debt, has matured into a fully-fledged fashion. Conspicuous Compassion says more about you than a Prada handbag ever could, and all for the paltry cost of a lapel badge.

It proclaims you as a caring, sensitive, discriminating world citizen, a twin soul to Bono and Sir Bob, and compared to the shallow buzz of appearing with the Birkin holdall in ostrich skin on your arm (when everyone knows there's a six-month waiting list for that bag), you get to feel like a very good person as well as a very, very cool one.

The snag for the charities that stand to benefit, though, is that the Compassion has to be Conspicuous. Nobody's much interested if the giving is to go unnoticed, which is something that the North West Cancer Hospice in County Sligo has just discovered. When Westlife's Shane Filan got married in Ashford Castle last December, he and his bride requested their guests to make a donation to the Hospice in lieu of a gift. It was a generous and decent gesture from a young couple who also eschewed the *Hello!* route to riches, and happily posed for all media, not just those with the fat cheque books, on their wedding day. In doing so, of course, they also furnished our Taoiseach with the opportunity to attend a pop star wedding at which he did not have to hide from photographers and skulk under tarpaulin for fear of being snapped by some paparazzo who hadn't paid up front. Which, as somebody amongst Bertie's team of demonstrably astute advisers seems to have decided, is the way to poll-topping popularity, and so over the past year the Taoiseach has become a sort of a walking photo opportunity for celebrity gigs.

This ingenious strategy can come a little unstuck, though, in the event of any unseemly fallout over the event in question, and this seems to be the case with the Westlife wedding and the conspicuous lack of compassion translating into hard cash from the glittering guests. A spokesman for the Hospice, which was to benefit from the wedding feast, came forward last week to express his disappointment with the level of generosity – they'd been expecting up to €50,000 in donations from the 380 guests at Filan's wedding, and instead they'd netted less than €10,000. Which might seem rather churlish from the Hospice folk – after all, as Filan's brother pointed out last week, it was ten grand more than they had before the wedding – but fund-raising is a relentless and competitive business, and no charity can afford the perception that they're rolling in it when they are not.

The Filan family are understandably hurt by the row, and have pointed out that most of their guests were ordinary family and friends, not rich stars and singers. Still, not even the most ordinary of guests would present a gift worth less than €100 per couple to a pair of newly weds from any background today, and by that reckoning the Hospice should have cleared at least €20,000. It may well be that most of the guests ignored the request for a charitable donation and opted for the conspicuous generosity of a traditional wedding gift, in which case the Hospice might perhaps brace itself for an avalanche of lattechino machines and smoothie makers from the couple who probably have everything.

It's been an entertainingly superficial little kerfuffle in a grim news week, which is why Bertie could probably have done without being drawn, albeit rather tenuously, into something so silly and frothy at this particular time. Footage from the wedding, showing him posing proudly with the happy couple in December, aired on the very same news bulletin last week as his rather baffling and sly attack on Gerry Adams. Juxtaposed, the two images of the Taoiseach might, perhaps, have shed some light on this administration's recent urge to undermine Adams at, almost literally, all costs.

Most of us certainly share Bertie Ahern's strong suspicion that Gerry Adams' connections with the IRA have not been limited to the opposite side of a negotiating table in a secret location. Adams' whole value to the peace process, his patent clout with the Republican movement and the status he has been accorded right back to the Lenadoon negotiations in 1972 is tacitly predicated on the understanding that he has singular 'influence', at the very least, with the IRA's army council. But it is evidently crucial for mainstream politicians to reserve the right to be intermittently horrified by his connections – just as they were publicly outraged when he carried Bootsy Begley's coffin after the Shankill bombing in 1993 whilst privately many would readily admit that there wouldn't be much use in talking to Adams if he'd been trailing, ignored, at the back of the funeral cortège. But all of us who voted for the Good Friday Agreement, which Bertie Ahern was instrumental in negotiating, also signed up to a suspension of disbelief and a sort of collective amnesia about the past history of the Troubles. In accepting that prisoners would go free and that previously reviled personnel on both sides had a legitimate role in the political process, we were taking a conscious and informed decision to leave the whataboutery and the tit-for-tat grievances of 30 years of circuitous violence to one side, at least.

For Bertie to come, suddenly, to a dawning realisation about Gerry Adams's past is irresponsible and disingenuous and downright cynical, and far more about damaging a political rival's popularity – and grabbing the attention from McDowell's 'vomit-making' headline-making outburst – than any plain-spoken epiphany. It is as though a player in a long-running and successful drama has suddenly turned on his fellow players and announced, 'You're acting, I'm acting, we're all acting', thus threatening the benign complicity that kept the show on the road, and all because one of the other dramatis personae has been getting better reviews than him.

Gerry Adams, for reasons that will keep political analysts busy as bees for decades to come, is the most popular political leader in the State. That is not withstanding the fact that a lot of people genuinely doubt his protestations of innocence in regard to an active service past. His popularity, the success of Sinn Féin in the recent assembly elections (to an assembly suspended over entirely unfounded and clearly politically motivated allegations against Sinn Féin) and the real chance of Sinn Féin advances in this summer's local and European polls, must be deeply worrying to Fianna Fáil and the PDs and Labour – all those who stand either to lose ground to SF or else to find themselves in the invidious position of having to negotiate with the Shinners after the next General Election. Which prospect has had the effect of laying bare the real priorities of the people currently in power – not the tantalisingly close possibility of securing peace for Northern Ireland, but the imperative of despatching the Shinners at whatever cost to that process.

On the main evening news, last week we saw (a) Bertie Ahern getting out of a limo at a glittering celebrity bash that's turned tacky and (b) Bertie Ahern getting into a row with Gerry Adams about his IRA links. Herewith a belated exercise in Conspicuous Covering of Exposed Political Ass, but perhaps some highly paid image adviser might just read the runes and advise that voters are simply hungry for just about anything resembling substance and idealism in a political leader. Love Gerry Adams or hate his guts, but you still can't picture him posing for the glossy magazines with Ronan Keating and Samantha Mumba at her star-studded 21st party.

April 2004

Abortion: you can only make a choice with your eyes open

WITHIN THE PAST couple of months, two newborn babies have been found abandoned in this country. In foster care now, they join a third unclaimed foundling who was forsaken by his mother a year ago. As a method of birth control, you'd have to conclude that the practice of dumping a newborn on the steps of a church is rather drastic.

And however disturbed the mothers of these children must be when they take the decision to leave them at the mercy of a passing stranger and a social care system, it must still be a harrowing choice. Almost invariably, these babies appear to have been well cared for in the first few days of their lives. The most recent foundling, the little girl called April who was left in a Marks & Spencer bag at the door of Leixlip parish church, had been carefully dressed in a clean babygro and warmly wrapped in a blanket decorated with cartoon characters. And a medical examination suggested that hers had been a hospital birth. So her mother, on departing the ward with her little bundle of joy, would have been given helpful advice about bathing and feeding and caring for her, along with little leaflets advising on her own health care and contraceptive choices in case she didn't want any more children.

And if you don't want children, there are plenty of options available to prevent pregnancy. But when an unwanted pregnancy is established, though, the options narrow, and none of them is easy. If you really don't want the child, it can be adopted, abandoned, or aborted. At one time, all three were considered almost equally dreadful, equally remorse-filled resorts of the most wretched women with absolutely no alternatives. And yet somehow, within the past half century, one of those options has ceased to be a desperate measure and become a lifestyle choice.

It may seem wryly facetious to describe abandoning a baby as a method of family planning, but it is arguably no more drastic and no more cruel than the abortion practices in some jurisdictions which permit the induced delivery of a viable foetus. At least the abandoned baby is alive, and available for tender photo opportunities in the arms of a caring nurse: those very pictures of baby April appeared in the papers last week, the images that make us all think of the countless childless couples who would do anything to have her, and wonder about her mother and ask, 'How could you ...?'

The aborted babies, though, don't make for nearly such cute photos, and it is thoroughly politically incorrect to look upon those images – as featured in a controversial Channel 4 documentary last week – and think, 'How could you ...?' We have become conditioned, through decades of freely available abortion, to view the procedure as a reasonable and conscious choice available to generations of informed and empowered women. Even the phrase 'the right to choose' suggests a fully functioning awareness of all the implications and processes involved in an abortion. We're big girls, we can handle this particular resolution of the conflicting rights of two lives in one body, we can deal with the details.

Except, from the outraged reaction to that documentary on Channel 4 last week, it appears we cannot, and we'll scream blue murder at anyone who attempts to make us face them. The most vocal opposition to the programme – which showed an eight-weeks pregnant woman having an abortion under local anaesthetic and then displayed the evacuated products in a Petri dish afterwards – came from the Right to Choose lobby. The programme was denounced as unfair, emotive and distressing to women who had had abortions, or were considering that course. So it would appear that what women have been demanding is not just the Right to Choose, but the Right to Choose without being obliged to confront the reality of our choice.

One pro-choice commentator argued that the portrayal of an abortion on television – the airing of a procedure chosen by many thousands of Irish women each year – was unnecessarily upsetting. She maintained that legalised abortion was sought only to take the procedure out of the backstreets and out of the hands of the unqualified butchers who regularly killed and maimed the desperate women who went to them in shameful secrecy. Nobody ever said it was a pretty thing, and so the unfortunate women who were obliged by circumstances to undergo an abortion shouldn't be forced to look at or even think about the destruction of the foetus.

Which would be a perfectly reasonable argument if only abortion had remained a last resort, as rare and harrowing as the decision to abandon a healthy baby in a shopping bag on a public road. Only a tiny handful of women are desperate enough to abandon a baby each year – yet hundreds from this country alone choose an abortion every week. So the argument that it is simply a barely tolerable alternative to backstreet butchery doesn't hold up – not when it is easily available, relatively painless and the doctors' legal obligations to satisfy themselves that it really is the woman's only option are a contemptible sham.

In Britain, late abortions – up to 24 weeks' gestation – are permitted in circumstances where the baby has been found to have a grave defect. At 24 weeks, almost six months, the baby is fully formed and entirely viable – there was a huge row in this country last year when a 24-week baby was born in an ambulance after her mother was turned away from a downsized maternity unit, and died shortly afterwards. Had she been born in a hospital she would have had a good chance of survival: in other circumstances, she would have been a piece of unwanted tissue to be destroyed. If you are happily pregnant, your 10-week scan will show a perfectly formed person, and you will be expected to delight in the sight. If you go for an abortion at 10 weeks, though, there will be no discussion of whether or not the foetus on the screen, being assessed to decide the best method of evacuation, has its daddy's nose. And at 24-weeks a baby can cry, and feed, and breathe unaided. Quite recently, in an English hospital, a 24-week foetus was aborted after an ultrasound scan revealed he had a cleft palate – this was considered a grave enough defect to permit an abortion. That decision is being challenged in the courts by a young female Church of England minister who was herself born with a severe facial deformity that was completely remedied by surgery. It is difficult to see how the decision to abort that baby was made on the grounds that the mother had absolutely no alternative. She would surely have been distressed to have seen, in detail, what happened to her 24-week foetus during and after the abortion – her decision must have been considerably easier, therefore, for knowing she wouldn't have to. And, to judge by the opposition to the images in the Channel 4 programme, we want that decision made artificially easy by the blurring, indeed the outright suppressing, of the inconvenient details.

A few years ago, some US research on the subject of abortion indicated that foetuses, even quite young foetuses, can feel pain during an abortion and the survey recommended that painkillers be administered to them, on humane grounds, in advance of the procedure. And that's another inconvenient detail that you won't find anywhere in the soft-focus magazine adverts for all those discreet and caring clinics that are just a phone call and a cheap Ryanair flight away.

If abortion was just the distasteful legal alternative to an illicit backstreet operation, we'd never get ourselves into such an indignant state about abortion in Britain being 'an Irish solution' – we'd accept, instead, that the circumstances in which it was truly justified were so rare that its availability in a neighbouring EU country was perfectly adequate, indeed that the more difficult it was to obtain, the better since then only the most desperate and determined would proceed.

So let's drop this pretence: abortion is no longer a last resort, it's a lifestyle choice, an acceptable birth control option, a legitimate solution if your amniocentesis (available in all Irish maternity hospitals) indicates you are carrying a Down's Syndrome baby, a woman's right. And that's perfectly fine, so long as you accept that, as with all rights, there is also a re-sponsibility – to acquaint yourself fully with what the exercise of your right entails. You certainly have the right to abort a foetus but that's not the same as a Right to Choose – you can only make a choice with your eyes open.

September 2004

A patently potty pose

I AM CURRENTLY in the process of toilet-training a three-year-old boy, who has yet to be persuaded of the merits of abandoning his perfectly comfortable nappies in favour of a cold and draughty potty out on the lawn. If he continues to resist all encouragement – I'm not sure he realises that it will never be so easy again to earn a round of applause from a supportive audience – I am going to have to resort to the tactic I used with his older siblings. Expensive, branded nappies are designed to remain cosy under all circumstances, so as to deprive a kid of the incentive to dispense with them, but the own-brand ones that come in large bales from the cheap supermarkets at €1.99 for 100 tend to chafe and thus concentrate the mind a little bit more effectively. Given that choice, the potty eventually becomes the more attractive option. For now, though, I can sort of see a rationale in his resistance – the current arrangement has the advantages of comfort and convenience, he doesn't have to interrupt his play or his television viewing or his mischief-making to trot off in search of a loo.

What he doesn't realise, of course, is that as a male person he will not, even as an adult, be obliged to interrupt his play or his mischief-making to go in search of a loo if he doesn't want to bother. He will never have to be the slightest bit inconvenienced in search of a convenience – it is simply not possible to walk a city street at night, or drive any distance of national public road, without being treated to the sight of at least one chap relieving himself copiously and without inhibition as the mood has taken him. At times, indeed, it looks like an enviably companionable activity, with rows of lads lined up together shooting the breeze. One thing it never appears to be, however, is a particularly traumatic experience for anyone involved. Even gents' public toilets are organised so that conversation need not be interrupted by proceedings – piddling in company seems an integral part of the male bonding experience.

Which makes the compensation claims by the former prisoners who were forced to 'slop out' from cells without flushing toilets an even more patent try-on than the normal run of spurious actions. One solicitor, who is willing to fight these cases, has reported that they are streaming in, so to speak, at a rate of 40 a week. The basis of the ex-prisoners' actions against the State is that they were 'traumatised', and their human rights denied, by the process of having to urinate into a potty and then empty it the following morning. The real basis of their actions, of course, is that a Scottish ex-con netted €3,600 from his own country's executive in largely similar circumstances, and these chaps have concluded that it's worth a shot. And if there are solicitors willing to run such cases on a 'no foal no fee' basis, regardless of the fact that defending these actions will cost the taxpayer a bundle, it's a fairly sensible punt. In a legal system which willingly and regularly compensates people for their own stupidity and negligence, it's a safe bet that you might pocket a few grand for the indirect injury of being dumb enough to land yourself in prison in the first place.

The compensation claims have prompted a curious debate about what, exactly, is the essential nature of the punishment involved in imprisonment. The very humane and compassionate Mountjoy governor John Lonergan has expressed the view that the denial of liberty alone is the hardship imposed, and therefore that conditions inside the prison itself ought to be as dignified and comfortable as resources allow. But if you pursue that argument to its logical conclusion then there really isn't any reason why prisons shouldn't be holiday camps in reality and not just in the fevered imaginations of tabloid headline writers. I have friends who regularly submit themselves to days on end of imprisonment on luxury cruise liners and appear to enjoy it immensely, even though there is very little chance of escape between stops in Grenada and St Lucia. And liberty itself is a fairly vague concept in certain socio-economic groups. If you can't get a job, afford a holiday, own a car, get a night out because childcare costs are so prohibitive, have the choice of going to secondary school just because of where you live, then the notion that you are free to make choices about how you live your life is entirely ludicrous. Another friend of mine – not the one who takes the luxury cruises, oddly enough – spent time in prison for a white-collar crime, and maintains that even in jail, money and connections give you options and opportunities that are denied to others inside. This particular chap hosted a cocktail hour in his cell every evening, and was able to order the precise ingredients for his entertaining right down to the colour and dimension of the olives required for the martinis. Even while Liam Lawlor and George Redmond were banged up they still had greater liberties, in terms of life choices and options, than many of those sentenced to bleak lives on ill-planned housing estates by these corrupt men's machinations.

So prison life has to be about more than the simple denial of liberty: it may not be a particularly edifying impulse on our part, but the desire to humiliate prisoners and dent their personal dignity is an undeniable part of the process of jailing them. In practice, a corrupt politician or a crooked official might well have an easier time in prison than your average ordinary decent criminal from one of the handful of deprived housing estates that supply the bulk of our prison population. He might well be able to use his contacts and his influence to get a nicer, more private cell with better facilities than his comrades in chains. The real blow to his image and ego, though, comes from the public perception that he is in there having a hard time, wee-weeing into a bucket and emptying it in the morning, stitching mail bags by day, tunnelling away with his teaspoon to escape a tyrannical warder by night.

So it is not so much the actual embarrassment or hardship of slopping out that is irking these ex-cons – it is more the public impression of what humiliations or hardships such a practice involves. And if that is the foundation of their compensation claims, it is difficult to see how such actions could succeed. Because going to prison ought to be a humiliating experience, rather than a couple of years' retreat from the world with time to read and study and learn a skill and write your memoirs. The crucial difference between the Irish claims, and the successful Scottish action, is that the latter prisoner was kept in overcrowded conditions without guaranteed access to a toilet, in circumstances where the Executive had expressly acknowledged that conditions were inadequate but had failed to fulfil a promise to improve them. In the Irish prison system, where some of the institutions date from Victorian times, the practice of keeping prisoners in cells without proper sanitation is not a specially devised cruel and unusual punishment, but rather an outdated situation that is gradually and expensively being phased out. In any event, all Irish prisoners are permitted to leave their cells at night to use toilets rather than their slop buckets if they make that request. And if they feel demeaned by having to ask to go to the lavatory, or embarrassed by having been short-taken at night and choosing to use their potties, well that is just tough luck – not even the most brass-necked counsel would dare argue that anyone had a legitimate expectation of life in prison, even with the most humane of governing staff, as a bed of roses.

October 2004

'Dear Failed Breastfeeder ...'

AS PART OF its tireless campaign to convince all women that breastmilk is an even better thing than sliced bread, the Department of Health and Children recently wrote to 476 restaurants asking them to support a new breastfeeding initiative. By the time the launch of the scheme was announced to coincide with the start of National Breastfeeding Week last Thursday, less than a quarter of those restaurants had replied positively. Now the hospitality industry was not being requested to facilitate live lunchtime sex-shows on the premises of restaurants and cafes – they were simply being asked to state a policy of welcoming and assisting women who wanted to nurse their babies while they dined out themselves. Just 105 of the premises approached are now backing the scheme.

Which means either the other 371 are pledged actively to discourage and inhibit nursing mothers, or they were afraid that explicit participation might just deter other diners, or else they didn't see the need for the initiative in the first place. It is reasonable to assume that the truth lies somewhere between the latter two possibilities. It would, after all, be a very foolhardy restaurateur who would take his life in his hands to tell a breastfeeding mother to cover up or clear out in these acutely politically correct and equality conscious times. Also, it is unlikely that any woman's decision about whether or not to breastfeed her newborn baby is going to be swayed one way or another by concern about being embarrassed or discommoded in her favourite restaurant a few weeks or months later. And lastly, breastfeeding mothers are so thoroughly and earnestly assured, from all quarters, that they have God on their sides that they are scarcely in need of any validation from any eating-house owner, thank you very much. Personally, I am sort of hoping that the 371 establishments that didn't back the scheme are instead planning to offer safe and sympathetic asylum, free from sneers and snide comments and rude stares, to failed mothers like myself who shamefully feed our babies on powdered milk out of plastic bottles and latex teats.

At the launch of the restaurant initiative last week, the Equality Authority chief executive Niall Crowley was quoted as saying that women were beginning to realise that breastfeeding was an equality issue, and he's certainly right there. It is indeed an equality issue, though not in the way he means, and not maybe the sort of equality issue he'd be so very keen to champion. Women who do not, for any number of reasons, choose to breastfeed are constantly made to feel less equal and less admirable as mothers than those who do. If you buy baby milk formula in your local supermarket, for example, you will notice a small sign telling you that it is one of the few products in the store – along, I think, with tobacco and alcohol – for which you will not earn any loyalty club card points. Stand by, perhaps, for the day when that sign will tell you that points will be deducted from your total for every box of formula you purchase for your unfortunate and neglected infant.

Us bottle-feeding mothers are constantly being bombarded with new surveys and studies telling us how much harm we are doing our poor kids by feeding them artificially – if they grow up to be obese psychopaths with learning difficulties and criminal propensities it will be all because we were too selfish, too busy or too inadequate to see them right in their earliest days.

A few years ago, a maverick report suggested that breast milk might not, after all, be quite so pure as contemporary wisdom had it, and in many cases was found to be contaminated with toxic chemicals from products like dry-cleaning fluid and sun creams. When I had the temerity to refer to this survey in a newspaper column, the wrath of a very substantial and vocal and political lobby came down upon my head. I was, it turned out, responsible for everything to juvenile delinquency to high infant mortality in sub-Saharan Africa: if style-setters like myself neglected to nurse, poor third world women would conclude that bottle feeding was the fashionable thing to do and their babies would consequently die when they were deprived access to clean boiled water and nourishing formula. Stumbling around my chaotic home, delirious from lack of sleep after three weeks of attempting to nourish a child who seemed to have a bottomless appetite and was struggling to satisfy it by feeding for up to 16 hours a day, I can't say I felt like much of a style icon for anyone at all when my first baby was born. But trying to get a sympathetic hearing from any of the professionals from whom I sought help at that time was next to impossible. I was simply instructed to stick at it, and advised that things would work out, even in the face of plain evidence that we were on a downward spiral where I was too tired to eat between feeds and the baby was consequently getting less and less milk each time. Eventually, one compassionate nurse whispered the name of a formula that was the closest in constitution to breast milk, and that night we all got some sleep.

In the months after I wrote that mildly controversial article, countless women got in touch, gradually and timidly even though some of them are quite prominent ladies, to say they had the same experience as me but were too scared to come out in support or even voice their own reservations at the time. The breastfeeding lobby, though, were on my case from the start and even to this day, maybe six years later, I will still get letters attacking my position on anything from the smoking ban to the situation in Iraq that begin, 'Dear Failed Breastfeeder . . .'

There is no more fulfilling feeling in the world than being able to feed your own baby – I realised that the handful of times it really worked for me – and there is much merit in the theory that human gestation is actually 12 months long, with intimate physical contact between mother and child in the three months after birth an essential continuation of the previous nine. But if you can't do it, for whatever reason, you can't do it, and hospitals and health professionals and the Equality Authority and even restaurateurs need to respect your position in that regard. Because when a mother feels obliged to persist with nursing, when it is clearly not working, the child inevitably suffers some distress. Against my own better judgement, last year, I dutifully fed my fifth baby, even though I insisted to the hospital staff that she seemed constantly hungry. By the time she was a week old she had dropped from a healthy birth weight to just five pounds and was in an incubator. At which point, to my astonishment, a midwife suggested feeding her formula but, to avoid spoiling her with a latex teat, she would have to drink it from a cup. With a saucer and two rich tea biscuits on the side, presumably.

Breastfeeding certainly is an equality issue. Mothers who cannot do it need to be assured that they are just as good, competent and caring parents – at a time when they are inevitably fragile and anxious – as those who can. Breastfeeding mothers, I have enviously noted, are usually so chuffed with themselves that they have no reservations about unveiling a nipple in public, but producing a plastic bottle in a trendy cafe, now, THAT is embarrassing.

October 2004

If money doesn't make you happy, begrudgery will

REASONS WHY WE should all admire Chris de Burgh: 1. He's rich and successful. 2. He writes nice, inoffensive, singalong, middle-of-the-road music. 3. Princess Diana loved 'Lady in Red' and the song made him a fortune. 4. He had an affair with a blonde teenager but he took his medicine and kept his marriage together. 5. His daughter is the first Irish Miss World.

Reasons why we all hate Chris de Burgh: 1. He's rich and successful. 2. He writes nice, inoffensive, singalong, middle-of-the-road music. 3. Princess Diana loved 'Lady in Red' and the song made him a fortune. 4. He had an affair with a blonde teenager but he took his medicine and kept his marriage together. 5. His daughter is the first Irish Miss World.

Begrudgery is just about the only human emotion that an Irish person is free to express without fearing a backlash from any quarter. Profess that you're proud of your child, you're happy that your marriage survived an infidelity or delighted that your work is appreciated – all recent crimes of poor old Chris – and nobody feels at all inhibited about taking a gloating potshot aimed at knocking you back into your box. At the time his daughter Rosanna won the Miss World title last year, mean-spirited rumours instantly began circulating about the presence of performance-enhancing substances in her bloodstream – the fact that she shared a genetic code with an international pop star whose ditties had won favour with the

Royals was whispered to have given her a head start on her rivals. Well, what a shocker! In a contest that's all about perception and presentation, and where there's little else to choose between the supernaturally flawless females who make it to the final, it's unlikely that a Unique Selling Point like a famous dad did her very much harm. Which is not to say that she wasn't the most beautiful girl there, it's just that Miss World is a package deal and she had the most to offer that year. But you can hardly blame her dad for being upset at suggestions that she didn't win fair and square – show me any father who hasn't gazed upon his baby daughter and concluded that if she wasn't in due course acknowledged as the most beautiful creature ever born then there simply was no God.

Cue much thinly disguised glee, though, when Chris complained in an interview last week that the year as Miss W. had not been as lucrative for his daughter as he might have expected. The sponsorships and endorsements and career breaks that she was entitled to expect, he said, didn't materialise. Now he didn't go so far as to blame their non-appearance on begrudgery, but he didn't have to. Advertisers simply didn't rally to Rosanna Davison's clear-cut win as eagerly as they might to, say, a dubious sporting triumph because there simply wasn't the same public goodwill towards the girl. If you've got wealth, privilege or exalted connections crowned with success, then in this country you are judged way too big for your boots and in need of an urgent reality check.

An audience member on *Questions and Answers* last Monday asked the panel if they felt that Cian O'Connor, the Olympic medallist at the centre of the latest Irish-sport-and-dope scandal, would be subjected to 'trial by media'. In the context, it was difficult to see what he meant by that phrase since O'Connor had primarily been subjected to trial by international drug testing authority, but 'trial by media' seems to have come to stand for any significant volume of coverage in the papers that might be subjectively unwelcome and uncomfortable. And no doubt Mr O'Connor feels he's getting a roasting from the media just at the moment, and if he is, then certainly nine parts of that sentiment stem from genuine disappointment and dismay from those who cheered the loudest for what seemed, at the time, a truly unimpeachable Irish victory. But there's also a small part begrudgery and Schadenfreude prompted by O'Connor's links with Sir Anthony O'Reilly, the proud godfather of the rider, sponsor of the horse Waterford Crystal, and author of a glowing tribute to the horseman for the front page of the *Sunday Independent* just after the Athens victory. Even for those most downcast by O'Connor's current troubles, you get the feeling that this cloud has a trace of a gold lining, if it even temporarily wiped the Cheshire cat grin from the face of the fabulously wealthy businessman, who was, curiously, uncontactable when asked to share his emotions on this latest twist to his godson's fortunes.

And the sight of the Minister for Justice sharing his emotions about the setbacks facing the completion of his rural idyll, his remote hideaway, his luxurious holiday home – depending on which newspaper description you prefer – because of planning permission hiccups hardly caused any great upsurge of sympathy for his difficulties, either. The sight of somebody usually so surefooted looking distinctly wrongfooted was one of the week's more memorable highlights.

And another person whose disappointments and personal setbacks made for faux-sympathetic headlines this week was the entertainer Twink, who was forced to issue a statement confirming that her 21-year marriage to her younger husband was over, as he had moved out to live with a blonde 20-something musician. And just about every report of the deeply private tragedy managed to mention, at least once, that Twink was now grieving alone in her 'one million euro house'. Considering the fact that €1 million wouldn't buy you much more than a reasonably nice semi-d in the greater Dublin area just at the moment, it seems the only point in juxtaposing evidence of the singer's wealth and success with her impending divorce and current heartbreak was to rub home the fact that money and fame and acclaim and brash confidence cannot, after all, guarantee happiness. Right up there with the suggestion that Rosanna Davison's pedigree might just have singled her out from the glamorous Miss World crowd, there's another shocker to ponder over your breakfast.

It almost seems as though we are more in need than ever of proof that material riches can't buy love and contentment. Begrudgery, envy of successful people and malicious delight in their misfortunes have always provided us with a bit of blameless diversion, but at least in the leaner, hungrier decades gone by those instincts were easier to understand. Now in our new climate of national affluence, wealth and all its trappings seem available to anyone determined enough to have them. A million-euro house is a reasonably commonplace acquisition these days, a brand-new car, a holiday home, a state-of-the-art home entertainment system, several foreign trips a year and an expensive wardrobe were all once the hallmarks of exclusivity and success – now you're just about nobody if you can't tick several of those boxes, even if it does mean sacrificing your quality time and commuting through the night just to keep up the repayments on your family debt. So we've got all the must-have items required to signal to the world our success and achievement, and all we need now is an explanation for why happiness hasn't come as part of the deal. Which is why celebrities, and their cheating spouses and their private disappointments and their public humiliations, have suddenly become so curiously relevant and newsworthy. They are our reassurance that we are not the only ones being cheated of our fondest expectations.

January 2005

A shallow grave

WHEN THEY FOUND Jean McConville's body, in its shallow grave on a County Louth beach almost two years ago, there was a rusted safety pin still attached to the rags that remained of her blouse. It was one of the few identifiable features to evoke the 30-year-old skeleton's lost humanity, a brittle token of the everyday cares and concerns of a widowed woman in her 30s with ten young children to raise in Belfast in the early 1970s. And it was a reminder of all the time that had passed since that group of brave warriors turned up at her small flat and dragged her away from the terrified clutches of the little children who tried their best to hold on to her. If science couldn't have dated her remains, the nappy pin would have done it, as a relic of a time before disposable nappies and scented wipes, when squares of cotton washed threadbare had to be soaked and scrubbed and sterilised and dried, and there was a real knack to folding a cloth nappy and pinning it safely onto a squirming baby. It was a reminder of all the labour-saving household advances she never got to see, automatic washing machines and tumble driers and microwaves and bottle warmers, all the nappies that still had to be changed for her babies after she was bundled out of her home just before Christmas of 1972, all the grandchildren she never got to see, all the clucking about how modern mums have it easy that she never got to do.

Last week Mitchell McLaughlin of Sinn Féin told us that the abduction and murder of Jean McConville was not a crime. It was wrong, he conceded, but it was not a crime. And it was not a crime, evidently, because it was a legitimate act of just war. And it was a legitimate act of war because of a belief that Mrs McConville, who had very recently been widowed, was an informer. And if she was an informer, that made her an ally of the hated security forces. And if she was allied to the security forces, that made her fair game for the freedom fighters who were taking them on. And if she was a legitimate casualty whose abduction and murder advanced the cause of Irish freedom, then her killing couldn't be a crime.

All of which makes you wonder why on earth Mitchell McLaughlin now considers it was wrong at all. Because, according to the foregoing reasoning, it wasn't just the right thing to do – it was a positive act of heroic obligation.

Perhaps it may be termed wrong, though, because it has since emerged that Jean McConville wasn't actually an informer at all. Sinn Féin sources have admitted that it was highly unlikely that she had, as alleged, been furnished with a transmitting device by the British security forces in order to grass on the boys. Why any military intelligence with a so-phistication beyond that of Dad's Army would trust a depressed, widowed, impoverished, exhausted mother of ten small children with a transmitting device in the middle of a cramped flat block is not a question that appears to have detained our heroes for very long at all. In all probability, Jean McConville was executed on foot of hysterical rumours that began after she went to the aid of a young British soldier who was dying on her doorstep. So presumably it was wrong, then, simply because of an intelligence hiccup. But the killing fails to meet the standard of a crime, even now, because Jean McConville's executioners believed they were despatching an enemy agent, and the integrity of that belief cannot be retro-spectively invalidated.

And this, after all, was what we subscribed to when we voted for the Good Friday Agreement and, specifically, approved those terms that provided for the release of prisoners on both sides. We accepted that they had done the things they had done in the honest belief that it was necessary for their particular causes, that if civilians died it was as unfortunate collateral damage, and that the killings for which they had been jailed were henceforth scoured of any grubby taint of base criminality. If the killers of Jean McConville had been in custody in 1998, they would have been perfectly entitled to have the slate wiped clean and their liberty restored. And so Mitchell McLaughlin is right – under the Good Friday Agreement that most of us endorsed, the killing of Jean McConville was not a crime, it was a regrettable act of war.

The question of whether or not the killers of Jerry McCabe qualify for freedom under the same agreement is one that has given rise to much public debate and disquiet in the past while. Even though it is difficult to see how the Detective Garda was abetting 800 years of English oppression by sitting in an unmarked police car in Adare in 1996, and thus became a legitimate target, it looks increasingly likely that his killers' liberty will turn out to have been a clause of the agreement. And if, in time, it turns out that the IRA was, indeed, behind the Northern Bank raid last month, you can bet that an obscure clause will be found to have anticipated the wrong but nonetheless genuine enthusiasm and conviction of the freedom fighters involved in abducting and terrorising the bank staff. And if we are to work the agreement that we supported in such numbers, perhaps these are conceits and fictions we are just going to have to live with in future. The Good Friday Agreement clearly means never having to say you are sorry. Effectively, it is increasingly beginning to seem, the Agreement was simply a mandate to redefine ongoing criminality as peace, and past criminality as justice. And the alternative, the consequence of disputing Sinn Féin's definitions of peace and justice, will be more of the same but without the reassuring labels. It's a bit like that old Monty Python inquisitor's line: if you don't confess you'll be tortured with unimaginable cruelty – if you DO confess, imaginable cruelty.

By even considering returning to talks with Sinn Féin in the aftermath of the bank raid and Mitchell McLaughlin's dismissal of Jean McConville's murder, by clearly planning to release Jerry McCabe's killers to sustain the process, our Government is interpreting our mandate to go much further than meeting Sinn Féin half way. But that is certainly not what was envisaged by a very trusting public back in 1998. We did expect that concessions would be made, but we were entitled to imagine that some would be reciprocated, and so far they have not.

If Sinn Féin has any genuine interest in advancing the peace process from here, it will concede that the killers of Det McCabe were cold-blooded criminals who deserve to stay in jail. It will clearly state that the Northern Bank raiders, even if they do turn out to be fellow travellers in disguise, should be locked away for a very long time. It will accept that the Columbia Three were not hapless ornithologists in need of a good map. And it will lay aside the obtuse semantics and admit that the murder of Jean McConville was not just wrong, not just a crime against common law but a crime against humanity, against the fractured and still grieving family she left behind, and, for those who still set some store by terms like this, a mortal sin.

Unless this happens, then we are required to accept that, along with the elastic definitions for terms like peace and justice, we also endorsed the retrospective validation of the abduction and murder of a defenceless widowed mother of ten children when we endorsed the Agreement. And that was never the case.

January 2005

Paid to stay single

IN ALL OF two brief lines in his Budget speech in 1973, Richie Ryan introduced a novel social welfare benefit called the Lone

Parents' Allowance. Unlike Noel Browne's Mother and Child scheme of some years earlier, this innovation was not denounced as heralding the end of the traditional family nor seen as a stealthy blow to the country's cherished moral values. Instead, it passed under the outrage radar because, at the time, lone parents were rare creatures and the number in the country at the time – less than 3,000 – would have just about amounted to a decent turnout for a club-level hurling final. The concept of an allowance for them originated in the Commission for the Status of Women report of the previous year, and it was a relatively inexpensive measure that pressed all the right buttons in a state that had just recently signed up for the Common Market and begun to look outwards towards European concepts of tolerance, liberality and inclusivity. Lone parents were a particularly vulnerable minority and the new allowance would afford them the economic safety net that their circumstances required.

Just over 30 years on, the number of lone parents in the country is heading swiftly for the 100,000 mark. And there is an increasingly compelling logic to the argument that, far from freeing single parents from one poverty trap, the Lone Parents' Allowance actually led them into a deeper, lonelier and far more effectively camouflaged one. There is also a view, to be expressed later this week by a leading academic, that the Allowance has led to the sort of social chaos and decline of family values that even its most strident critics could never have foreseen.

According to Professor Emeritus of Limerick University, Dr Edward Walsh, the combined financial package now on offer to single mothers amounts to a 'substantial inducement for abuse'. As a result, he argues, an increasing number of children are growing up without a biological father in their lives, and without the care, guidance and love that previous generations enjoyed. And, in a speech to be delivered next Wednesday, Dr Walsh points to a US survey which found that 72 per cent of murderers were raised by single mothers.

Addressing the matter of the Lone Parents' Allowance last month, economics lecturer Dr Ronnie O'Toole argued that the benefit had worked to distort the choices of those young women from deprived areas who have always made up the bulk of its claimants. The 'well-intentioned policy', he suggested, had 'warped the short-term prospects of a narrow stratum of society, offering them a fast track to an income and housing, on condition that they got pregnant without the support of a partner'. And it is easy to see how the allowance, and the comparative independence it brings, could hold out beguiling prospects for underprivileged young girls without much else to look forward to in their lives. Having a baby, an income and the chance of a local authority flat clearly confers a status on a poor 15-year-old girl that a mediocre Junior Cert and a checkout operator's job in the local cut-price superstore hardly ever would.

It is, perhaps, a classic example of the chicken-and-egg conundrum – did the numbers of single mothers rise because the allowance was there, or are the numbers claiming the allowance increasing because single parenthood, in an era of unprecedented sexual licence, was inevitably rising anyway? Except, of course, our national birth rate isn't increasing by anything remotely like the factor by which the numbers on Lone Parents' Allowance have grown since 1974. Now, clearly, marital breakdown statistics must be considered in calculating the rise in lone parents claiming benefits over the past three decades, but the rise in unmarried pregnancies is undeniable, and now almost one in every three pregnancies in this country occurs outside of marriage.

So there is increasing support for the view that the Lone Parents' Allowance scheme, along with all the other benefits and concessions for single parents, has had the effect of at best normalising, and at worst incentivising, single parenthood. Dr Walsh, who is to speak as part of a lecture series in the Cork Capital of Culture 2005 celebrations, takes up this point and argues that what he terms the very real financial incentives for single parents 'may actively encourage the formation of lone parent families'. Broad-ranging research literature, he points out, suggests that a wide variety of social ills can be traced to the growth of one-parent families, particularly where children grow up without a strong male role model in their lives – another study he quotes suggests that the number of lone-parent families in a community, and not its poverty level, is the best indicator of its rates of violent crime.

Dr Walsh contends that a single mother of two children, in a position to claim all the allowances and benefits that may come her way, could rely on an income of up to €25,000 per annum from the State.

On this point, though, there seems a slight contradiction in the arguments – if single mothers can potentially do so well out of the system, then how can they be trapped in consistent, corrosive poverty at the same time? If they have the chance of netting a tax-free €25,000 a year without having to work outside the home for it, how come their children are at a demonstrably increased risk of malnutrition, drug addiction and early criminality?

The answer seems to be that true poverty, of the kind that economist Ronnie O'Toole argues is perpetuated by the Lone Parents' Allowance scheme, is not solely financial. A life lived on benefits, on State handouts, on constantly contriving to stay within the qualifying requirements for the money leads not just to financial frustration but also to an impoverished outlook, impoverished expectations, impoverished self-esteem. A single mother who forms a stable, long term, cohabiting relationship with a partner – whether he is her children's father or not – is putting her allowances at risk. Extrapolating from British data on the same subject, O'Toole estimates that as many as 30,000 Irish children are being denied the influence of a stable male role model in their lives solely by their mothers' economic obligation to remain single. At the very least, then, it seems demonstrable that the Lone Parents' Allowance is incentivising the denial of a male authority figure in the lives of already vulnerable and disadvantaged children. Boys have a particular need for such an influence in their early years, and the alarming rise in suicide rates for young Irish men is unlikely to be entirely unconnected to the increasing number of young women trying to raise children alone.

In prospect, for sure, the Lone Parents' Allowance must have all the appeal for an aimless teenage girl that Dr Walsh suggests, but after she has spent a few years living with the reality of lone parenthood on a tight budget the novelty surely wears pretty thin. And that's when the real poverty of spirit and opportunity and initiative begins to kick in for herself and her children – parenting is a full-time job which doesn't always allow the time to cook healthy, nutritious and relatively low-cost foods, and so parents in these situations rely more heavily on processed or fast foods or ready meals which, according to a British study published just last week, impede them even more – it appears that attention deficit disorders and even conditions like autism can now be linked to children's unhealthy, modern, convenience diets.

That the way we deal with single parents needs an overhaul has been generally accepted for some time – a few years ago Tánaiste Mary Harney considered offering incentives for single parents to live with their families, in order that they could benefit from the extended family support system. It is, though, a hot political potato because of the perceived political incorrectness of targeting unfortunate teenage mums and their disadvantaged kids as the source of all society's ills. But tackling the dangerously misleading impression that single parenthood is a ticket to an easy life on benefits requires some urgent and courageous action. Economist Ronnie O'Toole suggests ending the Lone Parents' Allowance scheme for new applicants, guaranteeing the benefits of those already in the system until their children reach 18 so that there will be no disincentive to form stable new relationships, and pumping the freed-up resources into those communities, and even those families, most at risk.

In order that any such drastic move doesn't lead to social chaos in the poorest sectors, though, the solution has to be broader than the purely economic. It is perhaps blindingly obvious, but a hard-hitting educational campaign candidly spelling out the realities of teen parenthood, and the breadth of disadvantages for all concerned, has to precede any change to the relevant legislation. We have to shake off the fear of a backlash from those extreme feminist groups that will see any attempt to discourage single parenthood as a gross attack on female reproductive liberties and a return to the bad old days of the Magdalene Laundries: babies have rights, too, and the entitlement to be welcomed as a beloved addition to a stable family, and not conceived as a ticket to lifelong welfare benefits, ought to be among them.

April 2005

Branding the bullies

WHEN SHE STARTS secondary school later this year, my 12-year-old daughter recently announced, she will no longer need her lunch box. Not that she has any realistic hope of getting the cash to buy herself a meal every day in one of the school's cafeterias, but rather because it is the fashion there, apparently, to carry lunch to school in a brown paper bag.

This sounded to me like a perfectly routine and even harmless adolescent eccentricity, until we got to the bottom of it. It seems that lunch boxes are out because they probably contain – the shame of it – homemade sandwiches. And buying lunch in the cafeteria is uncool because it's sensible and boring, and for these kids it's no big deal to have twenty euro a day to spend on a curries and cokes and snacks. So the reason brown bags are in vogue is because they suggest you've left the school grounds to buy yourself a toasted ciabatta with salsa chicken and Caesar salad from one of the expensive and trendy little cafes nearby. And hot drinks, she explained, are only acceptable when sipped from paper cups stamped with chic coffee brand logos. As for bringing your own tea from home, I suspect she'd rather be found with a WW2 hand grenade in her schoolbag than my trusty old tartan thermos.

In other words, something as simple as the mode of transport for a lunchtime snack has become another ingenious means by which children may identify and single out the poorer, weaker, less clued in and so more likely targets for bullying in their midst. The need to assert themselves in a confusing world by picking on more inadequate peers seems to be a far more pressing imperative for pampered youngsters these days than it ever was before. And just like the more competitive adults in an increasingly affluent and consumerist society, children in well-heeled schools are finding it's not so easy to distinguish the socially inferior any more. This means they must devise ever more precise and insidious methods of fine-tuning the values and fads of their set to make sure that there are always some unfortunates outside the loop. Hence paper bags are in, lunch boxes are out.

And once isolated by sophisticated devices, the bullies' victims can now be persecuted by equally advanced means. No fewer than 34 second-year girls in Alexandra College in Milltown in Dublin had to be disciplined by various measures over the past few weeks for tormenting named classmates on a website by mocking their appearances, their mannerisms and their sexual naivety. The Hateboard website is an international one, but teenagers from the top college had seized upon it as a medium to vent their spite towards unpopular peers and the pupils of less glamorous educational establishments – or, as one entry on the site put it, 'U prob go 2 sum gay northside skul so f##k off – jus cause we can afford tings'. Charming stuff – even if the tings they can afford clearly don't include spelling grinds.

The essence of the taunts posted on the site seemed to boil down to two specific areas – the flaunting of wealth and of sexual nous. Particularly in the fee-paying schools, the need to weed the arriviste or, heaven forbid, scholarship chaff from your circle seems to be a relentless business – I know of one posh school where the 13-year-old 'in-crowd' have a custom of meeting for early dinner in a fairly expensive Italian restaurant every Friday night, and the kids live in dread of cruel exclusion from the weekly gathering on a ring-leader's whim. There's a sinister *Lord of the Flies*-style chill about the thought of mere children dreaming up ever more elaborate ways to torture and isolate those deemed weak or unworthy. And it's a real mystery where on earth these kids got the idea that it's acceptable to judge or dismiss somebody solely on the basis of a cheap jacket or an unfashionable address.

But events in the past week alone suggest that there is an increasing prevalence of childish misbehaviour based on sexual knowledge. And that's arguably even more alarming than old-fashioned snobbery. It emerged on Thursday, for example, that a group of girls as young as ten were suspended from a Dublin primary school for sending sexually suggestive text messages to a male teacher. These fifth and sixth class students had first blocked their own phone numbers and then bombarded the young man with raunchy texts, and were rumbled only when one kid panicked and feared that her number had been discovered.

Predictably enough, the response from teachers' and parents' spokespersons to both this incident, and the Hateboard bullying affair, has been to point the finger at technology. Text bullying is particularly popular with young girls, apparently, because it offers precision as well as deniability, and some schools have responded by banning mobile phones entirely. Similarly, the Alexandra College incident has been attributed to a lack of responsible monitoring of the children's internet access, which has now been addressed by 'firewalling' offending sites. There is, of course, nothing to stop these children catching up on their bitchy texting when they get back from school, nor from accessing any website they fancy on home computers in their bedrooms. But it is rather foolish of the adults, parents and teachers alike, charged with providing moral guidance to these youngsters to fall back on the argument that the phones and the PCs are entirely to blame for these nasty episodes.

Children don't need high technology to bully and isolate their peers – just carrying the wrong lunch bag can mark a kid out as prey. And children don't persecute others simply because it's a handy way to pass the time – they do it to deflect attention from insecurities and inadequacies in their own lives, and they particularly target those failings they fear in themselves. So the fact that sexual ignorance has evidently been identified as especially contemptible among such a young age group signals some cause for concern about the environment in which these children are growing up.

As adults we've almost become inured to sexual innuendo and imagery all around us, in advertising, in the words of popular songs, in all forms of the media, even on kids' clothes – despite promising that they'd abandon the juvenile FCUK logo, French Connection continue to flaunt it on sweatshirts designed for teenagers, to the point where it barely registers any more. We're desensitised to the fact that the vernacular of pornography has become acceptable advertising lingo – there has to be a statutory limit on the number of dull-witted ad agencies that can actually use the phrase 'size matters' at any one time. And we have given up the struggle against the coarsening of our cities and thoroughfares by unsavoury influences: there was almost another uprising on O'Connell Street when the Ann Summers sex shop opened its doors opposite the GPO some years back. Now Peter Stringfellow has got the nod to open a full-on strip club on Parnell Street and the only thing that seemed to bother local residents was that their property values might fall – just the Ruhama Project, which works with prostitutes, expressed any genuine objection to the venue on social and moral grounds. And nobody else was bothered very much at all.

If sex shops and strip clubs represent progress, then efforts to block them are probably doomed, but that doesn't mean voicing your reservations isn't worthwhile. These are sleazy, seedy developments and it's craven to keep quiet for fear of seeming oppressed and ignorant. If the grown-ups can't take a moral stand with any conviction, it's pointless to expect children to find their way through a maze of licentious influences and expectations. Instead, they're more likely to be troubled by a sense that everybody else is clued-in on sexual matters which, in turn, leads to taunting and bullying and promiscuity. Computers and mobile phones don't turn decent, secure youngsters into cruel cyber-bullies – the consumerist vacuity and sheer moral cowardice of those charged with their guidance is to blame for that.

May 2005

The Points Race

ONE OF THE highlights of my children's school year is the annual swimming gala. It's a wonderfully festive occasion, when all the daddies turn up with their camcorders and the teachers come along to watch them swim and everybody gets a most impressive-looking medal and a goodie bag of sweets and soft drinks and maybe a tee-shirt. Some of the kids are excellent swimmers and complete their lengths with ease, but it's always fascinating to watch the beginnings of the competitive instinct even in the smallest children who don't find the going quite so easy. My own three range between competitive, diligent and blithely unconcerned, but it doesn't make any difference because they'll all get medals and prizes anyway, which always seems to me a little unfair on the one who makes the effort to win her race, and really cares if she's pipped at the post. On the other hand, everyone goes home happy and the prevailing wisdom, especially in the case of preteen kids, is that it's the taking part that matters, and that everyone's a winner in their own way. Pointing up a child's shortcomings, making them feel inadequate or unequal to a challenge is now reckoned to be a Bad Thing, and all the child-rearing gurus will tell you that making a child feel incompetent or less capable than his peers is dreadfully damaging to his nascent self-esteem.

Which is perfectly good advice when you're dealing with young children. Nobody wants to see their toddler ticked off in playschool for constructing the least lifelike replica of the Eiffel Tower out of lolly sticks. Nor would you want your bookish and unathletic eight-year-old humiliated at the swimming gala because he's obviously never going to make the Irish Olympic team. But in our haste to be fair to all children and to make them all feel like winners, regardless of their gifts or strengths, we may be depriving them the benefit of one essential lesson that they need to take on board quite early in their lives – life isn't fair, we aren't all winners and the world won't reward you with medals and goodie bags for coming last.

There is, of course, a legitimate reluctance to place too much stress on young shoulders too early, particularly given the recent alarming rise in suicide rates and the suspicion that, primarily in the case of young men, it may be due to an inability to deal with the pressures and demands upon their role in modern society. But there may be another way of looking at this dilemma – it may well be that by pampering and protecting and cosseting our children from an early age, insulating them from stresses and challenges as best we can in childhood, we are denying them the tools to deal with the tough situations that life will inevitably throw in their way as they move out into the world.

It is generally agreed that the Leaving Cert examination, and the attendant points race, is one of the main sources of stress in the lives of our young people these days. There seems to be a consensus that it is much more stressful now than it ever was for generations past, that the pressure on students to achieve ever higher tallies of points is growing unbearable, and that the competition for university places is an untenable burden on teenagers who are still, for all their confidence and savvy, no more than children. Taking up this theme, Professor Donald Fitzmaurice of the Department of Chemistry in UCD has even gone so far as to suggest that the points system is a form of institutional child abuse comparable with the ill-treatment of orphans and abandoned kids in Church- and state-run homes in the last century. In a lecture to be delivered next Wednesday, Professor Fitzmaurice will argue there's a chance that, in years to come, our own children will demand to know why we kept silent and allowed them to be subjected to six years of narrow and intensive preparation for a State exam driven by the points race, on one hand, and on the other by self-interested groups with a vested interest in maintaining the status quo. He clearly believes that the system is abusive of the children in its clutches, and is in turn being abused and manipulated by teachers, third level institutions, employers and professional bodies to perpetuate a screening process that suits their requirements without giving any great consideration to the human by-products of this particular production line, and without much thought to the concept of education as an end in itself. Professor Fitzmaurice suggests that we look at the experience of other countries to see whether change is possible and how it might be achieved.

There is certainly plenty of room for improvement and refinement of the points system and the Leaving Cert exam, but are they inherently abusive devices because they impose stressful demands upon teenage children? On a purely academic level, for a start, the Leaving Cert seems to deliver the goods, as this country is considered to have one of the highest academic standards in the world, and our well-educated workforce has proved to be a major factor in encouraging foreign investment to this country over the past few decades. And this investment, along with the wealth and variety of employment opportunities it has brought, has arguably opened up career possibilities for the less academically gifted that never existed in recessionary times.

In the 1960s, 1970s and 1980s the Leaving Cert was just as tough an exam, loomed just as large in a child's life but, in those days, was a far more limited rite of passage into the world of work than it is today. Without the huge potential of the Internet Age, without the option of becoming a technological genius, a dot.com millionaire, a software specialist, a reality television celebrity instead of a doctor, a lawyer, a teacher or a priest, nerdy kids whose interests were rarefied and whose communication skills were poor had to settle for miserable lives on factory conveyor belts, when they could find the work. How would Bill Gates or David Beckham or Graham Norton or Sonia O'Sullivan have earned a crust 50 years ago? If you don't pass your Leaving Cert these days, it is no longer a big deal. You can repeat it, take an intensive grind in one of the colleges designed for that purpose, take a year out and backpack around the world, get a job, set up your own business selling bottles of Irish air once breathed by Bono over the internet to gullible Americans, start a rock band of your own.

Because so many people have had the same idea, though, you might find the market is a tough place to find your feet. But that's life, and it can't be soothed and cosseted and pampered away by the best efforts of parents and well-intentioned educators. The Leaving Cert is certainly a stressful exam, probably the toughest any student will ever sit throughout academic life – unlike later in college, you don't know the tutors setting the questions, you can't predict their form on marking, you can't factor their likes and dislikes into the process. It is certainly made doubly hard by the emphasis that parents and teachers place upon it. But get rid of it, modify it, and they'll simply find other ways of pushing the cream, clots and all, to the top.

For all its toughness, it is hardly comparable with the deliberate mistreatment of poor children in orphanages. Their early experiences blighted their whole lives – the Leaving Cert, by contrast, is democratic, all-embracing and about as good an introduction to the random injustices, caprices and unpredictabilities of real life as you can get. So it is stressful, but stress, particularly in a society that places such emphasis on material success, is inevitable, and rather than seeking ways to remove it from our children's lives we'd be better off teaching them to confront it, acknowledge it and deal with it. Not everybody will do well in the Leaving Cert, not everyone performs well in testing situations or fulfils their real potential in a high-pressure challenge or remembers everything they know when it really matters. That's how life is, too, but the difference is that the real world doesn't readily offer second chances. If the Leaving Cert doesn't suit you, it may be the most memorable way to learn that failure is not irredeemable but quitting definitely is.

So perhaps the stresses that crystallise for teenagers with the points race need to be addressed much earlier on. Applaud equally the toddlers' efforts to build aeroplanes with lolly sticks, by all means, but if one manages to construct a perfect working model of the new Airbus, that achievement has to be singled out for special praise. Making life as painless as possible, telling youngsters that they are all winners, and they are all brilliant, and they are all wonderful, won't spare them stress – it simply equips them with unrealistic assumptions about the world's judgements, and stores up misery for the inevitable day when they have to face the truth.

May 2005

Commodity trading

FULL MARKS FOR optimism, if nothing else, to those European governments who have cooked up an imaginative but, alas, surely doomed initiative to liberate trafficked prostitutes. It's perfectly simple – a number of Continental states have introduced confidential phone numbers for male clients who suspect that the woman they've just slept with for money might have been working against her will. Foolproof, you might think, after all, it simply requires a man, who has just paid a woman to have sex with him, to recognise that she mightn't have been wholly enthusiastic about the encounter, to view her as a vulnerable human being and not a piece of meat, and to show a little concern for her welfare. Well, how could that possibly not work?

Perhaps the reason the measure is doomed is because it flies in the face of the central male conceit that has kept prostitution flourishing for millennia. Men couldn't keep using the services of prostitutes if they hadn't managed to convince themselves that (a) they ARE actually pieces of meat, (b) they're making a really good living from it and (c) they definitely love it. Pops their corks every time, no doubt about it, and they get a fistful of tax-free cash into the bargain – what's not to love? And it's this same comforting sequence of joined-up delusions that has kept governments through the ages from acting on their stated abhorrence of the world's oldest profession and introducing the one measure that would crack down hard on it, once and for all: criminalising the clients.

If you're caught in possession of a drug like heroin, you face prosecution. Pleading that you're an addict, and you need a supply simply to keep going, won't necessarily cut any ice.

The theory is that if there wasn't a ready market for illicit drugs, then it wouldn't be worth anybody's while producing them, importing them, and killing rival drug gangsters in turf wars. If you're caught buying bootlegged DVDs, you face prosecution. Pleading that the kids would make your life hell if they weren't first to have the latest blockbuster movie won't get you very far with the beak. Again, the reasoning is purely logical – if there were no consumers for stolen, bootlegged or cheaply copied luxury goods, there would be no criminal empires built on supplying them. So far, so profoundly reasonable.

Trading in human beings, buying and selling vulnerable young woman, keeping them in sexual slavery through torture and terror and a very real threat of murder, ought to be viewed at least as seriously as flogging cannabis or wonky copies of *King Kong*, but it is not. Trafficking women for sex is not specifically outlawed in this country. Kidnapping a young girl, or luring her here with the false promise of a legitimate job, and keeping her captive while she is raped by a parade of Irish men who then pay her captors for the pleasure – that's not actually a specific crime here. We have, however, wonderfully watertight regulations governing immigration and asylum and work permits, and very precise requirements regarding the attendant paperwork. And so, as *Prime Time* revealed last week, when a trafficked girl called Maria was freed by Gardaí from the clutches of her pimp and the confinement of a grimy Dublin flat, she mistakenly believed that her horrific tale would ensure her some compassion and protection in a caring Christian country. Instead she was arrested for having no papers, despatched to Mountjoy Jail, and eventually deported. Full marks, there, to whoever drafted the relevant piece of legislation employed to expel Maria, it is obviously working most efficiently.

We do, undeniably, need to get in line with the rest of Europe when it comes to outlawing trafficking as a specific crime, but even those tough measures haven't come close to eliminating the problem elsewhere on the continent. Nor will they, while lawmakers continue to tiptoe around the source of the problem with ineffectual, cosmetic measures designed to make it look as though they give a damn. Asking men to phone a confidential number if they've had sex with a foreign prostitute who seemed troubled or reluctant is one such stunt – when has any 'john' given a flying curse about the real feelings of a prostitute? Such men would be far more likely to complain to her pimp, demand a refund, and earn her a hiding, if she didn't feign breathless enthusiasm with suitable conviction.

Obscene as it is, human trafficking is simply an inevitable by-product of a ruthless and lucrative criminal exploitation, just as the occasional gangland murder is a by-product of the trade in illicit drugs and, indeed, prostitution too. Young, vulnerable women are a commodity to be traded and sold to willing purchasers, and once that central transaction can be conducted with impunity, then it stands to reason that the suppliers will go to whatever lengths necessary to acquire the product. No surprises there.

Toeing the EU line and enforcing all those specific measures designed to hit the pimps and people-smugglers would be a very convincing and reassuring declaration of our commitment to ending human trafficking. My one small quibble with the notion is that it just won't make any difference. Throwing these scumbags in prison, if you catch them, if you convict them, may feel very good for the soul, but it won't save a single girl from their clutches. Closing down their markets by fiercely targeting their customers, though, now that would make an impact.

Unlike drug addicts, who tend not to care too much about their public image, the customers for the prostitution trade are often upstanding family men, professional chaps, pillars of the community. So they're more vulnerable to exposure, the prospect of being 'named and shamed' as consumers of peddled misery would act as a great deterrent to them. If they ran the added risk of being prosecuted as accessories in human trafficking – which is what they truly are – their enthusiasm for the services of prostitutes would surely wane dramatically. It's extraordinary, really, that downloading images of child porn is a crime, but effectively raping an abducted girl is not.

It's no defence, to a charge of handling stolen goods, to say, I didn't know the item was stolen, nor should it be an excuse for hiring a trafficked prostitute to say, I didn't realise she wasn't working willingly. Because here's the truth of another cherished male myth regarding prostitution – none of them is working willingly. No girl selects prostitution as a career option, not one of them would do it if she had any choice. And no, sorry, studs, but they don't enjoy it, you just pay them to make it look that way. Trafficked, coerced or just broke and in debt, every prostitute is a sad, desperate woman who once had proper dreams for her life.

One of the girls featured on the *Prime Time* programme had been based in a flat in Portarlington. She was pregnant when she returned to Romania, and now has an infant son. So there's a smug, probably married, most likely highly respected, pillar of the community somewhere in the midlands who has a baby son in Romania, an impoverished child dressed in hand-me-downs. Can't you just imagine the laddish sniggering in the pubs around the Portarlington area the night that programme screened, what a hoot, who's the daddy? That little boy is entitled to an Irish passport, he'll be eligible to play for our soccer team some day, not that he's likely ever to realise his birthright. Because like the crime and the misery, he's just another unfortunate by-product of a trade that no government on earth is willing to tackle. And his safely anonymous Irish father doesn't care a damn. Well, it's high time these men, these respected conspirators in the cruellest crime, were made to care, and made to worry.

July 2005

Return to the Dark Ages narrowly averted

THE VERY BOTTOM shelf of our local newsagents' stand regularly features a magazine that seems – apposite enough given its location on the shelves – entirely devoted to the nether regions of B-list female celebrities. It seems to pitch its wares particularly towards those folk who are fascinated by fleeting glimpses of Britney Spears or Charlotte Church's underwear as they get in and out of cars in unfeasibly short skirts – I suppose if you can have magazines aimed at lovers of model WW2 aircraft and origami, then a publication catering for admirers of nubile starlets' smalls is well within the bounds of possibility.

I do object, though, to the fact that this particular publication is laid out on the bottom shelf, so that my four-year-old has to lean across Jordan in a thong while he weighs up the merits of the free gifts on offer with this month's *Barney* magazine compared to the booty sellotaped to the cover of the *Tweenies* comic. In recent years, though, it seems as though the content of the so-called 'top shelf' magazines has migrated all over the news-stands, so that those publications still requiring to be quarantined high up out of kiddies' reach include some fairly raunchy stuff indeed.

Which may, it seems, be giving some retailers pause for thought. A few months ago I was presenting a radio series thrashing out modern-day moral dilemmas, and one such concern that came in from the owner of a large newsagents took me by surprise. He was a former teacher who had invested in a convenience store and newsagents along with his brother, and he was bothered by the fact that they were selling soft porn magazines in a shop where lots of kids shopped on a regular basis. He said he'd been involved in teaching the Relationship and Sexuality Education programme in school, and had formed the view that porn was exploitative and harmful, and that its use ran counter to the sort of messages about respect and commitment and responsibility that he had tried to impart in his teaching days. Surprisingly, perhaps, the bulk of the listeners who emailed the programme to comment on his dilemma sympathised fully, and made various helpful suggestions. They generally agreed, though, that if he didn't feel comfortable selling porn then he really didn't have to, and other retailers revealed they'd stopped stocking the stuff without meeting any storm of protest from disappointed customers. There was, of course, the predictable chorus of scorn from the liberal wing, bemoaning his single-handed efforts to haul the country back into the Dark Ages.

But then, any expression of a moral reservation about the pace or nature of social change in this country is often denounced as a threat to our treasured national image as a model of modern sophistication, not to mention a profound insult to the sensibilities of those foreign types who come here to invest their dollars. A shorthand guide to our progress over the past couple of decades usually includes a reference to how condoms were once only available to married couples on prescription, and the most exotic reading material readily accessible by consenting adults was *The Far East Magazine*. Predictably, then, there was widespread indignation when the Crisis Pregnancy Agency chairwoman Olive Braiden suggested that a number of pharmacies were refusing to sell contraceptives on moral grounds, and there were calls on the Minister for Health to make the issue of pharmacists' licences contingent upon their willingness to stock artificial birth control. One newspaper editorial ranted at great length about the 'fundamentalism' of these backward types, squarely laying the blame for the rise in teenage pregnancies upon their unenlightened and condom-free counters.

Unfortunately, though, this turned out to be a 'Small

Earthquake In Chile – Not Many Dead' type of story. A survey by *The Sunday Times* a few days later discovered that there was just one chemist in all of Dublin who refused to sell contraceptives to its reporter, but who did politely direct the customer to another pharmacy, two doors away, where all such requisites could be obtained. Phew! Return to the Dark Ages narrowly averted.

The headlines generated by this non-story, though, are far more accurate gauge of the depth and confidence of our cherished sophistication than any refusal by a handful of pharmacists to stock contraceptives because of their religious beliefs. A truly progressive and mature society could handle the fact that some people are willing to respect the fact that their Catholic faith prohibits artificial birth control. Pharmacists who take this decision are not actually foisting their beliefs on anybody, any more than newsagents who decline to sell naughty magazines are actively campaigning for the introduction of the burqa. Unfashionable an observation though it may be in our wonderful new multicultural Ireland, but the Constitutional assurance of freedom of religious expression also applies to Catholics. Funny how you won't find too many newspaper editorials railing at the reluctance of kosher butchers to sell good Irish pork sausages. If a chemist has a religious objection to the sale of contraceptives, he ought to be allowed express it without being lumped in with the London bus bombers as a religious fundamentalist. And if a newsagent doesn't want to sell X-rated magazines because they demean women, or objects to model WW2 aircraft magazines on the grounds that they glorify violence, or refuses to stock Barney comics in the belief that he is a large purple agent of Satan, our national self-confidence ought to be robust enough to absorb those blows, too.

October 2005

Protecting the brand: the Ferns Report

NOBODY WHO WORKED in the old *Irish Press* will ever forget Brendan Comiskey for one particularly pious and arrogant piece of grandstanding. *The Irish Press's* television reviewer had made a light-hearted comment about the then-imminent birth of the singer Madonna's first baby, and expressed the hope that this infant didn't cause as much trouble as the son born to a previous Madonna. Bishop Comiskey considered this remark to be blasphemous, and used the might and prominence of his role to demand a boycott by all God-fearing Catholics of the *Irish Press* Group newspapers. At that time the Press Group was in serious difficulties and did indeed close, not long afterwards, with the loss of many hundreds of jobs and hardship to many hundreds of families. Had Comiskey enjoyed quite as much clout as he hoped at that time, this would have happened sooner, and may even have been precipitated by his intervention.

Now we know that, at this time, the same Bishop who considered that hundreds of people deserved to lose their jobs and livelihoods because of one hack's throwaway quip did not feel that paedophiles and rapists should suffer any such fate as a result of their activities. Printers and copytakers and despatch drivers and all manner of people who had absolutely no input into the writing of the television column would have been put out of work in a tough economic climate, if Comiskey had had his way, while priests who corrupted and viciously assaulted innocent children could be redeployed with impunity.

Perhaps this is an insight into the value system of the man who hid himself away from the media he had once courted, in the wake of the Ferns Report last week, and issued a rather bland statement defending himself and describing his complicity in criminal activity for many years as simply 'human failings'. But it is also possible that Comiskey saw his attack on the *Press*'s blasphemous leanings to be entirely congruent with the effort to cover up and deny incidents of clerical sex abuse. In both instances, he may well have reasoned, the institution was under attack, and the institution had to be protected at all costs, even by the sacrifice of collateral civilian casualties.

It would be invidious to suggest that Bishop Comiskey, no more than his predecessor in the job nor his colleagues around the country and around the world, set out to do evil. But then, very few people do. Bank robbers, social welfare fraudsters, killers, even child abusers can all find justification in their experiences, circumstances and perceptions to justify and excuse their own particular brands of 'human failing' – that's how defence lawyers make a living. Had Bishop Comiskey's fingerprints been found all over the recovered Northern Bank raid notes, rather than the CVs of known child abusers, he could just as easily have pleaded 'human failings'. The fact that he'd have a far slimmer chance of fobbing the law off with that excuse if he'd been a party to stealing money rather than innocence is part of the reason why this obscenity persisted unchecked for so long.

As far back as the mid-1980s, the then Archbishop of Dublin sought legal advice as to the church's liability for clerical sexual abuse. He was told that any bishop who knew there were grounds to suspect a priest of abuse but nonetheless failed to withdraw him from ministry could be held legally, and expensively, liable for negligence. His sole response was to take out insurance cover against any resulting financial loss, and to advise every other bishop in the country to do the same. By 1990, most dioceses had this insurance in place. So they all knew this crime was prevalent enough to be a real concern, but their overriding instinct was to protect the institution from a financial hit, rather than to protect the children from the beasts who were raping and sodomising and terrorising them. Prioritising money rather than people may well be a human failing, but in this case it was also a very conscious, fully informed choice. By contrast, drunken driving causing death is a human failing but rarely a wholly conscious, coolly calculated decision. Nobody would expect to wash their hands of blame, in such circumstances, with the lame plea that they hadn't acted deliberately. And 'it could happen to a bishop' really isn't much of a defence anymore.

In 1988 Bishop Comiskey presided over a Confirmation ceremony in Monageer church in which he was assisted, in a grotesque insult to the sacrament, by a priest who had sexually abused some of the Confirmation girls just days before. Having specifically requested that James Grennan be absent from the ceremony, the girls' families walked out in disgust. When first asked about it Bishop Comiskey flatly denied the walkout had happened. When challenged with further evidence, he said he didn't see anyone walk out. He didn't notice a group of the Confirmation class of a small rural village walk out of the church along with their families and friends in the middle of proceedings. That is really difficult to believe.

So the evidence suggests that Bishop Comiskey, along with his Episcopal brethren, had reason to believe that children were being sexually abused by priests and acted deliberately to deny, and cover up, and minimise the effects, of this crime. There's now a proposal from Minister McDowell to make this form of 'human failing' into a statutory crime, but surely a Catholic churchman doesn't need legislative imprimatur to tell him the difference between right and wrong?

So what was it that stopped them from expressing a normal human response to the discovery that children were being sexually abused by priests? It can't be that they were all at it, although a friend of mine, a senior counsel who has represented many victims of abuse, reckons that in some institutions the view prevailed that the right to haul little orphaned boys from their beds in the middle of the night, rape them and dump them back with blood running down their legs, was something of a 'perk' of the job. It can't be that they didn't believe it or know it was wrong, or they'd never have gone to the expense of insuring against the costs of successful damages actions. And it can't have been that they expected divine mercy on the basis that their conspiracies were for the greater good of the church and its clergy – Jesus Christ took a surprisingly narrow view of scandalgivers and corrupters of innocence, and His solution to their failings involved millstones and ropes and lots of deep water.

The only explanation is that, somewhere along the way, the imperatives of the Catholic Church became less about what Jesus Christ thought of anything, less about people and more about power. Touchy-feely teachings about loving your neighbour and embracing humility weren't going to butter any parsnips. Vatican II may well have declared that the Church consisted of its flock, not its hierarchy, but within the world's oldest civil service – that of the Holy Roman Empire as absorbed by the Vatican – Pope John XXIII was viewed as little more than a meddling cabinet minister. And in the world's oldest civil service you can expect the world's most established 'Yes Minister' culture – the top brass come and go, but the system survives their well-intentioned tweaking and marches on. The rule of celibacy may have been designed to protect church wealth, but it also established a fortress of maleness at the heart of the Catholic Church, and it is a culture that simply cannot accept that the purpose of the institution could possibly be more important than the strength and endurance of its structure. So leaving helpless kids to the mercy of brutal paedophiles was about protecting the brand.

These bishops may have convinced themselves that they were doing the right thing, serving a greater purpose than mere transient humans, poor people's children, could possibly understand. But in their hearts they knew it was wrong, they knew they were turning a blind eye to the torture and corruption of innocents, they knew it when they checked the small print on their insurance policies and sought compliant new postings for their paedophile priests. They behaved like terrorists, blithely disregarding human suffering in pursuit of ends they believed would justify their means, and if the Catholic Church doesn't censure them, the law must.

November 2005

The Childcare Paradox

JUST BEFORE CHRISTMAS last year, my 9-year-old son arrived down to breakfast one morning and announced that he needed a camel costume. That day. Right then. There was, apparently, a dress rehearsal for the Nativity Play – a production so elaborate as to make Oberammergau look like improv – and he was a camel. I pointed out that strictly speaking the camels and Wise Men, weren't needed on set until 6 January, by which time I promised I would have secured a real live camel, but 15 minutes before school started was slightly short notice. Now it's at times like this that I really envy stay-at-home parents – not that they've all got the time to make perfect camels out of papier mâché, but because they miss out on the guilt that sent me scurrying around the house at twenty past eight in the morning doing unnatural things with a beige jumper, a pair of oven mitts and my best fringed belt. The whole childcare debate is centre stage as the budget approaches, and about time too, but there are elements of the dilemmas of working parents that no politician will ever resolve. No amount of legislation will ease the worry that, as a working mother, you're all losing out, that the extra money, intended to cushion your child's life and pay for his schooling, may be too hard won in the end. Childcare has to be reliable, first of all – a cheap understaffed crèche where they might just leave your kid behind after an outing to the park, as happened here recently, isn't much use. But it also has to be affordable, and when you think of it, buying childcare is in itself a paradox. You want to pay somebody to do the most valuable, most important job in your world, but you want to pay them less than you earn yourself. So almost by definition there has to be State intervention – the suggestion of childcare vouchers has some merit, but whether it is by tax credits, increased child benefits or supply-side subsidies, the cost of childcare has to come down – cheaper childcare will give parents the freedom to cut back on the hours they have to work to pay for the privilege of being able to work at all. And some initiatives could be relatively inexpensive – for many women those few hours between the end of the school day and the end of the work day are all that keeps them from the labour force, so after-school clubs, where perhaps local stay-at-home parents could earn extra cash by supervising children in an empty classroom, doing homework, watching DVDs or just texting each other all evening, would be an enormous help. I don't believe that kids need a parent with them all day long – but they do need a responsible and affectionate adult, and preferably other kids for company, if they're to grow into secure, sociable little people. No budgetary provision will change the fact that a working mother's life involves sacrifice – I consider it's important for my daughters and sons to see that an independent career gives a woman options and freedoms she might otherwise have to relinquish. But they don't always seem to appreciate this sacrifice when they beg me to stay home and make a jigsaw, or bake something for the school cake sale that I don't have to buy back myself, or produce a convincing camel in record time. But what innovative lawmakers can do is facilitate us in affording the most priceless commodity of all – time with our children.

2006

Sentencing Robert's killer
Box and Interview
Remembering the Stardust
Buy buy baby
'Turn that f***ing thing off'
The kitten in the incubator
'Plucking and stewing the golden goose'
Mollycoddling the KIPPERs
A nation of squinting villagers
Anger mismanagement
Keeping her feet on the ground in €29.99 shoes
Moral SWAT Team – 1; Peter Stringfellow – 0
When hanging is too good . . .
You can't unscramble an egg
Settling down

January 2006

Sentencing Robert's killer

A FEW DAYS ago in Britain, a group of teenagers who went on a murderous spree, that ended when they kicked and trampled a man to death just for fun, were all jailed for lengthy terms. Among the group was a 16-year-old girl called Chelsea O'Mahoney, who recorded the various attacks on her mobile phone for the entertainment of other friends. Even though some were underage, the judge ordered that the whole gang be named, and their photographs were released to the newspapers. And despite the fact that Chelsea O'Mahoney had been born to heroin addicts, abandoned to roam the streets of London from the age of three and spent all of her young life in care, the callous nature of her crimes cancelled out any leniency the court might have been inclined to show.

One of the gang's victims was a homeless man. Maybe they picked on him because they reckoned that nobody would miss him very much, nor make any fuss if he vanished from his usual patch. In that, they were probably right. The court reports carried no mention of a victim impact statement regarding the homeless man, there was nobody to say how much they loved him and how the gang's devilish cruelty had devastated their lives. But the fact that nobody cared too much what happened to this poor man didn't stop the judge getting all medieval with the teenagers, and putting them away for a very long time.

Entirely unrelated as they are, this case has some relevance to the controversy over the sentencing, yesterday, of Wayne O'Donoghue for the manslaughter of Robert Holohan. Because it illustrates the wisdom behind a principle of criminal law that victims and bereaved families find hard to accept – the law doesn't care how dearly you were loved or how badly you are missed, it doesn't matter if you were buried in a pauper's grave or if the whole country grieved for you – your life has an intrinsic worth to all humanity, no matter who you are, and your unlawful killing is a crime against all humanity, not just against your family, not even against yourself. As the victim of a crime, then, alive, you are just a witness, dead you're just forensic evidence – as a bereaved parent, you may have no role at all. Unfair though it might seem, Wayne O'Donoghue's crime was not 'against' the Holohans or even little Robert, it was against all of us.

There have been few cases in recent times that have engaged all of us like the disappearance of Robert Holohan in the early days of last year. A little boy cycling off on his shiny new bicycle, proud as punch with his new mobile phone, a whole week of the Christmas holidays still to enjoy. Until his body was found, curled like a baby in burnt swaddling robes of black plastic, it seemed impossible that the child could have come to any serious harm in such a safe rural community.

If he'd died exactly as Wayne O'Donoghue maintained, and if the young man had sought help immediately, it's actually unlikely that any charges would have been brought – accidents happen, after all. Instead it was O'Donoghue's subsequent deviousness that heightened the family's distress and now fuels their genuine suspicions of a more sinister motive. Why would somebody with a completely clear conscience go to such calculated, cool-headed lengths to cover his tracks?

For the Holohans, that question has not been answered by the criminal process. Instead, as the dead boy's mother explained yesterday, they have been left with doubts and unexplored possibilities that will torture them for the rest of their days.

It's hard to understand why Wayne O'Donoghue wasn't charged with concealing a body or obstructing justice, but since those charges weren't brought then he couldn't be sentenced for them. And he was not cross-examined about his version of Robert's death because he chose not to testify at his trial. As an accused person with a presumption of innocence, he had absolutely no obligation to do so. As a human being, though, as a friend and neighbour of the Holohans and as their dead boy's cherished hero, he should consider the true morality of this safe legal refuge. If killing little Robert was a crime against humanity, withholding details that might ease his parents' pain is a crime against mercy.

Until they know the truth, the Holohans will continue to endure nightmarish uncertainties about their child's last hours – did he suffer, was he fearful, did he cry for help?

And they also have to contend with the numbing finality of his loss. Robert was, by all accounts, a lovely little fellow, the kind of kid who fills every nook in the house with his laughter and his clutter and his exuberance – can't you just imagine the mess he made cooking those salty scrambled eggs for his mam?

However, the courts can't punish a killing more harshly because the victim was young and sweet and beautiful, or increase a prison sentence because he is so desperately missed. If so, then they'd have to deal more leniently with the killers of the old and lonely, the crotchety and forgotten.

If our lives were judged on our value to those left behind and not accorded an intrinsic worth, then Robert Holohan's killer would have been put away for the rest of his days. And the giggling teenage thugs who danced on the head of a homeless man would have escaped with scarcely a caution, all because there was nobody there to cry for him, or tell the court that he was loved.

February 2006

Box and Interview

IF EVERY SCHOOL in the country had a large deep pothole by the bicycle sheds, which routinely caused children to fall off their bikes and hurt themselves, you can bet it would be fixed pretty smartly. No matter how cash-strapped the school, money would be found to sort out the problem. The fear of serious injury, expensive legal action, and parental concern about the safety of their young children would ensure that the hazard was addressed as a matter of urgency.

Every single school in this country has a bully. No matter how proudly a school may boast of its anti-bullying policies, its 'tell-all' climate and its teachers' vigilance, every class at primary level, let alone every school, has at least one bully, and several victims. This may sound like an exaggeration, but it is true – according to figures recently released by Dr Mona O'Moore of the Anti-Bullying Centre (ABC) in Trinity College, almost one in three primary school pupils has been bullied at some time. At secondary level, the figure is 16 per cent. That means that around 200,000 Irish children are at present experiencing bullying. If you have a child at school in this country, in other words, you can be certain they are either aware of, have witnessed or are themselves victims of bullying.

And the effects of bullying are potentially much more serious and far-reaching than a tumble off a bike. At the very least, bullied children suffer stress, anxiety, fear of going to school each morning. As it goes on, they are prone to problems with their schoolwork and concentration, to insomnia and bed-wetting, to a loss of confidence and appetite, to mood swings, depression, stomach problems, and ultimately, according to ABC, they are at risk of nervous breakdown and suicide. The wonder is that this demonstrable catalogue of injury hasn't attracted compensation claims up to now.

And even those lucky enough to escape the bully's attentions don't come out of the experience unscathed. Children who witness bullying can also suffer feelings of powerlessness, stress, and deep upset at their own inability to intervene on behalf of a friend or classmate who is being persecuted. But at least small, scared children have an excuse for not putting a halt to the bully's activities – principals and boards of management do not. And now, thanks to a watershed case last week, school authorities may begin to realise that mere cosmetic solutions to the problem are not going to absolve them of responsibility any more. Just because you've got an impressive anti-bullying policy in place does not mean that you are tackling bullying. Unless it's followed through with determined action, such a policy is about as effective a legal defence as a sheet of Astroturf over your playground pothole – it may look neatly fixed, but if somebody gets hurt, the school will have to pay up.

Last week, a ten-year-old boy who was bullied and harassed at his primary school in Leixlip for two years was awarded €10,000 in compensation by a Circuit Court Judge. Given the possible effects of serious and sustained bullying, as identified by the Anti-Bullying Centre, the school got off fairly lightly in this case. The little boy suffered physical and verbal abuse from at least two other students. He was punched, kicked, spat at and pelted with stones. Cillín Ó Donnchadha's parents complained to the school, Scoil Chearbhaill Uí Dhálaigh in Leixlip, and were promised that the matter would be investigated, but nothing happened. Cillín told his mother that he didn't want a party for his seventh birthday. Nobody would come, he said, because all the other children in his class hated him. One day his mother found him doing press-ups, to make himself stronger so as to fight off the bullies. She raised her concerns with his teacher, but was assured all was well. The child began being ill in the mornings before school. In the afternoons he'd return home desperate for the bathroom, because he'd been afraid to use the toilets in school. His mother bought him a new Action Man jacket but he was afraid to wear it in school in case it drew too much attention to him. He began to suffer mood swings, sometimes quiet and withdrawn and sometimes violently angry with his older brothers. And all along, the school continued to assure his worried parents that nothing was amiss. Finally, Cillín's mother waited at the school gates one morning and watched her eight-year-old son walk into the playground. As she looked on, he was immediately attacked by two boys who thumped him without any evident fear of punishment. She took her child out of the school that day and never brought him back.

Personally, I think I'd have taken him straight to the nearest Garda Station to make a formal complaint of an assault occasioning actual bodily harm. No adult would be expected to run the gauntlet of kicks and punches on his way to his desk every morning, and there's absolutely no reason why a child should have to put up with it either. Physical assault is the most visible form of bullying, but it is by no means the worst. There's extortion bullying, where a child may be compelled to steal from home to satisfy the bully's demands, gesture bullying, verbal bullying, e-bullying by email or text, and, perhaps the nastiest, exclusion bullying, where the victim is isolated and humiliated by being told, as Cillín was, that he has no friends.

Often, the difficulty for both parents and schools is that bullying is sneaky and secretive, and the victim is fearful of the consequences of speaking out, and worried too about looking weak and cowardly. Victims of bullies don't always arrive home looking like the sad Billy Bunter kid of countless cartoon portrayals, with smashed specs and gashed knees and torn shirt. Your child may well be the bullies' target while you are obliviously attributing her mood swings, her withdrawn nature, her declining performance and her lost appetite to pre-pubescent hormones. Parents can easily remain in the dark about bullying but from now on it will be tougher for schools to plead ignorance.

Once a parent raises a concern, the schools are formally on notice of a problem and simply promising to 'keep an eye on it' is no longer good enough. With any luck, Cillín's case will herald a heightened obligation on schools to be proactive in rooting out and eliminating bullying. Up to now they could get away with protesting that they didn't know, especially if children were reluctant to come forward, but arguably now the law imposes a positive duty on school authorities to inform themselves about bullying on an ongoing basis. There's one cheap and simple technique, for instance, which should be common practice in all our schools, called the Box and Interview Method. Briefly, once a week every pupil is asked to fill and sign a form answering three simple questions: during the past week have you been bullied, do you know of anybody in the class who has been bullied, do you know of anybody in the school who has been bullied. The forms are dropped into a locked box, examined by volunteer teachers and the results passed on, in guaranteed confidence, to a nominated Anti-Bullying Coordinator, who will investigate all substantive complaints by interviewing victims, bullies, parents and other students. Crucially, children who don't fill in the form are interviewed too.

It would be time consuming, certainly, in already overstretched schools, but the system calls for the goodwill of volunteers from teaching staff. You'd hope that the incentive for teachers would be happier, more attentive, more confident pupils in the classroom, and not necessarily extra dosh in their paypackets.

At the very least, the system might alert the bullies to the risk of being rumbled. And while we are always assured that bullies have their own problems and need to be understood, often they're just nasty, cowardly brats who need to be identified and stopped. From now on, with the threat of compensation payouts looming before their eyes, school authorities might just discover they are not quite as powerless to discipline these sneaky little horrors as they thought.

February 2006

Remembering the Stardust

THE DRAUGHTY HALL, the hand-painted signs, the poor people in poor clothes and thin coats, the angry outbursts in working-class Dublin accents – everything about the Stardust drama's reconstruction of those early relatives' meetings brought me back more than 20 years.

In the mid-1980s I was a young freelance journalist, not long out of college, working for *The Irish Press*. Unlike the other papers at the time, they paid a shift rate for 'markings' – single assignments like a protest march or a council meeting, and they paid very well. And there were lots of council meetings endlessly rezoning the city in those days, and it being the 1980s there were lots of protest marches too, between the unemployed, the concerned parents against drugs, the pro-life crowd, somebody always seemed to be on the go.

Well-paid though it was, though, the one 'marking' you really didn't want was the Stardust Relatives' Committee meetings. You could walk to the council chambers on O'Connell Street, and doze in the heat while they droned on about amenities and green belts, and you could always catch the protest marchers outside the Dáil, but an assignment to cover the Stardust Relatives Committee was a real drag. It meant getting a couple of buses to chilly, grey halls in bleak landscapes on the Northside. It meant sitting in the cold for hours listening to the same angry, sad, defeated people endlessly pursuing their hopeless cause. There was no energy, there was no glamour, there was no news, there was no tea or coffee and worst of all, there was very little chance of seeing your story in the paper the next day.

You'd trudge back to Burgh Quay to write up the Committee's latest demands or their new action plan, and you'd know that at best your piece would end up as a couple of paragraphs on the bottom of a left-hand page. Everybody had Chrissie Keegan's phone number in their contacts books in the mid-1980s – I found it last week in an ancient diary alongside numbers for ACRA, the ground rents lobby, and the Divorce Action Group, and the Irish Anti-Extradition Committee. Those other issues were resolved, or won, or overtaken by events, but not the Stardust. They never got answers, they never got justice, they never won anything. They slipped from the headlines because we all got bored with the story, we stopped calling Chrissie Keegan's number because we'd never hear anything new, we stopped covering the meetings because there was nothing fresh to say. The Stardust was a major turn-off. We all forgot about them.

But now it's 25 years later and the imperatives of 'calendar journalism' require us to revisit them. There are a couple of generations of readers and viewers and listeners who never learned the details of the Stardust holocaust. We can watch and read and listen with our children or younger friends and say, I remember all that. Imagine it, 48 young people, with an average age of 19, burned to death at a Valentine's disco. Imagine the heartbreak in all those modest homes, and the financial hardship in households where those youngsters' wages helped make ends meet. Imagine that some of the firedoors were locked, and yet nobody went to prison. Imagine that the owner of the place got hundreds of thousands of pounds in compensation, and yet the families of the dead and maimed had to fight tooth and nail to get a few miserable thousand apiece, years later. Imagine that smart lawyers and cynical politicians bought them off so cheaply, knowing they were poor. Put like that, it has the desired effect on our children and our younger friends, who may have vaguely heard the name of the Stardust but never known what really happened. They are gratifyingly shocked. It's just a shame we stopped being shocked ourselves.

Now there are fresh calls for an enquiry, new interpretations of forensics have emerged, some doubt has been cast on the conclusion that the fire was arson. Sceptics may well ask, why now? If any new evidence really exists, then it has been available for years. How convenient that it turns up to coincide with a significant anniversary, a new wave of public interest, a controversial television drama. If the Stardust mysteries are truly worth reopening, why didn't we do it eight years ago, twelve years ago, six months ago?

The answer, obviously, is that it wouldn't have been a story then. No anniversary to hang it on, no valid excuse to drag out all those fading pictures of pretty girls with Lady Di hairstyles, no reason to replay that old footage of shocked blackened dancers being helped from the fire. So if journalists have, indeed, discovered a new cause for disquiet about the Stardust fire on its 25th anniversary, it's only because the story is sexy again. Not because that material wasn't available all along, but because nobody could be bothered looking for it until there was a newsworthy peg for the story. And that fact obliges all of us in the media to accept that we were the ones who let the Stardust victims down.

The public lost interest in the story, that's true, but that's because nothing new was happening, and outrage stagnated. And nothing new was happening because the media let the politicians off the hook. And the politicians, for all their bleating and posturing and haste to be filmed outside the smouldering wreckage that February, didn't give a hoot because there are no votes in dead poor people. In the mid-1980s our politicians, as we now know from the tribunals, had other fish to fry. They had all that zealous rezoning to do, they had little time to worry about Coolock and Artane when there were all those lovely new disadvantaged wastelands to be created. They had brown envelopes to collect, crooked lobbyists to meet, Parisian tailors to visit.

It is convenient, now, to blame the self-serving politicians of the day for what happened to the Stardust victims. It's easy to feel disgust for the cynical and smarmy legal advisers who devised a compensation scheme that effectively blackmailed those people into dropping their legal actions. But the self-serving politicians and the smarmy legal advisers were just doing what smarmy, self-serving, cynical types do. It's harder to forgive the media, to absolve all of us who were working as reporters and commentators and broadcasters at the time, for letting them away with it.

We were the Stardust victims' only conduit to the only leverage they might have had – public opinion. We knew they couldn't afford the best senior counsels, the slickest public relations officers, the comfortable hotel suites for their press conferences, as the State could. They couldn't even afford tea, or heat, or convenient venues, or photocopied press releases at their meetings. We all had Chrissie Keegan's phone number but we never called her as often as she called us, she phoned all the newsdesks all the time, her phone bill must have been enormous. We all sat through enough meetings to know they were getting a raw deal and that they hadn't the money or the clout to fight back. But time moved on, life began to improve and the Stardust victims simply evoked the angry, weary hopelessness of a decade we were anxious to leave behind. The public had no business growing bored with those wronged people until they got justice – we should have forced them down your throats until you lobbied your local TD for action just to make them go away. We should have championed them, forced them onto the national and political agenda, highlighted their shabby treatment at every election campaign and on every single anniversary until somebody listened.

Instead, we wait to revisit them on the 25th anniversary, when the passage of years puts them neatly back in the news. And we are astonished to find they are still bitter, still grieving, still looking for answers. Stranger still, we find them disillusioned with the media, sceptical about our interest. And you can't blame them. Watching that dramatic replay of those grim, cold committee meetings upset me like nothing I've seen on television in years. Because here's what I didn't tell my children: I was there, yes, but I wasn't angry enough. None of us was.

February 2006

Buy buy baby

WE'VE BECOME SO used to judicial decisions that seem at odds with common sense, or impervious to human emotion, that it's a major surprise when a judge does exactly what you'd like to do yourself. Well, maybe not exactly, but even to find a judicial ruling that comes pretty close to the ordinary citizen's instinctive concept of natural justice is a rare and wonderful thing. Fortunately for Joe and Lala Dowse, judges are not ordinary citizens, because most of us might well have considered that a spell in the nick for cruelty, abuse and neglect of their adopted son Tristan would have been proper order. Short of seeing this callous pair banged up, though, the financial obligations imposed on them last week by High Court Judge John McMenamin scored highly enough on the national clapometer to address the genuine anger that the Dowses' behaviour inspired.

Back in 2001, Joe Dowse, from Bray, and his Azerbaijani wife, Lala, bought a two-month old baby boy, however indirectly, from a poor Indonesian woman who couldn't afford to keep the child herself. You can dress the transaction up as a humane, inter-country adoption with the primary aim of giving an impoverished infant the chance of a life that his ignorant, inadequate birth-parent couldn't hope to offer, but it boiled down to a cold, crude cash deal. They wanted a baby and couldn't seem to have one. She had a baby and it didn't matter much whether she wanted to keep him or not. Harsh

financial realities and, allegedly, the intervention of a child
trafficker delivered baby Tristan into the fickle care of the
Dowses.

It being, then, a simple case of supply-and-demand in a
buyers' market, the Dowses appear to have decided that the
usual statutory rights of consumers applied as readily to a child
as to a toaster. Regardless of the guarantee provisions or the
retailers' particular returns policy, any item you purchase is
supposed to do the job for which it was advertised. If it does
not, you are entitled to bring it back. When the Dowses
acquired Tristan, they were looking for a contented, grateful,
low-maintenance baby who would love and appreciate them
from day one. But, as though he was a faulty packet of
wallpaper adhesive, he failed to bond, they said. Significantly,
this obstinacy of his emerged just around the time Mrs Dowse
discovered she was pregnant.

So there you are, muddling along with your new bog-
standard toaster, when you get a surprise gift of a top-of-the-
range model. Naturally, you return the first one to the shop
and tell them that you're just not happy with the thing. Which
is exactly what the Dowses' did with little Tristan. Suddenly he
was surplus to requirements, and far from perfect to boot, so
they dumped him back to the orphanage. They felt his interests
would be best protected, the Dowses told the court, if he could
be quietly re-adopted and the matter kept out of the public
gaze. Which was a heap of repulsively hypocritical rubbish.
Whatever chance a cute two-month old baby had of being
adopted in a country like Indonesia, the likelihood that a
lonely, confused English-speaking toddler might be satisfac-
torily recycled was obviously a long shot. Not that the Dowses
gave a damn. Ironically, it was the publicity that helped reunite
him with his natural mother, and had other couples
clamouring to give him a home. But the noble Dowses would
clearly have preferred if he'd languished quietly in that
orphanage, sharing a room with 34 other tots, and spared them
all this inconvenience. When they collected him in the

summer of 2001 the Dowses promised to care for little Tristan as if he was their 'own flesh and blood' but, as the judge rather delicately put it, 'what occurred is difficult to reconcile with that statement'.

Having returned him to the orphanage, they then made the princely donation of €1,175 to the place, presumably in the hope that this great bounty would soothe any quibbles from the authorities there. It certainly wasn't going to guarantee the little boy a comfortable life, it was simply conscience money. Obviously €1,175 is a large sum in Indonesia. How fortunate for the Dowses that the cost of assuaging their guilt was subject to the international exchange rate and measured in the national currency of a poor country.

Now, at least, the Irish courts have been able to apply a more realistic economic barometer to the situation. The financial package ordered by the High Court last week will have cost the Dowses almost €100,000 by the time Tristan reaches 18. It's a lot less than such a well-heeled couple would lavish on the pampering and clothing and educating of a child of their own over that time, and, while he'll be more comfortable than most in Indonesia, Tristan will undoubtedly have a lower standard of living and future prospects than the children who would have been his adoptive siblings if only he'd gotten his act together over the pesky 'bonding' business. Luckily for him, Judge McMenamin built in the possibility of redressing this imbalance in years to come – since he retains his succession rights as though he was still their child, Tristan will be able to challenge the Dowses' wills if they don't make provision for him that's considerably more generous than their bequests to their other children, given the clear inequality in the privileges they will have had. The Succession Act doesn't oblige you to leave something to each of your children in your will, but it does impose a moral obligation to treat your children fairly, taking all their circumstances into account.

So for little Tristan, back with his mother, financially secure and gradually recovering from the trauma of his abandonment, there is a happy ending of sorts. As there is, undeniably, for the many children of impoverished parents who find new homes with well-heeled families in the West, but this case casts a discomfiting light upon the hard facts behind such adoptions. Tempting though it may be to gloss over the truth, very few of these babies are 'unwanted' in the sense that some others, like Chinese baby girls, are genuinely unwelcome. Just because a mother can't afford it, perhaps because there are other mouths to feed or economic straits are truly dire, doesn't mean she wouldn't want to keep her child. Poverty doesn't necessarily immunise a new mother against a broken heart when she gives her baby away, even if it denies her any alternative.

In the very recent past, in this country, there were other factors that imposed this awful separation on new mothers here. As strong and independent a woman as the late Frankie Byrne was, one of thousands who had to part with her newborn baby in different, but not so distant, times. We know now that she brought that heartbreak to her grave, despite knowing that her little girl had a privileged and happy life. Our Western affluence, and a growing tendency to view babies as consumer goods rightly available to all who can afford them, is imposing that same grief on another generation of women. And now they're suffering, not because they've offended against morality, like Frankie Byrne, but against a far more implacable ethic. They've committed the unpardonable sin of being poor, and so people like the Dowses are free to buy their children, and ill-treat or discard them on a whim. It may be small comfort to such mothers, but last week's High Court ruling may at least ensure the likes of the Dowses will think twice before doing so in future.

March 2006

'Turn that f***ing thing off'

LAST SATURDAY EVENING, no less than two separate groups of walkers had to be rescued from the Dublin Mountains after they lost their way. They'd gone out for a trek, perhaps because the day looked promising early on, but Saturday turned rather nasty around six and the rain poured down for the rest of the night. Fortunately, according to reports of the incidents, disaster was averted because they happened to have their mobile phones with them, and were able to phone for help. Disaster, my foot. I've been in those mountains myself when it began to get dark and wintry, I suspect I've even been briefly lost there (men won't ask directions and never admit to being lost) but I'd have set my hair on fire for a torch before I'd have taken out a mobile phone and summoned some poor volunteer from his cosy fireside and out onto a dark, rainy mountain to lead me home.

It is not exactly the Amazon, after all, if you keep walking in a vaguely straight line you will hit what passes for civilisation in those parts eventually. Reading those reports of the dramatic rescues, I reckoned that our intrepid walkers found their little piggies getting cold when the rain came down heavier than they'd expected, the thought of a hot toddy in Johnnie Fox's sounded tempting, and the easiest thing to do was phone for help. What happened to mislaid mountaineers in the teeming tundra of south County Dublin before everyone had a mobile, I wonder? Did they just get on with it and find their own way down? Or are there still stray walkers trudging through the pines out there like forgotten Japanese soldiers, living off a baked bean a day and wondering why Taoiseach Jack Lynch hasn't sent in the troops?

In fact, how did any of us manage in the days before mobile phones? How did our nearest and dearest survive without knowing we were sitting on the bus and would be home in 20 minutes? How did we ever decide between two different brands of toilet paper in the supermarket without being able to phone home for help? How did we find our friends in a pub without being able to ring and check if they were in the bar or lounge? Which has to be the most irritating thing about being disturbed in public by somebody else's ring tone – you just know the call is unnecessary and the recipient just plain selfish.

Full marks for chutzpah, of course, to the woman whose mobile interrupted Ralph Fiennes in full flow in The Gate Theatre at the weekend. She tried to brazen it out, perhaps shot an accusing glance at her neighbour in the front row as the phone trilled on, but Ralph wasn't fooled. Abandoning his Faith Healer character, he shouted at her to 'turn that f***ing thing off', even if he did soften the blow with a joke as she fumbled, rumbled, in her bag.

Either stupidity or selfishness – both, alas, classic hallmarks of the inveterate mobile user – are to blame for that woman's decision to ignore the endless reminders you get in theatres and cinemas these days about switching off phones. The strongest proof, in fact, that these things do actually emit brain-frying rays is the indisputable dimness of their regular users. As well as making us stupid and forgetful, though, mobile phones have also made us inconsiderate, unpunctual, impatient and lazy. Nobody makes much effort to keep appointments any more – if you reckon your time is more valuable than somebody else's then it's easy to keep them waiting with a call to say you're running late. Better still, a quick text absolves you of actually having to bother speaking to them in person and coming up with an excuse. Mobiles mean nobody is entitled to down-time any more – just feel the rage when you call a switched-off phone. And it's high time mobile-using motorists were penalised, because they're a genuine menace on the roads.

Mobiles give parents a false sense of security about their kids' safety – the murdered Soham girls, as well as young Robert Holohan, all carried mobiles. Mobile companies tell us their products are connecting people – in fact, increasingly, they are distancing us from those around us, and irritating them, to boot.

Irish Rail is considering introducing a mobile-free carriage on its Dublin-to-Cork line. Presumably, the request to turn off phones will be made with polite little notices and announcements, just like the one they broadcast before curtain-up at The Gate. I suggest both places obtain a recording of Ralph Fiennes bellowing, 'Turn That F***ing Thing Off' and play it loudly and regularly for maximum compliance.

April 2006

The kitten in the incubator

SO, AS I was saying about kittens, anyway, I'm generally quite keen on them. Cute things, kittens. They look particularly good on greeting cards, or playing prettily with a little ball of wool, or curled up in front of a blazing fire. Useful, too, for keeping mice away. Can be quite amusing, sometimes, and they're the only animals I know that will actually bring you a gift as a sign of affection – I once had a small cat who used regularly present me with live baby mice, and always looked very crestfallen at my reaction. I hardly ever ate them alive, which I think was expected, and he seemed to think that was bad form.

In fact, I'm not in favour of eating any animals alive, or torturing them, or tying them to lamp posts and setting fire to them, or allowing them to die slow painful deaths entirely for my amusement, despite what a very large number of *Daily Mail* readers appear to have concluded. In fact my comments last week, about the open-heart surgery performed by an Irish vet on a 12-week-old kitten, generated quite an impressive mailbag, pretty much all of it accusing me of wanton savagery to small creatures and, in one especially intriguing piece of logic, of being a beast.

Perhaps you were among those shocked by the news that a farmer, of my father's vintage, wouldn't actually have summoned a team of surgeons to perform two hours of microsurgery on the ailing runt of a litter of kittens. Hard though it is to believe, he wouldn't have ponied up for the use of an incubator, designed for human babies, in which the patient might recover. But nor would he have left the animal to die slowly and miserably, as nature had obviously intended. Perhaps that's difficult to stomach but, well, that's the reality of a traditional, rural life for you. No farmer who makes a living from his animals would ever allow a creature to suffer. But most, that I know, have a healthy perspective on the value of an animal's life when compared to that of a human being. They can't afford to be too emotional about the creatures in their care — but, either due to our new-found affluence or the loneliness of modern lifestyles, a lot of us can. We spend un-conscionable fortunes on our pets. And I make no apology for wondering whether that is a good or moral development. Humans are more important than animals — build a bridge, as Sinead O'Connor would say, and get over it.

I admit I've given my share of cash to vets, over the years, for treatments and vaccinations and antibiotics and nail-trimming for dogs and cats and guinea pigs and goldfish (not the nail-trimming, obviously). And it always troubles me, quite a bit, because for days afterwards I have to turn away from news reports of children in disaster areas or war zones or third-world countries whose lives could well have been saved by the very drugs or level of medical attention I just shelled out on for an animal. And so that report of the kitten in the incubator really bugged me. Perhaps because it came in Holy Week, when we're meant to contemplate our priorities, and perhaps because of the general approving consensus, but that particular story seemed a profound insult to the principles that Christians are meant to honour at this time of year.

There are worse sins, you know, than coveting your neighbour's wife or lusting after his new car. We've all seen the heartbreaking pictures from Eastern European orphanages and bombed-out Iraqi hospitals – do you think any of them would refuse the gift of an incubator, even second-hand, even one formerly used to restore kittens to full health? I've watched one of my own newborn babies lying in an incubator – the thought of a kitten in the same machine while there are infants dying for want of such equipment strikes me as downright sacrilegious. Black mass rituals sometimes use pigs instead of babies to parody the baptismal rite – operating on a cat, swaddling it like a human child and placing it in a paediatric care unit doesn't seem to me a million miles from that.

It is, of course, cruel to allow an animal to suffer needlessly, though subjecting a 12-week-old kitten to two hours of surgery wasn't necessarily the most humane course, either. But the simple fact is that somebody had the money to pay for this operation, that's why it happened. If you've got the cash and you want to spend it on microsurgery for your cat, good luck to you. It's morally more admirable than forking out five grand on a handbag from Brown Thomas. And it's morally less admirable than sending that money to Trócaire. Be very clear that's the choice you make.

April 2006

Plucking and stewing the golden goose

THESE ARE THE dying days of 1975, you are a very senior civil servant, and you are locking that year's state papers away to be re-opened three decades later. Being so senior, you are earning more than £4,000, which means you are paying 77 pence in every pound in tax, in a depressed economy where inflation is running at 21 per cent. Before you go home to your houseful of children, contraception being illegal and you being a devout Catholic, and settle down to watch *Fawlty Towers* on your black and white television, you might get into musing on the Ireland in which those sealed papers will once again see the light of day. The prospects, you'd have to say, do not look very good. The Northern situation is hopeless. The economy is banjaxed. You are, in the words of an angry young punk from Blackrock, living in a Banana Republic. The country, as that Boomtown Rats ditty put it, is run by the black and blue uniforms of police and priests. It is impossible to imagine how any of this might begin to change.

Over a pint in a smoky pub that evening, you try to conceive of an Ireland about as different as it could possibly be from your daily reality. You imagine one of the world's richest countries, with so much technological savvy that eight-year-olds carry phones the size of Marietta biscuits around in their pockets, where hundreds of thousands of us own foreign holiday homes, where the Tánaiste – a woman – recommends emergency contraception for 11-year-old girls, where the IRA has given up its weapons and disbanded, where smoking is banned in pubs and where Sir Bob Geldof is a multimillion-aire advising the British Conservative Party on its anti-poverty strategy. You wouldn't dream of sharing this fantasy with even your nearest and dearest, for fear that the State Papers were not all that ended up being locked away for a very, very long time.

On that reckoning, it is fair to assume that the State Papers from this new year of 2006 will themselves be opened in a vastly different country to the one we now know, just as the Ireland of 30 years ago is all but unrecognisable now. Viewed from the lofty heights of our 21st-century sophistication and prosperity, the citizens of 1975 look like a dumb and docile bunch, dull and inward-looking, lacking ambitions and imagination. The pinnacle of our cultural aspirations back then was, apparently, a concert that could star both Frank Sinatra AND Morecambe and Wise – such an event, a Stormont official suggested, would be so blindingly star-studded that the youth of the North would be inspired to renounce paramilitarism forever. Teen drinking was a growing concern, to the extent that one alcoholism expert recommended to the Taoiseach Liam Cosgrave that drink be banned at state functions so as to set a good example. Back then we must have respected and even believed our politicians – how quaintly naïve that now seems.

So, in 30 years' time, what will future generations and commentators make of us? Will we appear as we fondly imagine ourselves to be – clever and knowing, discerning and worldly – or will we just look cynical, greedy, shortsighted and self-absorbed? And from that remove, will 1975 look as it does now, like a time of impoverished despair, or rather as the beginning of the last era of genuine Irish patriotism and national unity, one that was long dead by 2006?

We are undeniably richer now, more prosperous, more globally envied. There are jobs for all who want them, including the 100,000 foreign workers who came here last year. We also seem to be living proof that money can, indeed, make you happy, as just last week we topped yet another international survey to find the most contented nation on earth. We are far more liberated and educated, and wouldn't dream of tolerating the sort of political and religious imperiousness we lived with in 1975. And we have so much stuff! There isn't a designer vehicle or garment or household appliance that we can't afford – we even have a waiting list for 06 reg Ferarri sports cars and €1,500 Vuitton suitcases. If the people of 2036 are exponentially shallow and acquisitive, they will certainly be impressed when they look back at us.

But it's just as likely that they'll look back and wonder why we couldn't see how recklessly we were squandering our good fortune, and their heritage. We're just not listening to the warnings from the ESRI about the need to rein-in consumer spending and pay demands, and there isn't a single political party with the courage to say that we can't go on living beyond our means. Next year, for example, public sector pay is going to cost us an additional 7 per cent, more than twice the rate of inflation, even before pay increases are negotiated. Meanwhile the sectors that actually bring wealth into the country, manufacturing and export businesses, are being squeezed because growing labour costs and ever-increasing pay expectations are making it difficult for them to compete. But no political party has the guts to cool consumer spending – on the contrary, daft measures like the Budget's additional €1,000 allowance to parents of under-fives, not to mention the impending SSIA payouts, will only whip it up. Thanks to Eddie Hobbs we know we're being ripped off right, left and centre and we don't much like it, but it doesn't stop us doing it to everybody else. Tourists, employers, customers, all can expect to pay more and more for shoddy service, cut corners and downright shameless scams. We may fancy ourselves sophisticated and worldly with our designer goods and our holiday villas, but our instincts are pure gombeenism: we're throttling and plucking and stewing the golden goose without a thought to where next year's eggs will come from. No wonder we're happy – those *Titanic* passengers who played deck football with chunks of iceberg thought they were having a ball, too.

Compare this with the Ireland of the late 1970s and 1980s.

At least then we knew we were banjaxed, and we pulled together to do something about it. Say what you like about Charles Haughey, but at least he had the sheer chutzpah to tell us to tighten our belts at a time when he was letting his own out a notch or three. You can call it patriotism, or put it down to the sheer force of blindingly obvious reality, but there was a genuine sense that the country's good required wage restraint and public spending cuts and partnership cooperation. But we stuck it out and it worked, we even clawed back the cynical reverses of Jack Lynch's 1977 election profligacy, and the result was the boom that began in the late 1990s. But if fleecing tourists, exploiting foreign workers and ripping off hapless consumers is the best we can do to keep profits up, then it's clear we have no insight into how we became rich and not a clue how to sustain it. Take the Taoiseach's justification for wanting to spend the price of several hospital wings on the Bertie Bowl project a few years back – the money wouldn't last forever, he explained, so we might as well lash it around on useless vanity projects while we had it. That's the spirit! Instead of analysing and consolidating our gains, we've decided to spend, spend, spend, and the devil take the hindmost. And like all spendthrifts, we've nothing much to show for our good fortune. Our health service is still woeful, our roads are gridlocked, the Dublin port tunnel is going to cost over a billion and looks set to emerge in Brisbane sometime in the next century, we have a hopeless public transport system, and if it wasn't for the EU we wouldn't have a decent stretch of motorway in the country. And we stubbornly refuse to listen to, let alone elect, any politician who tells us that the good times are winding down, which is why we get election budgets that keep us feeling happy and rich, and an opposition too timid to point out the approaching storm.

So when they open this year's State papers in 30 years' time, will the folk of 2036 pity or envy us? Or with the effort of paying off our debts, rebuilding our export trade and luring back our tourists, will they even bother opening them at all?

May 2006

Mollycoddling the KIPPERs

I BLAME THE Prodigal Son's father for the price of property in Dublin. If only he'd said, 'Inheritance? What inheritance would that be?' when his lad asked for an early cut of the will, then we might not have this ingrained sense of filial entitlement to the proceeds of a parent's life's work. And if kids weren't anticipating that windfall at some stage in the future, they wouldn't feel a real and present claim on their parents' nest eggs or a right to a slice of the idle equity in the family home. And if they weren't able to put the squeeze on the parental units, then they wouldn't be running about the place snapping up smartly appointed shoeboxes for half a million euro and pushing prices through the roof for the rest of us.

Young adults are greedily eyeing the inflated value of their parents' homes, calculating the share that's heading their way, and dining out – literally – on the strength of it. Our recent economic boom has brought a general sense of entitlement, but young people seem particularly cavalier about this assumption of enduring good fortune. When they see others apparently having it all, they know of no good reason why they shouldn't have it all, too. They want property, certainly, but they want the flash, pampered lifestyle, too – and something has definitely got to give. The alarm bells have been growing deafening lately – the OECD estimates that Irish houses are overvalued by up to 20 per cent, but all the signs are that Dublin values will rise by another 15 per cent in the coming year. And there's no doubt that this scary escalation is fuelled by that frenzy of demand – people are desperate to get on the property ladder, whatever the cost or evident lunacy of their frantic purchases, simply because everybody else is doing it so it must be a good idea. Lemmings heading for a cliff edge seem positively cautious by comparison. Last week 62 houses in a new development in Rathfarnham sold in a single day, and potential buyers camped out for ten days for a chance to buy new homes in the €400,000 bracket in Blessington at the weekend – all 30 sold out in a couple of hours, mostly to young couples and first-time buyers.

Who exactly is whipping these young people into a state of panic about property ownership? Actually, I do blame the parents. They're the ones remortgaging their own homes to provide deposits for grown offspring, they're the ones mollycoddling the KIPPERs – that's Kids In Parents' Pockets Eroding Retirement – by allowing them to stay living at home until they've nailed down a property of their own. But the arguments that persuaded middle-aged folk to buy rather than rent are no longer so strong. Yes, rent may be dead money – but a 40-year-mortgage on a tiny 'starter' property you'll never actually own, and the vast sums you'll pay in stamp duty and fees for the privilege of trading up to silly money status in a few years time, doesn't make much sense, either. Lots of investors have bought to let, so there are actually plenty of really decent properties available from owners who'd be happy to sign a secure and lengthy lease – even a bedsit doesn't have to mean a wonky Baby Belling cooker, a candlewick bedspread and a poster of Che Guevara covering the damp spot anymore.

But the parental encouragement to buy also fuels this sense of material entitlement – young people don't see why they can't have the car, and the clothes, and the holidays and the lifestyle, once the parents are worrying about the deposit for the apartment, and even doing the queueing for them. The evidence of programmes like *I'm An Adult, Get Me Out of Here* suggests that young people don't see any possible connection between self-denial and reward. And why should they, when they can live at home, live it up and leave the folks to fret about confusing stuff like interest rates and square footage and where and when to buy?

The irony is that frantic buying for fear of ever-spiralling prices becomes a self-fulfilling prophesy – unless we calm down and cool it, then the housing market and the entire economy will overheat, with disastrous results: if it all comes crashing down, then there'll be a generation of home owners looking at serious negative equity in their properties, paying off massive mortgages for homes worth a pitiful fraction of their purchase price.

And if that happens – and some sort of a readjustment is pretty much inevitable soon – there'll be some real bargains to be had by the smart ones who held off and rented for a few years. Which is surely what the Prodigal Son, broke, disinherited AND stuck living with the da for good, must have wished he'd done himself.

May 2006

A nation of squinting villagers

A FEW YEARS ago, around this time of year, a priest in a small County Kerry village caused a bit of a stink by airing his views on couples 'living in sin', as the wonderfully impartial phrase used to go. It was the First Communion season and he warned that the unmarried parents of the young Communicants had no business approaching the altar along with their children, as they would be denied the sacrament, and a refusal often offends. He did, however, make the distinction between unmarried couples who continued to cohabitate, and single parents who were alone. The latter group would be welcome to participate in the sacrament, because of an assumption that they regretted their sin and were not openly and brazenly repeating it by continuing to reside with the other party. In other words, unmarried couples who stayed together to raise their kids as a family were recidivist sinners, while, say, single fathers who had legged it would be welcome as the flowers of May at the altar rails on First Communion Sunday.

Being of a naturally contrary disposition, this struck me as a tad unfair. I duly wrote a radio column about it, and made reference to the fact that the village where it happened had some ironic significance to the substance of the issue. Of all the places of Ireland, I said, that might have learned the dangers of stigmatising unmarried parenthood, wouldn't you think it might be Abbeydorney?

For those old enough to remember the Kerry Babies saga, the name of Abbeydorney has a resonance gloomier than Granard, more bizarre than Ballinspittle, more alarming than Abbeylara. It was the homeplace of Joanne Hayes, the young woman at the centre of the tale, who gave birth in secret, smothered her baby and buried it in a field, and subsequently confessed to the murder of a second baby who had been stabbed and washed up on Cahersiveen Strand around the same time. The matter took on an inconvenient complexity when it emerged that Ms Hayes couldn't possibly have been the mother of the second murdered infant, and a tribunal was set up to establish how the series of unfortunate events played out.

I was a trainee reporter on *The Irish Press* at the time and was sent to cover the tribunal one day. Since that afternoon more than 20 years ago, the very mention of Abbeydorney recalls for me one of the most nightmarish sights I've ever seen. I was sitting behind one of the tribunal barristers when he took off for lunch, carelessly leaving a book of evidence open on his desk. The open page bore a near-lifesized photograph of the Cahersiveen baby, taken shortly after he'd been washed up on the strand, with all 23 stab wounds visible on the tiny corpse. The tribunal never established who murdered the little boy in such a frenzy, although it did find that Joanne Hayes had certainly killed her own child by clutching its throat to stop it crying.

There was, and remains, huge sympathy for her. She was young, she'd been involved with a married man, she was frightened and she panicked, for rural Ireland of the early 1980s was no clement climate for pregnant single women. We had a brief chance, then, to confront our own consciences, and address the cause of this lethal shame, but we let it slip away. The tribunal duly reported, the case was closed and the furore stirred up by the Kerry Babies subsided into guilty silence. And 20 years later, when I mentioned the matter in a radio column, I got some clue as to why that occurred.

Because RTÉ immediately received a written complaint, signed by around 70 citizens including Joanne Hayes. There was outrage that the matter was being alluded to again, when folk wanted it forgotten. Well, of course they did, since nobody had much to be proud of in the whole affair. But the fact remained that two helpless babies died, and we allowed ourselves to hush up the matter out of deference to the sensitivities of the adults involved. By failing to act on the lessons of the Kerry Babies, we behaved like a nation of squinting villagers, safe behind our twitching net curtains.

Now two separate filmmakers are planning to revisit the Kerry Babies story, and Joanne Hayes and her family have begged them to desist. For everybody's sake we must hope they write her sympathetic but firm letters, and press on with their projects. Because if we'd squared up to the issues raised by the Kerry Babies 20 years ago, if we'd truly tried to make amends, we might not still be finding dead, abandoned infants in remote sheds in the spring of 2006. Joanne Hayes may well want her story forgotten – sadly, though it was never just her story.

June 2006

Anger mismanagement

TEN DAYS AGO, a man was walking along Dublin's O'Connell Street in the early hours of the morning, on his way home from a night out in town. He'd had a few drinks, as had most of the punters strolling through the city at that hour, he was in good spirits and maybe engaging in a bit of horseplay with a friend. He was carrying a soft drink and he may have flicked some of the liquid at his mate as a joke. Some of the drink may have splashed a passer-by, maybe some comments were made. Whatever the trifling provocation, the man was punched square in the face by a complete stranger. Because the blow was so unexpected, the man had no defence, he fell straight back, cracked his head on the pavement and died in hospital a few days later.

The incident has passed cleanly under the radar of national attention. You might have heard an appeal for witnesses, but otherwise the story aroused very little interest because it aroused very little surprise. Drunken fights are a common sight on the streets of towns and cities across the country at closing time, it's inevitable that sometimes they end badly. Except this doesn't appear to have been a drunken fight: there was no sloppy brawling or rowdy goading, the whole thing was over in five seconds. Two strangers pass on the street, one says or does something that irritates the other, he gets punched and killed, and nobody bats an eyelid. So here, then, is a modern caveat that we accept without quibble – take care not to annoy a stranger or you might end up dead. Uncontrollable anger isn't a cause for shame or censure any more, it's a legitimate defence.

For some reason frustration, impatience and anger have become everyday features of modern life. Maybe it's because we all live in bubbles of personal isolation, alone in our cars with our mobile phones and our iPods and our multiple distractions, that other people have ceased to be human and just become pesky obstacles. Stop and think how many times, in the course of a day, you have to deal with somebody else's temperamental incontinence. Delay for more than three seconds at a green light, for example, and another driver will shout and hoot. Slow down to look out for a parking space and some red-faced yob will roar abuse through his car window.

And it's not just on the roads, either – jump the queue in the bank or block a supermarket aisle with your trolley and you'll face a lynch mob. It used to be just toddlers in buggies who threw tantrums in crowded shops – now you hear grown adults loudly whingeing that the lady in front has eleven items in her basket in the 'Ten or Less' line. Wherever you go, it seems an outburst of temper is now the automatic response to the most trivial slight or imposition.

And maybe it's a boy thing, but temper tantrums by prominent individuals, almost invariably males, are generally indulged and rarely criticised any more. Sport is supposed to teach self-control, but hot-headed pettiness is a much more prominent feature of professional games. The only reason David Beckham was roasted for his sly kick at an opponent in the last World Cup was because he got himself sent off, not because it was a sneaky and unrestrained gesture unworthy of a sportsman representing his country. And when Wayne Rooney flung his boots about, after being substituted in a recent game, that was seen as an understandable response to frustration – not the childish and undisciplined sulk it really was.

The plea that 'I was angry and I lost my temper' should compound an offence, not mitigate it, but it seems an episode of rage is an excuse for almost any excess. When he foamed at the mouth and called Richard Bruton a Nazi, Justice Minister McDowell's explanation was that he lost his temper. Last week, the Taoiseach lost his rag when Joe Higgins needled him about all the rich builders in the VIP corral at the Haughey funeral, and denounced the socialist TD as a 'nitwit' and a 'failed person'. Most likely the Taoiseach was suffering other pressures, just then, and Higgins was in the wrong place at the wrong time. But that's the problem – we shouldn't have to tiptoe around other people, whether they're work colleagues or passers-by, for fear that they've had a bad day or a few drinks and are just reaching boiling point. But we must, and it diminishes everyone's quality of life. Just yesterday, a strutting teenage lad flung a cigarette box on the street as he passed me by. I should have told him to pick it up, of course, but I didn't. Would you?

July 2006

Keeping her feet on the ground in €29.99 shoes

So it seems we are the second richest people in the world, runners-up only to the Japanese in terms of our spending power and disposable loot, not to mention our fondness for dinky gadgets and smart motors. Nobody seemed remotely surprised by this revelation, brought to us last week courtesy of Bank of Ireland and the 'They-Would-Say-That-Wouldn't-They' School of Feelgood Economics, and apparently based on our 'courageous' borrowing and investment patterns. Hmmm. Anyway, it wasn't ever thus, you know – once upon a time there were only about three or four rich people in this country, and we knew all their names. And one of them was Michael Smurfit and some years ago, when rich people were rare and wondrous enough to be objects of awestruck curiosity, I was sent to interview him.

He was most pleasant and charming and, though he struck

me as quite a shy man, he talked with particular feeling about the loneliness of extreme wealth. When you are very rich you're never quite sure what people want when they befriend you, and so you tend to keep the more economically challenged of your acquaintances at arm's length. I was just as interested, though, in the daily realities of being loaded, and had always wondered whether rich people carried money with them, and what they might need to buy. So, towards the end of our interview I asked Michael Smurfit, do you have any cash on you at the moment? At which point he stood up abruptly, patted his pockets and said, no, no I don't, and we carried on.

It was only later, listening back to the tape, that I realised, to my intense shame, that he thought I was asking him for money. And I reckoned that this must have finally clinched his suspicion that everyone he met really was on the make, if a journalist at an interview could try to hit on him for a few bob. But it struck me, too, as a sad and stressful way to go through life, always having to be on your guard against friendly overtures that really are just a way of parting you from your cash, just because folk think you can afford it.

I really do hope that the same isolating worry hasn't beset Dolores McNamara, who has just notched up one year as the 72nd richest person in Ireland following her Euromillions win last summer. Being filthy rich, of course, is a lot commoner now than when I interviewed Michael Smurfit back in the early 1990s, with something like 30,000 millionaires in the country and more than 70 of them being worth more than Dolores' €115 million. So much money, so much to worry about. A famous journalist I know, who spends a lot of time as a 'trophy guest' at wealthy folk's parties, says they're genuinely uncomfortable amongst ordinary people – it seems they can't bitch so freely about the design of the latest Lear Jet, or enthuse about the quality of Frette bedsheets at €800 a pop, when in the company of lesser mortals whose idea of affluence is a gazebo bought with the SSIA funds.

Dolores has, according to recent reports, been keeping her head down of late and seems to have distanced herself from the local community in her native part of Limerick. Apart from buying a swish, but not excessively splendid, new house on the shores of Lough Derg, new cars for her family and some top-level counsel for a nephew with some rather tricky legal difficulties, she hasn't gone on a massive spending spree.

At the time she won the money she promised she would keep her feet on the ground. Should we worry about her because she hasn't done the chat-show circuit, extended her hair with the shorn locks of some impoverished Ukrainian, run off with a Premier League football player, turned up on *Celebrity Love Island* or destroyed her nose with a cocaine habit? Is her reticence necessarily a sign that she's not dealing with her altered state very well? Is the fact that she still shops at Penneys and Champion Sports a sign of some pathological denial of her new reality?

Actually, I doubt it. Because Dolores has this advantage over her colleagues on the Irish rich list – she had her friends, her family, her routines and her personal tastes long before she had her money. She doesn't actually have to question the motives of the mates she's known forever, so she can surely spot the ones on the make from a mile away. A few months ago it was reported that the most expensive accessory she'd bought herself with her money was a €38 handbag. There's every reason to believe that Dolores is, indeed, keeping her feet on the ground – in €29.99 shoes, at that. Let's not worry about her just yet.

July 2006

Moral SWAT team - 1;
Peter Stringfellow - 0

EVEN MORE NAUSEATING than Peter Stringfellow's oily grin and matching mullet has been the orgy of gloating and self-congratulation since 'people power' sent him packing. For the second Sunday in a row, I've heard, the Prayers of the Faithful at Masses around the country have included thanksgiving for the most noble defeat of the English corrupter, for the faith and fortitude of the ordinary people whose moral courage sustained them through the great battle, for the liberation of the misguided and unfortunate women enslaved by Stringfellow's evil empire, and for the restoration of the virtues of decency and chastity to the threatened capital city. It's a shame, really, that none of it is true.

Just for starters, it wasn't really the pure force of moral righteousness that closed the lap dancing club on Parnell Street after just a few months in business. Indignation was certainly an element, though it mostly reflected the outrage of young urban investors who had bought themselves swish new apartments in the newly gentrified north inner city and were most appalled at a possible impact on their property values if the place turned into a glorified red light district. Indeed, the fact that property prices would suffer was a quietly stated element of the campaign to close the place down, even if the more admirable veneer of good old Irish Catholic values conveniently masked a more pragmatic concern for another type of valuation altogether. Discreet and dingy clubs are no real concern, apparently, but one as brazen and up-front as Stringfellows? Please!

This was truly a win-win situation for many of the protesters with that dual agenda – they could despatch an undesirable commercial neighbour under the guise of a selfless interest in the very souls of vulnerable family men and poor exploited women. Of course there's no harm in objecting to a business that may not fit with the tone or aspirations of a particular area, but mobilising the moral majority effectively to defend the value of your property is cynical and hypocritical.

None of us would fancy living next to Stringfellows, it's hardly the landmark you'd want when directing potential tenants to your gleaming new duplex apartment, but living in the centre of a bustling European capital city requires a certain amount of compromise – you really can't expect to be woken by birdsong every morning. And as these places go, Stringfellows has a certain quasi-respectability about it – being so prominent means their standards and hygiene and pay structures and employment policies are fairly well scrutinised, so it probably is true to say that the girls in his clubs are there by choice, that they're well rewarded and that the only real suckers in the deal are the drooling men who pay them €30 or more a pop for a peremptory, hands-off jiggle.

And as the owners of these places go, Stringfellow himself is probably the Del Boy of the adult entertainment industry – more successful, of course, but take Del Trotter out of Peckham, hand him the keys of a lap-dancing joint and try to spot the difference. And Stringfellow's harmless, buffoonish and caricatured image probably suits the purveyors of the really hard, really nasty stuff in this country at the moment, because it suggests that the wicked scandal-givers are always so easy to spot.

And the fact is that they're not, that most of those men and women who traffic poor Eastern European girls to be gang raped on a nightly basis in anonymous Dublin venues are moving amongst us without a hairy chest or a leopardskin accessory between them. Stringfellows closed because the well-heeled men who frequent these places didn't want to be spotted and photographed patronising the place, as such were the tactics used by the objectors. That doesn't mean, though, that they went home to their wives and kids and repented the error of their ways. No, they took their repulsive and remorseless business elsewhere, to places where the girls aren't nearly so safe or so free to make choices. They drove their swanky cars right past Stringfellows and on to shadier and more sinister locations which had the big advantage of an absence of protesting busybodies and amused journalists patrolling the front doors.

Because the folk who routed Stringfellows have no real concern for the poorer areas of the city where the local residents lives are genuinely blighted by crawling johns and sleazy traffic. Let's wait and see if they take their campaign to the doors of those grimy clubs where the working girls speak no English, are strung out on drugs, regularly beaten and living in fear of vicious pimps and peddlers of human misery. It's a fair bet that you won't see the Moral SWAT team descend on Benburb Street any time soon, they're too busy toasting their victory in Parnell Street and patting themselves on the back for upholding the Christian values of a decent community. Oh, and if the property values stay buoyant as well, isn't it a grand little bonus?

September 2006

When hanging is too good ...

WHAT DO YOU do with the kind of person who could walk up to a car containing two tiny children, dowse it with petrol, and then wait until their mother arrived to toss in a flaming firelighter? How should the law deal with the kind of evil that can justify, to itself, an act such as that? I'd just recently been lecturing my 11-year-old son on the barbarity of capital punishment, and how it was never excusable in any circumstances, when he caught me poring over the pictures of those two poor little kids and debating the merits of piano wire over hemp as the most lingering means of despatching the culprits. How can you say you're against the death penalty, he wanted to know, when you'd even think about making the odd exception?

I very much doubt that I was the only person in the country last week who could be simultaneously capable of being horrified at the prospect of executing Saddam Hussein, considering it a shameful capitulation to medieval vengefulness, and still think that hanging would be far too good for anyone who attempted to burn alive two innocent little children. I'd be hypocritically critical of any rabble-rousing politician who even hinted at restoring the death penalty for such crimes, and genuinely appalled if it was given any serious consideration.

But from time to time there are crimes that really try your patience with the enlightened objectives of a modern criminal justice system, all that business of rehabilitation, understanding, accountability and remorse, and make you want to cut straight to the punishment bit. It just doesn't seem a fair vindication of the rights of those children, whose beautiful baby skin has been burned off their bodies and whose lives will be forever blighted with surgery, skin grafts and stolen glances from curious strangers in the streets, to bang on right now about the deprivation, isolation and marginalisation that motivated their attackers, and how best to reintegrate them into society.

And yet, it would seem, the culprits may be little more than children themselves. And it is arguable that their own rights to a normal childhood, a healthy adolescence and a legitimate expectation of a peaceful, productive life were taken from them long ago. The perpetrators of this act are clearly the inhabitants of a twilit, parallel realm with a set of rules, values and standards entirely incomprehensible to mainstream society. The real question is whether they are victims of an indifferent social and political system that left them to their fate, or willing and conscious players in a hierarchy of terror and intimidation that gives them status and power.

There are more than two million people currently in employment in this country, many tens of thousands of them foreign nationals who came here in search of work. We have, of course, desperate pockets of long-term unemployment and disadvantage in decrepit estates around the country. As the rising tide lifted most boats and the rest of us sailed away to affluence, comfort, liberality, these people stayed mired in their grim, hopeless, unchanging lives. But whose fault is that, and whose purpose does it really serve to maintain pockets of lawlessness, no-go areas for the forces of law and order, territories uninhabitable by ordinary decent people who want no part of criminality or anarchy?

In his fascinating new book, *Lies In A Mirror: An Essay On Evil and Deceit*, criminal lawyer Peter Charleton maintains that deceit is the dynamic of evil, and there is a lie at the heart of every crime. People who perpetrate evil live in a myth, and they gather around them people who will reflect back to them their own disordered view of themselves. They construe scenarios in which they are the actual victims, and the crimes they commit are about levelling the score, defending themselves, exacting justice and respect from the object of their hatred or envy. 'Playing at being a victim is a feature of many of the personalities that I have seen drawn to violence.' he says, and within a group or gang 'it is easier to maintain a self-supporting fiction'.

Limerick has been riven with gangland violence in recent years, and it appears to have become more extreme as the country developed and prospered. Inevitably, alongside legitimate business opportunities, the possibilities for lucrative illicit trade grew. Even the most disadvantaged young people now have unprecedented opportunities to make good, but there are clearly those whom that doesn't suit. Gangsters need runners, mules, enforcers. So they need to lure youngsters into their underworld with promises of easy money and a feared status within their cowed communities.

The lie at the heart of this contract is that they are all equal victims of a greedy, avaricious and uncaring society, that they have to look out for themselves and one another and take what they can get: that they have no chance of succeeding legitimately because of their backgrounds, addresses, paltry educations, that they are disrespected. That the only ones to show them due status and respect are other gang members, and when this status is challenged or undermined, either by rivals or by unwitting members of the public, that they are entitled to punish this insolence.

The father of the two burned children has claimed that the arsonists were in the pay of a gangland leader whom either he, or the children's mother, had inadvertently slighted in some minor way, and that the attempted murder of the children was about teaching them a lesson. Writing about such attacks in his book, Peter Charleton says, 'Gangland killings are usually not so much about broken drug deals and lost money, as the challenge to the authority of the boss-figure. His ego is so enormous that no one will cross him without being crushed. Like nations on the verge of aggressive warfare, those who order others to murder for them are twisted up in notions of their own prestige, and how their authority might be diminished unless they strike down their enemies. They want control, because being in control allows a person to think what they choose about themselves without challenge. Any fundamental loss of control risks the total deflation of people who have constructed their lives in this way.'

It has been suggested that the children's mother may have refused a lift to a gang member. In the above scenario, this was an unpardonable insubordination. It threatened the authority of the gang member, and potentially undermined the entire gang structure right to the very top. These gangs couldn't function as they do, and keep their communities in such gratifying terror and fearful silence, if they didn't slap down every act of insolence immediately and decisively. They cannot allow the bubble of their own awesome, all-sustaining self-importance to be burst by a mere woman with her own errands to run. The killing of rival gang members or even innocent strangers has lost its power to chasten – we now file these murders under 'gangland executions' and we turn a blind eye. So it was inevitable that they would up the ante by turning their murderous attentions on children – after all they've been doing it to their own, indirectly, for years.

It's clear that the only way to tackle the sort of institutionalised criminality that led to this week's unspeakable attack on Gavin and Millie McNamara is to target the kingpins, close them down in the way that police attention frustrated The General's operations in the early 1990s. The lies these people tell to themselves, and about themselves, sever their connection with reality and allow them to inhabit a world where it is proper order to burn two children alive. It will take enormous Garda resources, but they need to be hounded, humiliated and exposed for the grubby, violent, mindless little thugs that they are, if their power structures are to crumble and their awesome reputations are to be punctured. Their cowardly, strutting little henchmen need to be stripped of the excuses and justifications that sustain their self-serving victimhood. I read that one of those questioned about the attacks on the children, when shown pictures of their injuries, burst into tears. Which is the most predictable, self-pitying reaction of a newly deflated little demigod.

So what do you do with people who can justify incinerating two children? Hanging really is too good for them – instead you peel away their 'self-supporting fictions', force them to confront the reality of their actions and then make sure they live, for the longest possible time, with that knowledge and guilt and inevitable self-disgust.

November 2006

You can't unscramble an egg

A MARRIED COUPLE have difficulty conceiving so they seek fertility treatment from a private clinic. They both willingly supply the necessary components for new life and a number of embryos are created and frozen. Some time later, the couple split up. One of them has lost all interest in the notion of having children together; however, the other spouse is still desperate to become a parent. The biological clock is ticking, and this person doesn't want to wait too long for a baby. The broody spouse goes to a solicitor to seek advice on the chances of having the embryos thawed and implanted, against the wishes of the other party.

When the solicitor has finished laughing and picked himself up off the floor, he gently explains to the husband that, no, there isn't a court on earth – at least this side of Sharia law – that would order the restraint of a woman so that she could be forcibly impregnated at the behest of an estranged partner. That situation is, of course, a mirror image of the case that has detained the High Court at length over the past number of months and may well be appealed to the Supreme Court in the near future. But the fact that the reverse situation is so utterly improbable shows just how ludicrous it is for men ever to try to claim an equal role, either legally or practically, in the reproductive process.

The real life version of the embryo case may have appeared to have accorded the man some legal say in whether or not his biological child came into the world. The reality of that process, though, makes any such paternal embargo a logical impossibility. If men really think this case means that they can call the shots over whether or not they become fathers in any other scenario, they've been sold a pup. The sad, singular circumstances of this controversial case are probably the only ones in which a man has even the remotest chance of a veto in the process, and even then it is a legally constructed illusion. The fact is that once the man in this case had fertilised the egg, his work was done. Once he'd made his contribution to the process, he was surplus to requirements and so, certainly nature considers, was his consent or even his opinion.

Once those embryos were created, Mr Roche couldn't possibly opt out of being their father – he already was their father. He may have succeeded in preventing the implantation of the embryos in his wife's womb on a fine legal point, but he cannot undo the fertilisation simply by changing his mind. And it is blindingly obvious that fertilisation is the starting point for the creation of life – the fact that these little cell clusters have not crossed the hurdle of being deemed 'unborn' within the meaning contemplated by Article 40.3.3 back in 1993 doesn't mean they're not each unique individual scraps of human life. The mother's body, consent and ongoing active participation is required to bring them to independent life – the father's is not, whatever the law says.

Tragically, though, this case seems to have given some comfort to those men who just can't get their heads around the fact that their role in the reproductive process is little more than a walk-on part. If you doubt that, just check out the internet sites that offer those DIY donor kits for women who've decided they want a baby without even finding out the identity of the father, let alone bothering to pursue a relationship with him. Get over it, guys, there is no corresponding service so far available to you.

Tragically, too, there are other men who view this biological reality as an excuse to take an equally minimal role in their children's lives. The plus side of this equation, so an alarming number of irresponsible fathers seem to reckon, is that men are free to renounce their responsibilities and walk away from their kids long before they're even born – women can't do that. Consider, even, the vernacular sense of the different terms involved – fathering a child denotes a brief physical transaction, mothering, on the other hand, conveys a life-long caring commitment.

Having decided, in the present case, that the father could withdraw his consent to be a father after the eggs were fertilised, the court probably had no real option but to hold that the embryos were not 'unborn' humans with legal rights and protections. If he'd been prevented from changing his mind on the perfectly reasonable basis that the embryos' very existence confirmed that they had a father and a mother, then their claim to human status and constitutional protection would have been much stronger.

Viewing the process through a laboratory microscope, then, it makes complete sense to say that these embryos are potential humans with a father and a mother. The view through the scientists' microscope, though, was only one of the many perspectives the law had to consider in deciding this issue.

Contorted as the reasoning of this case may be, the effect of the ruling is to reflect a more sophisticated and profound concept of fatherhood than the strictly scientific and coolly logical conclusion could have done. In a nutshell, it says that there's much more to being a father than just doing the necessary deed. In the physical act of creating a child, fathers aren't needed beyond their initial contribution, and like it or not, that's true – but for the creation of fully rounded, balanced, functional human beings, they're absolutely essential.

Hard though it may be for Mrs Roche to accept, and illogical though the route by which it was reached, this judgement effectively declares that a father's commitment, involvement and willingness to be part of his child's life is even more important than the mere contribution of half the genetic jigsaw. It was perfectly clear that Mr Roche had no intention of being such a father to those three potential people. Very many men don't, either, and the grim statistical evidence of the lot of so many children raised by lone mothers suggests that many suffer poverty and deprivation as the price of this rejection.

Whatever the more bullish male commentators may insist, the father's role in the actual reproductive process is becoming more, and not less, tangential with the advance of science – a man can, after all, literally mail in his contribution to the procedure these days. So once he had donated and labelled and signed his particular contribution in the IVF clinic, Mr Roche could indeed have been forced, on entirely logical legal grounds, to become a father against his will. But he could never have been forced to be a dad.

December 2006

Settling down

'TRAVELLER UNEMPLOYMENT HIGH, Study Finds'. What's your gut reaction to a headline such as this one, which appeared in a national paper last week, which happened to be National Traveller Focus week? Do you think, oh, how terrible, shame on me for being smug and settled and having a job? Or is it more like, there's a surprise, most of them don't want to work, anyway. Or somewhere in between, as in, do I look like I give a damn?

The one thing you probably won't ask, though, is what exactly are the travellers' champions doing to change this? That question won't cross your mind because the single biggest success of the travellers' apologists, over the past forty years, has been to dump all responsibility for the miserable lives and paltry life expectancies of the nomadic community firmly upon your doorstep. Travellers have hard lives, you don't, so it must be your fault. Travellers' kids rarely make it to third-level education and most drop out of school before they're fifteen, you must be to blame because your kids go to college. Travellers can't find jobs or GPs or pubs that will host their weddings. You take all these basic services for granted, clearly you are responsible for the travellers' plight. And you're so busy beating yourself black and blue from sheer guilt that it never occurs to you to ask – how come the travellers themselves, and their vocal, well-funded, endlessly-indulged advocates, are never accountable for any of this mess?

Apart from commissioning one whingeing report after another – this most recent one, with those jaw-dropping tidings about traveller unemployment, is from the Galway Traveller Movement – and apart from following these reports with stroppy statements demanding 'positive discrimination' and 'affirmative action', as they duly did last week, what practical efforts do the travellers' champions actually make to improve their charges' chances of finding decent jobs? The answer is little or none, of course. Because if travellers really wanted jobs, rather than victimhood, they'd make one simple, blindingly obvious lifestyle change. They'd stop travelling.

They'd accept the houses that the local authorities bend over backwards to provide for them. They'd send their children to school. They'd stay in one place long enough for the next generation to get the education that is available to them. They'd abandon their anachronistic, indefensible, ludicrous existence in order to give their kids the chance to enjoy the rights, the services and the respect that they demand for themselves. And if their spokespeople were doing them any favours, they would be devoting all their energies towards persuading travellers to give up the road, rather than berating the rest of us over the utterly predictable effects of a rootless, selfish, nomadic lifestyle.

'Traveller Unemployment High, Study Finds'. Well, what do you expect? A shiftless, nomadic way of life is entirely incompatible with the sort of work that offers prospects and potential. It is quite difficult to get to be head of General Motors if you've got no fixed abode. The kind of work that instils self-esteem and earns respect can never be the result of 'positive discrimination', and no able-bodied person is entitled to expect such a concession in an economy that has had to import a quarter of a million foreign workers just to keep ticking over. Collecting and selling scrap and old cars is not a job – meaningful employment or a life on the road, it's a straight choice.

And a nomadic life doesn't tend to foster civic obedience and community spirit, either. If you don't have roots, a sense of place, an attachment to an area, a connection with a locality, you're less likely to care about staying on good terms with the neighbours or to take a proprietary interest in the local environment. Settled folks aren't all saints, but the real possibility of penal sanction is a major factor in keeping us on the right side of the law – but if you can invoke your quaint cultural characteristic of nomadic behaviour, and scarper under cover of darkness after you've caused trouble, then you're less likely to be caught and punished.

The travellers' insistence that they should be free to move around the country at will, with fully serviced halting bays wherever they choose to hang their hats, imposes unrealistic demands on local authorities and taxpayers alike. Exactly how many bays are we required to provide per family? The travellers' spokespeople insist that such facilities are a human right deriving from their unique culture, but the nomadic life is completely incompatible with any reciprocal responsibility towards public amenities and resources.

Responsibility, though, is not a concept which their advocates are comfortable discussing. Try to pin them down on accountability for a ruined scenic site or a trashed school sports pitch, and you'll end up being complained to the Equality Authority – I know, I've been there. If a traveller couple have produced fifteen children in circumstances where they live in a caravan by a roadside, that is not a matter of an unconscionable personal choice. That's your fault, and their culture. I know settled couples with two jobs who agonise over whether they can afford, feed, educate, clothe a second child – these concerns never seem to detain travellers for a second and, again, nobody dares raise this patent irresponsibility for fear of being called 'racist'.

On radio recently I asked a travellers' representative how they could realistically gripe about their employment difficulties and their kids' educational challenges when they were the ones who rejected continuity by insisting on a nomadic lifestyle. His response was that they do most of their travelling in the summer. But so do the rest of us – we call it going on holidays, we pay for the privilege, and we ensure that we are available for work and schools when the holidays end.

The days when the travellers' lifestyle supported a genuine contribution to rural communities, when they were welcome purveyors of news and skills and goods for sale to remote townlands, are long gone. Their travelling now serves no real purpose, other than to remove them as quickly as possible from an area in which they've worn out their welcome. If they really want respectable jobs for themselves, an education and prospects for their kids, they have got to stop travelling. If they have a culture worth preserving, it has to be based on more than an itinerant existence – their language, their folklore, their customs and traditions can be fostered just as well in a settled environment. Moreover, they've a better chance of engaging the support and understanding of the settled community if they show respect for the customs and values of others. Economist Felim O'Rourke recently pointed out that forty years ago, when the travellers' traditional means first began to disappear, the emphasis initially was on integrating them. But when the notion of a separate 'traveller culture' emerged in the 1970s and 1980s, they were willingly segregated and isolated by the liberal enthusiasm to embrace their diversity. They were sold a pup. The result of that trendy daftness is that the travelling community is now being kept in poverty, ignorance and disadvantage by a small group of professional advocates who refuse to acknowledge that they got it wrong.

2007-2009

February 2007

Putting the Frighteners on
Those Uppity Wimmin

ALL GOING WELL, and barring any unforeseen change of plan, I'm going to die on the 8 January 2042. I think it's a Tuesday, but to be on the safe side, I won't make any plans for that whole week. It is morbid fun, checking out your check-out date on the on-line Deathclock.com — you just fill in your date of birth, some health details, weight and height, and wait to see when your number's going to come up. A warning, though — don't try it if you're an overweight smoker of a certain age, or it will insist that you actually passed away sometime back in the mid-1990s.

I have to admit I'd been hoping for a slightly better innings, given that we're told the current crop of baby girls can expect to live to be 100 or more, but it still leaves me with a good 35 years to kill. By January 2042 my youngest child will be 38 and, I hope, well past the age when she'll need me for anything more than my Christmas cake recipe and the occasional spot of light babysitting. If, that is, she has actually found a window of opportunity in her career plan to reproduce at all by then: according to ESRI statistics published last week, the average age at which women have been giving birth has been steadily increasing over the last decade or so. Two years ago it was up to 30.6 years, so by 2042 there's every chance that a 38-year-old woman might well be considered a mere slip of a girl with many fertile years ahead of her, and far too young to be thinking about tying herself down. For her sake, I do hope so.

The trend, certainly, is towards older motherhood. And since women have unprecedented control over their reproductive functions these days, it may be safe to assume that these changing patterns are a product of enhanced options. When women have the choice, in other words, they'll have their babies later on in life. So why has it become generally accepted, socially as well as medically, that older pregnancy is Not A Good Thing? I'm sick to death of moving personal testimonies from high-flying career women and glamorous celebrities lamenting their selfishness in leaving it too late to start trying for a baby. Invariably, wouldn't you know, they run into all kinds of difficulties when getting pregnant doesn't turn out to be the cakewalk they'd always expected, spend vast reserves of cash and emotional energy on sophisticated but ill-fated interventions, and end up warning blithe younger women of the dangers of assuming you can have it all. Their sob stories make for great copy, of course, but they're far from the experience of most healthy and normal women, and it always seems to me their true subtext is to put the frighteners on those uppity wimmin who make the subversive error of forgetting their true biological purpose on this earth.

If you were minded to be of a paranoid nature, you might suspect that the consensus on the benefits of youthful motherhood is a male plot to keep women safely constrained by the glass ceiling. All the indications, both here and in Britain, suggest that women are poised to take control of the professions and the upper echelons of the business world over the next decade. Girls consistently outperform boys in the State exams and outnumber them at graduate level in law and medicine, for example. The imbalance has become so pronounced in Britain that the MP and commentator Boris Johnson warned last week, only partially tongue-in-cheek, that all these thrusting females are going to have problems in future in finding suitable mates even close to their own level of achievement, let alone locating a single superior Alpha male. It's all doom and gloom, then, unless these pesky ambitious birds can be persuaded to get themselves knocked up in their early twenties – the sleepless nights, the school run, the dental appointments, the million other daily distractions of motherhood are fairly guaranteed to halt the gallop of the most single-minded female executive, for a couple of years at least.

The truth, of course, is that there are probably more advantages to older motherhood than drawbacks. The health concerns that would have made later pregnancies high risk a generation ago have largely been allayed by medical advances. Your chances of having a Down's baby increase as you age, for sure, but then, as a doctor once put it to me, your chances of winning the lotto increase tenfold when you buy ten tickets instead of one – it's still a very long shot, though. If it's not happening naturally, then a new breakthrough in IVF announced last week is likely to double that procedure's success rates. Once she gets pregnant, an older mother is probably more likely to have informed herself of the optimum dietary regime, the best supplements to take, the foods and environments to avoid. She's probably put more thought into the entire process and its long-term implications than a dizzy twenty-something who quite fancies playing mummies and daddies.

Young mothers will tell you that they're looking forward to reclaiming their lives, while still young enough to enjoy them, when their children are reared. That sounds great but it is, alas, mere wishful thinking. Your children will always be your children, a lifelong concern and worry, and they don't stop being a concern the minute you sign up for those skydiving classes. Whether you have them at 17 or 47, you'll still lie awake at night waiting for them to come in, whatever age they are, you'll still fret about their first tooth/

job/relationship/car/baby. You might as well have a bit of a life of your own, for as long as you can, before they arrive to take it over, because you ain't getting it back afterwards.

I know women who've had their children while they were very young, and those who've given birth later in life, and nobody seems to be entirely without their regrets. The ones with the grown-up kids are no less broody when they see an older friend with a new baby – I always get the impression they'd like one more shot at it, a chance to relive the experiences they were too young, or too poor, or too resentful, or too immature to relish and wonder at the first time around. The older mothers, though, may well have less energy to run after an active toddler, but the running-around years are short enough. They might possibly find themselves mistaken for the granny at the school gates, but they won't be alone in that, and gravity catches up with even the yummiest mummies eventually. And the older mums will have had a life and experiences that will enrich the relationship with their children as they both push on in years. At the very least, I hope I'll have the material wherewithal that will keep them interested in visiting me in the Sunnyside Golden Years Home as January of 2042 edges closer.

May 2007

A spell on the bold step for Bertie

HELP ME OUT here, Bertie, because I want to believe you, I really do. I'm perfectly happy to accept that your finances were all over the place 15 years ago because intimate difficulties had left you scattered and distracted. I even believe that you had a bunch of good-natured friends and enthusiastic admirers who were willing to bail you out because they didn't want your political potential compromised by irregular personal circumstances. Like the rest of the nation I sat transfixed in front of the six o'clock television news last September, lump in throat all present and correct, as you paused for composure while explaining how your marriage breakdown had taken a financial and emotional toll. Even then, the facts didn't really stack up but the wave of warmth that buoyed you in the polls after that performance didn't surprise me at all. Because underlying our communal response was the fundamental perception that Bertie was an honest bloke who was trying his best to put us straight. He was hardly to blame if friends and supporters took a misguided course of assistance in a different political era, and now he was left trying to explain his way out of a maze of financial transactions he probably never fully understood even at the time.

And lots of people still want to believe that, but by now even that hard core of Fianna Fáil supporters, who will go to their graves believing that Charles Haughey was a maligned beacon of propriety, must be beginning to question their own grip on reality. Because in order to absolve Bertie here, and to accept the Fianna Fáil line that this is nothing more than a dirty tricks campaign by desperate political rivals, you have to accept a whale of a yarn that would test the self-respect of the most imaginative junior infant.

Imagine you find, in your five-year-old's schoolbag, the remnants of a giant, family-sized box of sticky toffees. First he tells you that you didn't really find them at all, since his pocket money of one euro a week would never stretch to such a purchase. Then he tells you that they may well have been there, but that you're being most unfair in asking him about them and it's clear you're just looking for an excuse to put him to bed early without any supper. And then he tells you that while it may appear that the toffees were in his bag, and that the evidence indeed suggested that he'd eaten them all himself, in fact they were given to one of his friends by a child from another school altogether. His friend was minding the toffees for the other child, it was a completely separate arrangement between the two of them and you had a cheek quizzing him about what two other children chose to do with their own stash of sweets. And he's not entirely sure how they ended up in his possession, and in what circumstances they came to be eaten by him, but at the time he got them he would have sworn they weren't toffees, at all, they were three packets of Tayto and some bubblegum. And, anyway, he really doesn't have to explain a thing until he is 18 and legally an adult, but at that point he'll be happy to supply all the detail you need, and in the meantime it would be most unfair to punish him, and could he kindly finish his sweets in peace? Full marks for sheer ingenuity, I guess, but he'd still do time on the bold step, right?

I really wanted to believe Bertie, last September, for a whole variety of reasons. It was clear there were anonymous leakers behind the story, there was obviously a bid to bring the Government down, and you don't like feeling manipulated by a hidden hand. And I wanted to believe that nobody would really use the intensely personal circumstances of a marriage breakdown as an emotional flak jacket, an exclusion zone of discomfort, to ward off legitimate enquiry. But most of all I really hoped we'd put those days, when we had to doubt and wonder and quiz a Taoiseach about where he got his money, well behind us. We've been there, done that, worn the witty tee-shirts, and it's not even remotely entertaining any more. Which is one possible reason why Enda KenBarlow suddenly looks like a realistic alternative Taoiseach – he might still have his Communion money, but it is HIS Communion money, and I reckon he's had the same bank account since then. And it also explains why the sight of P. J. Mara trying to silence Vincent Browne's persistent financial probing at a Fianna Fáil leader's press conference was one of the most dispiriting and defining moments of this election campaign so far – for God's sake, not even the personnel has changed. Can we turn the page?

The PDs asked Bertie to produce a 'credible' account of his financial intricacies by Friday. It really is hard to imagine any explanation that will tie up all the dangling loose ends and allow Michael McDowell to profess himself satisfied and convinced at last. I reckon he must be pinning his hopes on a *Dallas* type denouement, where Charlie Haughey emerges, hale and hearty, from the executive shower room on the fifth floor of Leinster House, Bertie is still Minister for Finance and he himself is still safely ensconced in the Law Library, a flight to New York costs more than a house and we just dreamt the last 15 years. That would just about do it.

June 2007

Don't mention the Communion

THE OTHER DAY I called into a big newsagents in town to pick up a First Communion card for a friend's son. It's one of the dafter rituals that the parents of Communion kids go through at this time of year, sending cards to children whose parents will take one look and think, oh God, we forgot about her, give me that €20 so I can send it straight back, now I have to go to the bother of getting a card and a stamp, and what's their house number, again?

As we all know well by now, the money is the only thing that the newly sanctified little souls care a hoot about – I heard of one little girl, opening envelope after envelope, extracting the cash and tossing the cards into a heap until she came to one with no money inside and chucked it away saying, 'this one doesn't work'.

But there's a chance that the parents may just notice the card, so you've got to put some thought into your selection. Something tasteful, thoughtful, not too garish, not too flippant, not too God-botheringly pious but solemn none the less – we do, after all, live in the hope that some of the innocence and beauty of the ceremony will stay with them long after the new Nintendo DS console or the pink flip-up phone is history. With all of this in mind, then, I set about picking a suitable card from the large variety on display. A few of them caught my eye, nice colours, stylish art work, and it took a while to dawn on me why these perfectly pleasant cards struck a jarring note.

At least half the cards bore absolutely no reference to the event they were designed to celebrate. They looked more like birthday cards, in fact, than tokens to mark the child's initiation into one of the most profound ceremonies of the Catholic faith. They were either chic and stylish, with vague line drawings of wistful children on ivory linen paper, or else cheerful inoffensive scenes showing happy boys playing with footballs or computer screens – reminders, I guess, of the good times that lay ahead when the cash was all in and the pesky faffing around in new suits and haircuts was done and dusted. It took a while, in fact, to find a card that dared to mention prayers or blessings or the sacredness of the day, and Jesus Christ's role in the whole thing seemed to have ended up on the cuttingroom floor.

Back home, I had a look through the cards my own girl had received and found much the same pattern – about half her cards were just cute greetings with the word Communion apologetically tagged on, sometimes in the small print of the little verse inside. What is this about? I can understand perfectly the trend for Christmas cards that don't use the word Christmas or feature any religious symbolism – there's a lot of weight in the argument that Christmas is an ancient pagan festival celebrating the turning of the year, the lengthening of the days and the approaching end of winter, and that it was hijacked by Christianity for its own ends. It's also a time of family reunion and celebration; whatever your creed, at the very least it's a few days off work in an atmosphere of general good cheer, so it's an appropriate time to reach out with a card and a few lines of greeting to a friend or relative you rarely see. A neutral card makes sense because you can't assume that a new acquaintance or a work colleague shares your religious beliefs, and they are just as entitled to be included in the celebrations whether they've any or none at all.

And even neutral christening cards have some slim justification – despite the clue in the name, christening ceremonies can be fairly secular these days, with parents and sponsors scripting their own readings and pledges, and no fear of scaring the older children or getting a snigger from a sceptical gathering with all this renouncing Satan lark. Again, if you didn't know the couple well you might not risk sending an overtly religious card to a christening ceremony, just in case.

But a First Holy Communion card that tactfully avoids the religious element makes no sense to me. If a friend tells you his son is making his Communion, aren't you on fairly safe ground assuming they're Catholics? If you're invited to a party to celebrate a First Holy Communion, are you really going out on a limb if you buy a card that mentions the Body of Christ? Is there really a chance that you'll offend your friends by presenting a greeting that emphasises the spiritual element of the celebration? Or is it the donor, and not the recipient, that these cards are designed to mollify?

Because I suspect that the card manufacturers' target market for non-religious Communion cards are the conscientious objectors that we're all expected to tiptoe around these days: the touchy Muslim workmate who's always primed to be offended by religious expression in a Christian country, the lapsed Papists who ferry their own kids to non-denomi-national schools in the next province rather than subject them to the taint of a Catholic school, the trendy affluenza victims who reckon this whole God business is just quaint superstition. A neutral card allows these folks to turn a discreet blind eye to your primitive or ill-informed credulity, while reserving the expectation to be invited to the party afterwards.

I'm sure that the friends and relatives who sent these cards to my daughter picked them because they were pretty and stylish, and probably didn't even notice the absence of a religious message – it's the fact that they're available at all that irritates me. Nobody else is expected to apologise for their religious observance, so why should Catholics? If you're invited to a Communion ceremony then send a proper card, whatever your feelings, because that's a question of basic courtesy, not faith. Of course you're not expected to share the beliefs of all your friends and workmates in new, multicultural Ireland – but why is Catholicism the only religion you're not required to respect?

July 2007

Happily ever after?

BROWSING A RACK of humorous birthday cards recently, I noticed one hoary old theme that seems to have survived the onslaught of political correctness. Race, disability, mothers-in-law, they're all pretty much off limits now, but if greeting cards are any sort of a social barometer then we still find the idea of marital strife an absolute rib-tickler.

You don't see as many rolling pins and frying pans awaiting drunken cartoon husbands when they lurch home in the wee hours any more, that's certainly true. Andy Capp's nudge-nudge name might have escaped the PC censors but his famous dust-ups with wife Flo have long since mellowed into verbal attrition. Black eyes and throbbing duck-egg bruises aren't nearly such a hoot now that we know the extent of serious domestic violence, and that men are even less likely to expose their victimhood than women.

And yet the kind of feelings that can erupt into violence are somehow an acceptable subject for comedy. Married couples in greeting-card land are either cheesy soft-focus honeymooners from the Newly Wed section, or else bitter enemies glaring murderously across the no-man's-land of the dining table. One card I saw last week showed a man calmly reading his newspaper at breakfast while his seething wife leans over the tea and toast to make a rude gesture unseen. 'I know what you're doing,' the chap is saying. My favourite ran, 'It's better to have loved and lost than to live with a psycho for the rest of your life'. They were all quite amusing, actually, though you'd have to be quite careful about whom you sent them to – the funniest jokes are the ones that hit quite close to the bone, resonate with us, even scare us a little. And the sad thing is that quite a lot of apparently contented couples might easily recognise the impotent, grinding, frustrated hatred those pithy little gags convey.

That unspoken reality is the reason, for instance, why the chief suspect in any murder enquiry is always the bereaved spouse. Even if they have no previous convictions, even if there's no history of violence, even if outward appearances were fine, we almost casually accept that the very person who loved the deceased enough to vow fidelity and commitment before God is also the most likely to hate them enough to kill them. The term 'crime of passion' suggests an overwhelming brainstorm of intense, sexual jealousy, but I suspect most domestic tragedies are triggered by pent-up years of irritation, frustration, exasperation with a partner who leaves tea bags in the sink, or overfills the wheelie bin, or puts the empty milk carton back in the fridge, or butts in when you try to tell a joke. And it's this accretion of grievances that the comic cards, and sit-com clichés, mine for laughs.

Long-married couples in soaps and comedies are a fount of lazy humour – they grate on each other, they stay together out of mutual spite, and it's so long since they've had sex they're even impervious to innuendo: funniest line in Coronation Street for many a year had to be Jack Duckworth observing to a gobsmacked young neighbour, 'A man should know his own bird without even having to look at the ring'. He was talking about his pigeons, and the double entendre went right over his head.

So the longer the relationship, is the sniggering secret behind all this humour, the more likely it is to be unhappy, rather than cosily contented. So I was a bit taken aback, last week, at the media coverage of new figures from the family courts which suggest that long-married couples are the ones boosting the divorce statistics, rather than younger pairs suffering the seven-year itch. Couples married from 21 to 30 years, according to Dr Carol Coulter's analysis of a month's decisions in Cork Circuit Court, made up the bulk of those seeking divorces in that period. Of the 48 cases decided in that month, some 31 were sought by couples who had been married at least 16 years, but some were in their 70s and six couples had more than 30 years on the clock. I'm surprised we're surprised at this.

If we accept, as a comic truism, that long marriages are frequently miserable and unfulfilling, why are we amazed when the parties decide to end them? I don't subscribe for a minute to the notion that divorce has been the death knell for family life in this country, or that people who would otherwise have rubbed along happily for the duration are suddenly filing for divorce because it's fashionable or easy. But I think it has probably empowered folk who might have stayed trapped in awful marriages to consider their options.

Divorce has a ring of finality about it that separation just does not. If you've been lonely, abused, bullied, deceived or dominated in a marriage for years, then you want to deliver it a *coup de grâce*. Separation sounds impermanent, more like a temporary geographic reality than a fundamental life change. Divorce is the end, and if you really want out, it has an appealing certainty.

But why would you really want out if you've managed to survive up to 30 years with the same person? This is the question that exercised commentators when Carol Coulter's figures appeared last week? Why would you not hang in there – how bad could it be, and it's not as if there's much left to endure, your life is nearly over anyway, why go through the trauma and scandal of a divorce when you're on the home straight?

Well, pshaw to that – why not? I'd point the finger at the Celtic Tiger for the rise in 'grey' divorce much more than at the vote for constitutional change – I reckon we've all had our eyes opened, in the last ten years or so, to the lives that we could be living. And older people, who lived through tough recessionary times, are probably more entitled and more eager to explore the possibilities of a changing culture than a complacent generation who have grown up with unprecedented liberties. And if anything, in fact, waiting until the children are grown is more responsible than selfishly chucking it all in because you're feeling a little unfulfilled as a parent of toddlers.

And why shouldn't 'grey divorcees' make the most of the opportunities that are out there – try on-line dating, take up hot-air-ballooning, join a singles travel club? Why should we see divorce as an acceptable option for dissatisfied 30-somethings, as the response to those figures suggests we do, and yet expect 60-somethings to subside into mutual antipathy until they potter off to their single-sex old folks' homes?

Is it because we still have difficulty accepting that older people still have hopes, and unfulfilled ambitions, and an appetite for sex, and a better than ever chance of realising all of the above? We should be encouraged by these statistics, not tut-tutting over them. Which would you prefer – to spend your golden years watching *Countdown* in a private nursing home, or cruising the Med with the proceeds of your well-invested SSIA, your racy new lover and a manual on Tantric sex? Thought so – sixty really is the new forty, so suck it up.

September 2007

The glib vocabulary of Grief Lite

A COUPLE OF years ago I bumped into a friend, a married man about my own age, whom I hadn't seen for a while. He looked a little under the weather so I asked him how he was. 'Not great,' he said, 'we lost our third child a few months ago.' As you'd expect, I was deeply shocked, and upset that I'd been so out of touch I hadn't even known they had a third child. So I apologised for not having heard about this awful tragedy, and asked was it an accident, an illness, a cot death, what happened? No, he explained, it was a miscarriage, at seven weeks. Seven weeks. But they were having counselling and coming to terms with it, he said, they both had their good days and their bad days.

I distinctly recall wanting to slap his self-pitying face. I was furious at him for engaging my most profound parental dread – the death of a child – for what was little more than a false alarm. A miscarriage at seven weeks is hardly comparable with the loss of a child you've held and dressed and played with and fed. Most women scarcely even know they're pregnant at seven weeks, so they've hardly time to bond with and plan for a baby by then. Whatever about the woman's feelings in the situation, and she was sure to feel deep regret if not actual bereavement, but it seemed to me that the man couldn't honestly have had much more to deal with than concern for his wife and disappointment for himself. And yet he'd been counselled into a state of inconsolable anguish. He'd been encouraged to articulate feelings that he was truly unlikely to be experiencing.

At the time I remember thinking this was a manifestation of what one commentator dubbed Grief Lite, to explain the communal keening that followed Princess Diana's death. It's almost a pagan instinct, a way of loudly reminding the gods that you've had your share of woe, thanks very much, that it affected you profoundly even though it might have seemed vicarious, and that in all fairness they should look elsewhere when dishing out the next round of misfortunes.

But I now suspect there was also a far more modern influence prompting my friend to oversell his tragedy. I think he felt under pressure, from his wife, from the counsellor, from uncertainty over his role in the whole process, to express the 'right emotions', to satisfy everyone that he was 'in touch with his grief', to demonstrate his liberation from traditional male reticence about 'women's problems' as part of the admirable process of introducing Irish men to their deepest feelings. But surely being encouraged to express emotions that you're not, in fact, experiencing is even worse than stifling the ones you actually feel? Isn't that more likely to lead to emotional confusion and a sense of inadequacy, rather than relief?

A generation ago, a man would scarcely know his wife was pregnant by the seventh week, much less be expected to wail and cry into his pint if anything went wrong at that point. In such circumstances, thirty years ago it would have been the man's job to be sympathetic and understanding, and to defer completely to his partner's distress. Now, he's expected to claim part of it for himself, and to act as though his experience is equal to hers, even though it patently is not. A father's love for a living, breathing child is just as strong as a mother's, but his attachment to an unborn foetus is entirely different. That's one of the mysteries of the whole process that we're going to have to live with, and accepting that situation is far more honest than telling men they're Neanderthal savages if they don't suffer miscarriage in precisely the same way as their partners.

The bizarre case, a couple of weeks back, of the soccer player Stephen Ireland rather neatly summed up the confusing pressures on a man when his partner suffers a miscarriage. It seems the player's girlfriend rang, just before the Irish team took on the Czech Republic, and summoned him home from Prague on the pretext that his grandmother had died. Inconveniently, both grandmothers were alive and well and keen to reassure the media that reports of their deaths had been a little exaggerated. Eventually it emerged that the couple had cooked up the 'dead grandmother' story because they didn't expect that the truth – his girlfriend's miscarriage – would have been enough to earn him compassionate leave.

And it would, of course, because every single wounded emotion is elevated to the same status these days for fear of causing offence or appearing discriminatory or heartless. If Steve Staunton had refused to let him leave to comfort his girlfriend and the team had still lost, imagine the fallout then. I can understand Ireland's girlfriend wanting him with her at the time but, nonetheless, a generation ago she'd have turned first to other women, to a mother or a sister or a girlfriend for consolation because miscarriage would have been seen as a realm entirely outside of male understanding. Just because that was the custom of an earlier time, though, doesn't make it wrong.

A new book, by an Irish couple affected by miscarriage, recounts their different reactions to the event. At one point, the man admitted, his wife impatiently told him to stop his crying, because the loss was primarily hers. I imagine that lots of women – and pretty much everyone who's had a successful pregnancy has had a miscarriage too – could relate to that.

One of the reasons I was so impatient with my male pal and his 'lost child' was that, at the same time, a close female friend had suffered a miscarriage, a few weeks later on in her pregnancy, and was dealing with it extremely practically. Unlike him she'd confided in very few people and didn't canvass sympathy at all. She had decided that this was wise Mother Nature's quality control system at work, that it was almost certainly for the best, and that the next baby would be perfect and all would be well. She'd been almost floored by a well-meaning nurse, at the maternity hospital, who told her to 'go home and grieve for the little one', but had managed to convince herself that all the grieving was for what might have been, rather than what was. She believed that her husband, in his response to the loss, would take his lead from her and, because she knew the limits of her own endurance in the situation, but not his, she never repeated that nurse's comment to him. And just about the last thing either of them needed, I reckoned, was to meet a chap like my maudlin friend with his over-counselled woe and his glib vocabulary of received emotions.

I know Irish men have been led a confusing dance, over the years, about the feelings they should and should not express, and there's a fear that our suicide statistics reflect that bewilderment. But I'm afraid that insisting that they articulate emotions they really can't share, and plumb losses whose depths they can't really fathom, may do more harm than good.

October 2007

Short shrift for dead gangsters

A FEW YEARS ago a Kerry priest cast a bit of a cloud over the First Communion preparations in his village by announcing that he'd be refusing the sacrament to any unmarried parents of the Communion class who dared present themselves at the altar. Which was controversial, of course, but not especially inspired – no, the real genius of the stance lay in his decision to refuse Communion only to those unmarried parents who were still together. Lone single parents, in other words, would be welcome because of the assumption that they had seen the error of their ways and renounced the sin of fornication – those who lived with the other parent, though, were presumed to be enjoying on-going occasions of sin and thus couldn't possibly have repented. And if, so the priest's argument went, he had reason to believe they had not repented then he couldn't give them the sacrament.

There was outcry, of course, at the ludicrous implications of this attitude – unmarried couples who were striving to give their children a stable home were to be singled out as sinners, while feckless dads who'd done a bunk on a pregnant girlfriend could waltz up to the altar without a care. And there was a climb-down, of course, and the whole thing blew over. But it is, nonetheless, the case that fornication is a mortal sin in Catholic doctrine, and that priest was doing no more than enunciating that teaching. So it's not just the feeble flock who can be à la carte Catholics – at times the Church seems easily cowed into backing away from its core principles when they prove unpalatable to a modern secular society.

Remember, as an example, the Church's response to Fr Mossie, the priest whose young girlfriend gave birth to their baby a couple of years back? Senior members of the hierarchy called for tolerance and understanding, space and privacy for the couple and their baby. Very laudable, of course, but celibacy is a rule for priests, not an optional extra. And in line with those rules, Fr Mossie really should have been censured in some way, excommunicated, defrocked, packed off to his very own Craggy Island, not mollycoddled with touchy-feely psychobabble like he was Britney Spears in rehab. He broke the rules, as, indeed, do cohabiting couples who take Communion. A Kilkenny priest who implored the faithful to pray that same-sex marriages never darken our shores came in for some stick recently, and there seemed very little support for his initiative amongst senior churchmen. But again, he was just articulating the Catholic Church's age-old teachings and rules. So you either change those rules, or you implement them. But just ignoring them when they are inconvenient or embarrassing is a craven cop-out, and weakens the Church's ability to take a stand when it really counts.

In the next couple of days we will see a funeral for John Daly, the notorious gangster shot dead early yesterday morning in Finglas in Dublin. In 1999 Daly robbed a petrol station and jammed a sawn-off shotgun into the faces of terrified staff. It was for this crime that he was behind bars, earlier this year, when he was dumb enough to ring *Liveline* to bitch about a journalist's exposés of his criminal connections. As a result, cells were raided, phones were confiscated and I'd say quite a few criminal operations disrupted as jailed masterminds suddenly found themselves out of the loop. Daly was probably a dead man walking since that hot-headed blunder, though it is probably fair to assume that he made enemies prior to that in his criminal career. It's probably also fair to assume that the serious offence for which he was jailed wasn't his only brush with the law.

If it is theologically sound for a priest to assume that a cohabiting couple are unrepentant sinners with every intention of resuming their errant ways the minute they get home from church (as you do when you've got young children around the house) I wonder if anybody might make the same assumption about the late lamented Mr Daly and the associates who will crawl into the daylight for his funeral later this week?

Churchmen justify officiating at a criminal's funeral by pointing out that you or I have no way of ruling out a deathbed conversion – John Daly, or Marlo Hyland, or any other murdered gangster might have seen the light just hours earlier and resolved to go straight, or perhaps made a heartfelt confession with their dying breaths. I've discussed this apparent dilemma with priests in the past and they've also pointed out funerals are not actually celebrations of a life just ended. Instead, the purpose of a funeral is to beg forgiveness for a flawed soul, even if it has become the norm to give thanks for the loved one's life and to humour the grieving relatives if they simply must conclude the proceedings with a blast of 'Stairway to Heaven'. That's fair enough, and I doubt there's any priest who's going to wear the prospect of Daly's mates delivering resounding eulogies from the pulpit and presenting his trustiest customised shotgun at the offertory.

But even so, I'd love to hear a priest at a criminal funeral asking those with blood on their hands or vengeance in their hearts to stay away from the altar at Communion. Wouldn't it be awesome to see a priest, in those circumstances, warn that he will refuse the sacrament to anybody he honestly believes to be involved in ongoing criminal activity? The priests in affected parishes across the country must know these guys, or could at least make it their business to find out who they are, so the threat need not be an idle one. If it is fair to assume that unmarried parents are sinners, why not make the same leap in the dark about a jobless young man with an expensive car and an ostentatious lifestyle and a string of previous convictions?

Unmarried parents, homosexuals, girls who've had abortions were very easy targets. These days, we are more compassionate towards them, and yet they still suffer discrimination and intolerance informed, in some part, by the long-held perception of their sinfulness. Perhaps the Church could now lead the way in channelling this level of opprobrium towards the really bad guys – will we ever see known gangsters turned away from Masses, refused Communion, threatened with excommunication? 'Short shrift' was the abbreviated absolution given to murderers on their way to the gallows – how about offering brief and pared-down obsequies to dead gangsters? Instead of hitting on gays and psychics and desperate girls, the Catholic Church could do wonders for its bruised status in this country by picking on an enemy its own size for a change.

November 2007

Suicide and the Workplace

AFTER ALL THESE years of wringing our hands over the spiralling suicide statistics across the country, we're still no closer to answering a central question that might just shape a successful response to the problem – is suicide ever somebody else's 'fault'? If one person deliberately ends his own life, could that ever be the direct and reasonably foreseeable result of another's negligence, cruelty or criminality? Or is the decision to select suicide from amongst other available options always a profoundly personal choice?

Recent legal developments both here and in Britain would suggest a shift towards the former attitude. Earlier this year in our own courts a sex abuser was found legally liable for his victim's subsequent suicide, while in Britain an employer has been held accountable for the suicide of a worker who developed a depressive illness after an accident at work. And last weekend a conference in Galway heard that employers' liability for suicide is pretty much inevitable in this country too.

It is impossible not to sympathise with those families whose loved ones' suicides were clearly linked to avoidable external stresses. There is very little doubt that Jane Roberts, who took her own life years after she was sexually abused as a child, would be alive today if not for the actions of her abuser. His statement admitting guilt was a crucial factor in swaying the civil action taken by her next of kin, and in the absence of a criminal conviction that judgement and award of compensation has offered some vital comfort to her bereaved family. There was clearly compelling evidence to suggest a causal link between the abuse and the suicide – these were exceptional circumstances, a classic hard case.

But hard cases shouldn't be allowed to make bad law. And

legally enshrining the notion that a third party can be held to blame for a suicide would be a bad law. Instead of illuminating the whole fraught issue, it would be a depressingly retrograde step both in terms of understanding suicide and preventing it. It may well be a foreseeable and even proportionate reaction to exceptional trauma, but we must hold fast to the view that suicide, in an otherwise mentally intact individual, is always a personal choice. To suggest otherwise would be to validate and even licence suicide as a legitimate response to injustice, as an objectively justifiable last resort rather than an entirely subjective solution.

Only last week on the radio a caller told me he'd considered suicide, in the throes of a difficult child custody battle, but rejected that course because he feared his bereft son would never forgive him. Shift the blame onto somebody else, though, and you remove that impediment. It is no longer your fault, it is your employers', your ex's, your abusive parent's doing. And I don't believe this is the case. Even where the other options are limited and unappealing or indiscernible, they always exist nonetheless.

Some years ago I interviewed a man called Pat Tierney, an angry, damaged poet who was planning to commit suicide and wanted to explain his reasons to a newspaper reporter. He felt they were good and valid reasons and he feared that a suicide note could be misinterpreted or even ignored, and his act of ultimate protest dismissed as the tragic and irrational act of an unstable mind.

Briefly, he'd been reared in Letterfrack orphanage, beaten and starved and sexually abused and farmed out at the age of seven to a local family who treated him like an animal and put him sleeping with the cattle. He'd tracked down his mother and was rejected; he had contracted Aids from drug abuse, and had learned the news only when an angry doctor accused him of endangering hospital staff with his tainted blood. A book he'd written to tell his story had failed to find a publisher and he'd spent all he had on publishing it himself to an overwhelmingly indifferent response. At the age of 39 he was jobless and alone and broke and in the advanced stages of Aids and absolutely determined not to pass his last days as he'd spent his early years, a charity case in chilly State care. Suicide was a final act of defiant autonomy, Pat's way of saying, 'Fate, you can't fire me – I quit'. And he also wanted somebody to tell his story without judging or interfering, which I did.

I did not alert a Garda or a social worker or a priest or a psychiatrist – he was pretty adamant he'd had his fill of the lot of them – but I did try, for what my efforts were worth, to point out those other options. I know it's a quaint journalistic quirk, but over ten years later I still have the tapes of our hours and hours of conversations. I pointed out that he had good friends, a keen intelligence, an extraordinary amount of energy and personal charisma, and, with proper medication, years still to live. He listened very politely, and argued his position. He'd had no control over his coming into the world and he wanted some hand in the manner of his leaving it. It was a strong and persuasive argument, and I don't think I've ever met anyone who seemed to have so little to live for.

After he'd hanged himself, under a full moon as he'd wanted, I came in for enormous criticism for not intervening. But I was fiercely certain that I'd done the correct thing, and that nobody had the right to deny him his drastic but reasoned choice. And I still believe that, and suspect he would have killed himself eventually whatever I'd done. But with a decade's hindsight I've come to the conclusion that everyone has a reason to live, even if it is sometimes oblique or even tardy in showing itself. In Pat Tierney's case neither of us saw it coming, but it was coming just the same.

Less than a year after he died, Christine Buckley went public with her Goldenbridge memories, and the damburst of institutional child abuse stories swamped the whole country. It was the very issue he'd been trying for years to raise, with his anger and his poetry and his one-man campaigns for the forgotten Magdalene women, and he would have loved to have been around to see it explode.

He'd have enjoyed being a pain in the ass for the church, he'd have revelled in the media attention, he'd have been the Simon Wiesenthal of the child abuse holocaust, hunting down abusers in their cosy retirement homes and pursuing their prosecutions. He'd have had a reason to live, and new Aids treatments would have done the rest.

December 2007

It had happened before

WHEN HER BODY was found in the burnt-out shell of the family home in Omagh last month, Caroline McElhill was holding her mobile phone in one hand and her rosary beads in the other. Caroline was 13 years old, the eldest of the five children who died along with their parents in the house fire that was most likely started by their father. Just about every detail of that diabolical incident – from the fact that screams were heard inside the house as the flames took hold, to the ghastly delay in locating the smallest baby's body in the charred dwelling – was uncommonly harrowing, but the revelation about the child clutching her rosary beads has haunted me more than anything else I've heard this past year.

When you hear of a fatal house fire, particularly where children are involved, you hope that the smoke got them before the heat ever did and, if it happened at night time, that they just slipped into a deeper sleep without a moment's fear or pain. There's something profoundly harrowing about the thought of terrified children trapped in an inferno – I remember standing outside the house where the three little Quinn boys were burned to death in Portadown after a petrol bomb attack on their neat terraced home during a tense marching season some years ago, and feeling physically ill as neighbours described seeing the small brothers huddled at a window crying for help: the lawns in the estate had just been cut and ever since then smell of freshly-mown grass reminds me of the sickly reek of burnt things that tainted the innocent summer scent that day.

Whatever about her siblings, there's no doubt that young Caroline McElhill was awake and alert when the fire started in her home, and most likely witnessed whatever ructions preceded it inside that house as well. And in those unimaginably fearful and desperate moments she'd reached for her mobile phone and her rosary beads. I don't know any 13-year-old who carries a rosary beads – if it wasn't for the gifts of kindly relatives at First Communion time I don't suppose any of mine would have a clue what rosary beads even looked like, and would probably identify them as the piece of jewellery that David Beckham occasionally wears around his neck.

They all know how to use a mobile phone, though, because pretty much every child in the country owns one of those before they reach their teens. And the argument that most of us use, when we buy a phone for a child, is that it will help them stay safe. If they get stranded, or frightened or threatened in any way, then they will be able to ring for help. You can even buy phones designed for toddlers these days that just have two buttons, one showing a little figure of a man and the other of a woman, so that they can call mammy or daddy in an emergency.

This whole marketing tack is based on the presumption, of course, that mammy or daddy will always be able to save them from the fear or the harm. For Caroline McElhill, though, as for lots of child victims of domestic violence, that was clearly not the case. The very people who should have been protecting her, and her little brothers and sisters, from harm were the source of their greatest danger. The fact that the child had her rosary beads to hand that night suggests to me that she knew well, from past experience, that she was going to have to look somewhere else for help. Most 13-year-old girls don't sleep with a rosary beads to hand these days, not unless they are accustomed to clinging to it in despair when there is no earthly comfort to be had.

Whatever grieving relatives and well-intentioned neighbours may insist, the row that led to this mass murder and suicide was hardly the sudden and catastrophic disintegration of a previously functional and peaceable family. The child simply wouldn't have had her rosary beads in her hand if she wasn't used to listening to this carry-on, the rows and the pleas and the threats, and praying for it to end. And the inquiry into those deaths needs to ask hard questions about who else knew, or pretended not to know, or hoped that turning a deaf ear would make it all go away.

Every now and then the various mens' and womens' lobby groups go head-to-head over the latest domestic violence statistics – the men resent the suggestion that they're always the perpetrators, the women insist that they are the victims in most cases. Children, though, are victims in every case. The complexities that keep intelligent and otherwise functional adults together in violent relationships often boil down to matters of personal choice.

I've spoken to women who have stayed with aggressive men for longer than was safe or wise and they are often able to explain their behaviour with reference to childhood experiences or personal shortcomings or even financial circumstances that held them back from leaving. Other times, though, they'll admit that they loved the man and needed the feedback of violent, jealous rages to confirm his passion.

A couple of years ago a frustrated judge threatened to jail women who called the Gardaí after they'd been beaten up by a violent man and then scuppered the prosecution by withdrawing their witness statements at the last minute. Such a heavy-handed approach would never work – you can't punish victims of domestic violence for being fearful of the consequences of testifying in court, or even for being foolishly optimistic when the aggressor wears them down with pleading and promises. Alternatives, such as allowing a police officer to present the witness statement in sensitive cases where it has subsequently been withdrawn, work in other jurisdictions and should certainly be considered here. But giving evidence against a partner who has beaten you up is simply not comparable with testifying against a stranger who assaults you in the street. You don't, after all, have to take your children to prison to visit that stranger, or even try to explain to them why you helped send him there.

But neither do you have to subject your children to the sights and sounds of domestic violence, particularly as study after study confirms that makes them more likely to grow up to be victims or aggressors themselves. Where there are children in the home, then the dynamics of a dysfunctional, tempestuous relationship are not simply the discrete concern of the adults involved. No matter how charming or persuasive or contrite an aggressive partner may subsequently be, and no matter how overwhelming the practical restraints on leaving a violent home, there is very little excuse for continuing to expose children to domestic abuse.

People stay with violent partners for all sorts of reasons, but very few are good enough to justify the harm such an upbringing does to innocent children. Both parents have a duty to protect their children, and we need to question the mythology that portrays adult victims of domestic abuse as pervasively helpless, powerless, cornered casualties of an inescapable fate. Often they are competent, intelligent, professional people, holding down a job and determinedly keeping the good side out. Often they tacitly conspire with their abuser to deflect inquiry and suspicion, which in turn absolves relatives and concerned neighbours from the obligation to delve further. Last week the family of Arthur McElhill said they've been crushed by the speculation about his role in the seven deaths, and pointed out that nobody knows what happened in that house before the fire began. That's true, nobody does – but the fact that a 13-year-old girl was clutching her mobile phone and her rosary beads in the small hours of the morning strongly suggests that it had happened before.

March 2008

Chummy lawyers, matey judges and Guards in civvies ...

WE'VE JUST SPENT a great week in a large, modern and totally child-friendly hotel in Killarney. They'd thought of just about everything that might make a break with children that bit safer, more comfortable and even fun – buffet breakfasts till nearly midday, well-supervised kids' club activities from first thing in the morning until after ten at night, crèche facilities if you wanted them and, if not, nobody batted an eyelid at the sight of small children romping around the foyer bar until one in the morning. Well, alright, Elvis looked a tad put out as the night wore on and the under-tens began to outnumber the adult audience for his tribute act, but Neil Diamond took it all in good part. And I have reason to believe that if you happen to mislay a child in this hotel – say you forget to do a head count as you round up the crowd after a game of indoor soccer, just for example – the kind lady on reception will give him a dinosaur egg to stop him crying while she phones your mobile, and will not betray even a hint of disapproval when it becomes clear that you hadn't even missed him yet. Or so I've heard.

This whole 'child-friendly' concept is a relatively new one

in this country. It's really only in the last five years or so that 'family' hotels and restaurants have come round to the idea that families occasionally include children and that, if you want the adults to feel relaxed and welcome and inclined to return, you'll do some serious buttering up on the nippers.

And the 'child-friendly' concept has spread beyond hotels and restaurants into other areas of activity in which children are likely to engage. Children's hospitals and dental surgeries are now routinely designed to prevent young patients feeling intimidated, with pastel colours and scaled-down furniture and books and murals all thoughtfully located. Even the Catholic Church has stumbled to the child-friendly concept as a way of ensuring return business from parents and investing in the parishioners of the future, and lots of parishes around the country now offer family Masses, having short sermons in simple language and children doing readings, leading prayers and bringing up Offertory gifts.

In fact, we've all become so conditioned to the notion that child-friendly invariably equals good and positive and desirable that we see nothing bizarre or dysfunctional in the extension of the concept into one venue that should be anything but friendly and welcoming to children – the criminal court.

While reading a news report last week on a court appearance by one of the youngsters accused of the Drimnagh stabbings, I spent several minutes looking at a sentence that included the phrase 'child-friendly criminal court' and trying to figure out why it jarred so much. Child-friendly means welcoming and hospitable to children, doesn't it, someplace unthreatening and homely in which they feel perfectly comfortable and at ease? Should this really include the dock of a criminal court?

The report described how the normal protocols of a criminal court don't apply in the Children's Court – the language is kept as simple and informal as possible, the lawyers wear casual dress rather than wigs and gowns, the judge is equally dressed-down. I know this sounds hopelessly 'hang 'em and flog 'em' but I really do believe that the only dressing-down that should go on in a criminal court – any criminal court – ought to be the roasting that a convicted defendant can expect from the bench.

I was vaguely aware that the Children's Court was tailored to accommodate young defendants, but had never stopped to question the absolute lunacy of 'child-friendly' criminal justice. In the same week that we've heard of drunken boys of 10 and 12 years joining in the Finglas rioting, terrorising neighbourhoods, stoning Gardaí and burning cars, isn't there something utterly bonkers about the criminal justice system bending over backwards to make accused children feel relaxed in the surroundings of a court?

Youngsters who face the terrifying prospect of testifying in an adult criminal court aren't guaranteed anything like the same concessions – they can still endure cross-examination from lawyers in wigs and gowns, even if the case involves a sexual assault. And harsh as that may seem, there is a strong argument for observing procedures regardless of the age or vulnerability of the participants. Justice is meant to be blind, for a start, not peeking out from under her blindfold to check that the defendant's feet reach the floor when he sits in the dock. And the case for retaining the wigs and gowns in general is that they convey the ancient authority and gravity of the whole process of administering justice: it's a reminder to all parties, not least the defendant, that this is a very serious business and they'd be foolish to take the proceedings lightly.

But what message, do you suppose, would a 12-year-old rioter take away from the 'child-friendly' atmosphere of the Children's Court? Chummy lawyers, matey judges, Gardaí in their civvies or shirt-sleeves for fear of looking remotely stern, all of it calculated to convey the impression that this is no big deal, nothing to be scared of, something all children go through, like a state exam or an inoculation or a visit to a boring relative – is it at all likely that a young offender will leave with a cheery goodbye to the friendly beak and resolve never, ever to set foot inside the place again? Or will he come out and tell his mates what a doddle the whole thing turned out to be?

I'm all for child-friendly hotels, Masses and dentists, but not courtrooms. Now that the guards despair, the teachers are terrified to say boo, and parents are their mates, the courtroom is society's last chance to instil some respect for authority on wayward children and should, quite properly, scare the living daylights out of them. Or am I missing something here?

April 2008

Joan of Arc at the Mahon Tribunal

A FEW MONTHS ago Eddie Hobbs nearly got himself lynched when he dared to suggest that a working mother was less valuable to an employer than a single colleague. And just recently, and to even greater howls of outrage, Sir Alan Sugar came out and said the same thing – that between maternity leave, parent–teacher meetings, dental appointments, medical emergencies and the emotional and practical wear and tear of motherhood, you couldn't blame any boss who hired a single young man instead of a working mum, however impressive her credentials.

I happen to agree with this point of view. I reckon women are pricing themselves out of the jobs market by demanding ever-enhanced maternity packages, first call on holiday leave and the right to down tools and go home without notice – and without objection – if a child is ill or a nanny cries off. I don't know any working mother who would say, 'My children come second to my job'. So it's hardly fair to insist on absolute equality with childless, single colleagues who have indeed prioritised their careers, while at the same time demanding special concessions in the workplace to accommodate your personal lifestyle choice. Any time I express that view, though, I'm barraged with indignant letters and emails from men and women practically accusing me of incitement to hatred.

If anything, I'm told, working mothers are far more productive and conscientious than single colleagues because they realise they've got to be so much more competent and capable to stay in the game. How dare I peddle the line that mums in the workplace are frazzled, fragile, hormonal wrecks, pining for their children, endlessly distracted by domestic crises, and liable to burst into floods of tears if the boss dares to look crooked at them? Motherhood and homemaking don't rot your brain, you know, and don't turn you into a weak, weepy, helpless ninny who needs to be rescued from her own dizzy ineptitude by a big strong bloke. Whether she has children or not, a woman is just as competent and accountable as any man, and this 'weaker sex' lark is an insulting, outdated myth.

So where have they been for the last few weeks, all these outspoken champions of multitasking feminine capability? Why haven't they been up in arms at the coverage of Gráinne Carruth's evidence before the Mahon Tribunal? Why aren't they absolutely incensed by the suggestion that Ms Carruth, who gave deeply dodgy evidence to the tribunal and only changed her mind when threatened with criminal proceedings, should have been treated more sympathetically because she's a woman and a mother?

Under very uncomfortable cross-examination – necessitated by inconsistencies in her own previous sworn testimony – she broke down in tears and bleated to the judge that she just wanted to go home to her children. Instead of being rebuked for playing the 'hit me now with the child in my arms' card, Ms Carruth was cast as a modern-day Joan of Arc, immolated by the cowardice of scheming, powerful men. And the tribunal lawyers, who are paid to winkle the truth out of some very slippery and recalcitrant witnesses, were vilified as cold-hearted bullies picking on a mere woman. I'm sure there were times when Frank Dunlop would have preferred to be sitting at home in the bosom of his family as well – why didn't that plea work for him?

Let's imagine a parallel scenario where Bertie Ahern's former constituency secretary is a strapping chap called George Carruth. Back in 1994 our George, who is related by marriage to the then Minister for Finance, has a path worn from St Luke's to the Irish Permanent Building Society branch in Drumcondra. Each time he lodges substantial bundles of cash, each one many multiples of his own take-home pay at the time. In total, George lodges £15,500 for his boss, the Minister. Nothing about any of this strikes George as the least bit odd, to the extent that he forgets all about it.

In December of last year, George goes before the Tribunal and states, on oath, that he was simply making lodgements from the salary of his boss, who preferred dealing in cash. Then, last month, George is recalled to the Tribunal and asked to explain documents which indicate, beyond any reasonable doubt, that he was actually converting and lodging sterling on his boss's behalf all that time. George says he is upset at this revelation, and insists that he still doesn't remember handling all that sterling. When the judge reminds him that he could go to jail for lying to the tribunal, George starts to cry and says he wants to go home to his children. Does George need (a) sympathy, (b) counselling or (c) a chat with the Gardaí?

Unless the fact of her motherhood and femininity addled her brain in some way, then there is no reason to doubt that Gráinne Carruth knew exactly what she was doing when she went before the Tribunal to trot out patently mendacious evidence last December. She now says she 'accepts' that she lodged sterling for Bertie Ahern but still can't remember doing so. So she was certain enough in her memory just a few months ago to assert, on oath, that the money was Irish currency, salary payments, but when suddenly faced with evidence to the contrary, like so many other Tribunal witnesses, she's been felled by amnesia. I have no idea why Ms Carruth went to the deceptive lengths she did to back up the Taoiseach's tall tales. All I know for sure is that, like her former boss, her evasions and memory losses have added considerably to the tribunal's expensive enquiries. And I really don't believe her gender absolves her of all responsibility for that.

November 2008

Walking into doors

SITTING IN HER bedroom nursing her newborn baby, about ten o'clock one morning a few years ago, a friend heard footsteps outside on the landing. She was alone in the house at the time so realised instantly that this was not a good thing, but she didn't panic or scream. Instead, she put her baby back into his cot and went out to find a strange man standing in the corridor brandishing a screwdriver.

She's still not sure where she found the strength, and puts it down to some heavy-duty postpartum hormones, but she managed to bundle the man into an empty bedroom. She turned the key and then, still in superhuman mode, dragged a heavy chest of drawers across the doorway. It took two strong Guards to lift it away, in order to arrest the intruder, when they eventually arrived – 45 minutes and three phone calls later, even though she lives just a few hundred yards from the nearest Garda Station.

After they'd removed the burglar, and found that his screwdriver had been sharpened to a deadly point, my outraged and adrenaline-charged friend stormed round to the station and tore a strip off the duty sergeant. Why had it taken so long for them to come, she demanded to know? Why did she have to make three phone calls pleading for help, when she was alone in her home with a tiny infant, before the cavalry arrived?

The sergeant hummed and hawed and looked sheepish, and finally admitted, under pretty relentless cross-examination, that her call had been logged as a 'domestic'. In other words, they believed that the man menacing and terrorising a new mother in her own bedroom, putting her in such fear that she rang the police begging for help, was her partner. And in that case, somebody reckoned, it might be best to hold back and see if it all blew over. Even though far more women are killed in this country by their partners than by strangers, they still figured on waiting it out.

And the awful thing is, you can't really blame them for that. Nobody wants to get involved in a domestic – not the neighbours, not the doctors, not the kids' teachers, often not even the victim's family, so you can hardly fault the police for their reticence. And the fact that their first response was a 'wait and see' approach suggests that jaded experience has taught them that this is often the most practical course. It must be demoralising to answer a call, find a woman beaten to a pulp, arrest her partner and process a prosecution, only to have her withdraw her statement and drop the charges because he's promised he'll never do it again and she desperately wants to believe him.

Domestic violence must be the only crime in which the victim can also be a co-conspirator, an accessory after the fact, helping to cover up the offence with false statements and alibis. We have all known the woman who walked into doors, or suffered the mystery allergy that caused her face to swell, or wore sunglasses in winter or tightly wrapped scarves on the hottest days. And if it's difficult for police to break down these protective facades when they've actually been summoned to a dispute, think how much harder it is for families and friends to make an unsought, and almost certainly unwelcome, intervention. If your sister or daughter or friend really wanted help, then she'd ask for it, wouldn't she? And nobody really knows what makes another marriage tick, do they?

It's four years last week since Rachel O'Reilly was bludgeoned to death by her husband Joe. Though her family had no reason to believe she was at risk, her mother's gut instinct told her straight away that the stricken widower was the murderer. It's easy to be wise afterwards, though – strains in a marriage are hard to conceal, but blundering in to take sides can do immense harm if a couple are working things out. Nobody will ever know if Rachel herself felt under threat and hid it from her family, because that's such a difficult question to ask.

At the trial of Dermot McArdle for the killing of his wife Kelly-Anne last week, the accused's sister implied that drunken rows were a feature of the marriage. To the disgust of the dead woman's relatives, she claimed this was common knowledge amongst the extended family, and that Kelly-Anne's father had comforted McArdle, immediately after her death, saying, 'Son, I know what she was like with drink on her'. Kelly-Anne's family, however, insisted that she had suffered violence at her husband's hands in the past, and say they'd known he was an aggressive and domineering man. Lots of families, living with those same whispered suspicions, must have read that evidence hoping to God they never have to air their secrets in the witness box of a murder trial.

This is clearly an issue that troubles President McAleese, because she has spoken out many times about the evils of domestic violence and the need to acknowledge its toxic legacy for generations to come. Again last week she called for a national debate on the subject, and it's a timely plea – the tough economic times ahead will cause tensions in even the most peaceable of households, so heaven help those who are already at risk.

But who are they, actually, these families at risk? Whatever your suspicions, they couldn't really be people like us, could they? Even though we all know a woman who walks into doors, even though we've read of the nice, familiar lives of the women battered, stabbed, strangled by partners, domestic violence doesn't really happen to decent families, does it? It happens in sink estates, with cheap furniture smashed around shabby kitchens while grubby children cower in damp bedrooms, not in the glossy designer homes of plausible, successful men, right?

I was struck by the President's use of the world 'loneliness' to describe the misery of the victims. With life and limb at risk, you might think, loneliness should be the least of their worries, but in fact it's the most critical of all. Because loneliness is more about emotional isolation than physical solitude, and when you're lying to your family and your closest friends then you're really on your own.

And it is shame, more than loyalty and as much as fear, that makes victims lie. It is shame that denies the bruises, shame that assists the culprits, shame that frustrates the Gardaí, and shame that stifles debate. The first step, then, has got to be about convincing victims that they are not the ones who should feel shame, and persuading families to ask the awkward question where their suspicions are aroused. Only when victims find the support and the courage to speak out can this debate really begin.

May 2008

'The Ballad of Bobby Sands'

ON A CYCLING holiday in Corsica some years ago, we stumbled upon a tiny little village in the middle of the island that wasn't marked on any map and had just one road leading into it, but none leading out. There was no hotel in the village, but the shifty-looking bar owner led us to a small room in an empty old house which, he told us, he kept for tourists who had gone astray and needed a bed for the night.

After a rather uneasy sleep – the whole set-up was a bit too *Deliverance* for my liking – we were disturbed, before dawn, by unnerving noises outside the bedroom window. On the street below, we were rather alarmed to see a group of whispering rustics gathering with shotguns and torches but, just when we were wondering if they'd at least be sporting enough to give us a few minutes' head start, they all climbed into a truck and disappeared.

Over breakfast later we were told that the men of the village had gone on a wild boar hunt because there was a wedding on that evening and spit-roasted 'sanglier' was the traditional fare. And as rare and honoured guests we were persuaded to stay for the feast, which involved lots of roast pig, sweet little beignets and endless champagne toasts to the happy couple and to the enduring warmth of Corsican–Irish relations. And in the small hours of the morning, the wedding band wrapped up their set with a rousing encore that brought the whole place to its feet – 'The Ballad of Bobby Sands'. The locals sang along with gusto to lyrics that compared the Corsican secession crusade with the Republican cause – this number hadn't been included for our benefit, though they were proud as punch that we were there to hear it.

I'm sure those Corsican revellers would have been astonished to learn that 'The Ballad of Bobby Sands' isn't quite the sure-fire crowd pleaser at any Irish wedding and could, indeed, be pretty much guaranteed to bring proceedings to an embarrassing halt. I've seen a walk-out at a function at which an instrumental version of 'The Merry Ploughboy' was played – even the tune to the words 'I'm off to join the IRA and I'm off tomorrow morn' was enough to cause offence – so I don't expect to hear the Ballad of Bobby sending 'em home sweating in my lifetime. The French towns of Nantes, St Etienne, Le Mans Vierzon and St Denis all have their Rues Bobby Sands and, of course, the Iranian Government famously renamed Winston Churchill Street, the location of the British Embassy in Tehran, in honour of Bobby Sands for the sheer pleasure of seeing that address on the Ambassador's stationery. It will be a while, though, before we see a Bobby Sands Avenue in Dublin city.

Because even after all these years, even after all the leaps of faith and the compromises made and the bitterness set aside, even after we've seen polarised bogey men like Ian Paisley and Martin McGuinness chuckling together in Stormont, the mention of Bobby Sands is still as divisive and inflammatory and provocative as it was 27 years ago. You're safe enough assuming that most people share the same views on Bloody Sunday, on Enniskillen, on Omagh, these days, but even after almost three decades there's something raw and unresolved about the hunger strikes.

It's like a shameful family secret – we don't like to talk about it, ourselves, we change the subject if a stranger brings it up, all that pain, all that anger, all that unruly passion, so intense and messy and barbaric that we still haven't managed to decide how we feel about it, nor found a place for it in our collective memory.

Now a harrowing new movie about Sands' agonising death, after 66 days on hunger strike in the spring of 1981, may finally force us to acknowledge the subliminal battering so many smug certainties took that year. Up to then, you see, we in the South were fairly unanimous in how we felt about the thugs and the rabble-rousers in the Republican movement. The brief outrage that followed Bloody Sunday had long since passed, the Provos and their supporters were widely regarded as criminal scum and the Northern conflict a tedious international embarrassment.

And then ten young men starved themselves to death for the right to be treated as political prisoners – and suddenly you couldn't write them off as hot-headed, brainwashed, numbskulled louts any longer. The cynics said the hunger strikes were more about shaming and discomfiting Britain than winning the right to wear civvies inside, not that it mattered – either way, you had to feel pretty convinced by your cause to watch a friend die in unimaginable torment from hunger and then embark on the same course. There was as much visceral anger towards the strikers – we were a modern, civilised nation, for God's sake, we'd just won the Eurovision for a second time – as there was towards Margaret Thatcher. I remember being outraged by rumours that polite applause would break out at posh London dinner parties when another hunger striker died, and yet equally furious at these men leaving behind small children and wives and mothers to die as martyrs for an absolutely hopeless crusade.

There was murky manipulation and profound cynicism at play within the Republican organisation at the time, and that has helped poison attitudes towards the episode, but perhaps it is time to consider that maybe those men's lives weren't lost for quite as hopeless, or selfish, or fanatical a purpose as the fragile consensus holds. A leaked British Government briefing document of the time revealed that the hunger strikes had opened British eyes to the appalling vista that these men were driven by an ideology rather than by venality and so would never be defeated by counter-criminal measures. It may be entirely coincidental, of course, that within a decade the first moves towards the talks that led to Good Friday 1998 had begun, but I don't think so.

The film *Hunger* will polarise and galvanise opinion about the hunger strikes all over again, and it really is high time we eyeballed the skeletal figures in that particular closet. I still don't expect I'll live to walk down Bobby Sands Boulevard in Dublin city or to dance to 'The Ballad of Bobby Sands' at an Irish wedding, but I'd quite like to hear that name mentioned in sane, calm, informed debate so that the generation, for whom he truly believed he was giving his life, can make up their own minds.

September 2008

Bubblewrapped kids

THERE'S A DEVICE you can buy to fit under the bonnet of a car that will monitor its speed and send a notification, by text, if it goes above a prescribed limit. So say you've agreed to buy, tax and insure your teenage son's first car, but only on the condition that 60 kmph is quite fast enough for a 17-year-old lad in a second-hand Micra. You fit it with one of these speed monitors, and then the minute he hits 61 kmph you get a text grassing him up and, just so he knows he's been busted, so does he. At this point, as a responsible parent, you have a couple of options: do you confiscate the car on the spot or do you give him another chance and a final warning?

You have, of course, always got a couple of other options as well. You could omit to fit the widget in the car in the first place and trust the young adult, who is legally old enough to drive without this high-tech form of aversion therapy, to behave sensibly on the roads. Or you could always refuse to buy a car for your teenager, offer instead a lecture on how you managed when you were his age, point out the benefits of bicycles, public transport and delayed gratification, and make him wait until he can afford a vehicle of his own.

The bewildering question, though, is which of these four options does a conscientious parent choose these days? Is it really appropriate to deny your son a car when all his friends are driving, he's got lots of heavy books to ferry to and from college, plus he'll need a licence when he goes for his first job? On the other hand, where's the incentive to work and save if his every desire is handed to him on a plate? But even if he helps pay for the car himself, isn't it simply responsible to train him to observe limits by checking his speed with the help of an electronic sneak? Or does growing up not involve an awareness of risk and an acceptance of personal accountabil-ity? After all, if a parent assumes a role in supervising a young adult's behaviour – in this case driving habits – aren't they also implicitly undertaking to make it all better if things go wrong?

Yet more and more, it seems, parents are choosing the 'bubblewrap' option, as one British parenting expert termed it in a recent lecture to preschool teachers here. We are, he suggested, in danger of churning out a brood of 'battery kids', hot-housed from early childhood by anxious parents who dance attendance on their every whim and fret over remote hazards. These youngsters are growing up 'street-stupid' rather than smart because they have so little exposure to risk that they subsequently fail to recognise it until it jumps up and bites them or, more likely, pulls a hidden blade in a petulant brawl.

And it is not, it would seem, just in terms of their ability to deal with the unexpected that this generation is being handicapped by over-anxious and indulgent parents. We're also producing a generation of wide-eyed Pollyannas, convinced that the world owes them an exceptionally good living and will deliver it just as promptly as their parents stumped up for iPhones and gap-year holidays and sweet sixteen parties.

The latest Graduates Careers Survey found that one in five of the current crop of final-year students expects to be earning at least €100,000 by the time they're 30. Despite the still-prohibitive cost of property, almost 70 per cent of them believe they'll own their own homes by the age of 30, a majority expect to have spent a period living and working abroad by that advanced age and almost half reckon they'll have holidayed in at least ten different foreign countries before the end of their 20s. All told, then, not exactly a generation that anticipates keeping its nose to a poorly paid grindstone over the next decade or so.

And why should they? They have, after all, come of age in full view of their parents' enjoyment of the fruits of the boom, and have been the beneficiaries of their 'kid-in-a-sweetshop' largesse. The 40-something parents of these undergraduates would have weathered their own teens and college years in far more straitened times. And when you splash out on your children you are, I suspect, also buying that car or that holiday or that desirable designer gadget for the hard-up youngster you used to be.

But maybe we need to get over the fact that we didn't have the car, or the expensive gym membership, or the Harvey Nicks charge card when we were 17, since we somehow managed to survive. Twenty years ago you spent your summers bussing tables in cheap seafood restaurants in Cape Cod to earn spending money for the next college term, but also to remind yourself why you were slogging out those college years in the first place. Hard work and study were a way out of menial labour and second-hand clothes shops and packed lunches in the canteen. You had a legitimate expectation of better times, if you were a college student in Ireland in the 1980s, because there wasn't much scope for things to get a whole lot worse.

But how do you improve on an upbringing that considers stretch Hummers to First Communions and foreign holiday homes and hired domestic help to be fairly basic necessities? For a variety of reasons, and despite their high-flying aspirations, the undergraduates of 2008 are probably the first generation in the past century who cannot reasonably expect to do better than their parents. They are unlikely to be educated to a significantly higher level – indeed, if anything, standards have been dumbed down because the proliferation of for-profit colleges means that even the most average Leaving Cert will get you an impressive-sounding qualification. If they do own their homes by 30 they're likely to be boxy apartments rather than suburban semi-ds, nice cars and foreign holidays and luxury goods won't be the novelties they previously were and, if 20 per cent of today's final year students are indeed earning €100,000 within the decade it'll only be because inflation will have rendered that sum worth precisely the square root of sweet FA.

The truth is that today's bubblewrapped, mollycoddled, over-indulged youngsters are singularly ill-prepared for either a general economic downturn or a specific personal disappointment. In the year since Madeline McCann disappeared 'responsible parenting' has crystallised as the obligation to anticipate and head off even the most outlandish possibilities with ever more paranoid precautions, and I'm as guilty as the next parent: my 12-year-old son took a bus into town alone for the first time last Saturday, to buy himself a goldfish, and there was more synchronising of watches and scale maps and contingency plans than attended the Normandy landings. I know it'd be a hardy paedophile that'd chance snatching a strapping 5'11" adolescent complete with bag of goldfish, but you can't be too careful.

But you can, actually. You can be too careful, too indulgent and too fierce a firewall against harsh, disappointing reality. Optimism is wonderful and essential for success, but it does need to be based on something a little more substantial than the fact that rewards and approval have always come easy. It's no bad thing that we have equipped this year's graduates with a sense of entitlement to the best life has to offer – but they also need a leavening pinch of reality to cope with the possibility that the parents won't always be there to kiss things better.

October 2008

Stop animal testing ... why?

FAKE FUR IS having a fashion moment this autumn. The shops are full of coats and jackets and wraps in man-made pelts, all so beautifully soft you'd be hard pressed to tell them from the real thing. This is great news for me. It means I can finally wear the lovely silver fox coat I invested in a couple of winters back, when we were all rich, and nobody will be any the wiser. At a glance you'd swear dozens of adorable little acrylics had given up their lives to keep me warm and, though it seems a bit daft to buy a real fur and insist to everybody it's faux, darling, you never know where those PETA types might be lurking with a pot of red gloss paint.

I wish I could say I agonised over the ethics of buying the coat but, honestly, the price was the only thing that made me dither. Fur is probably the oldest animal product in human use, since we haven't had much insulation of our own for at least a hundred thousand years, so it's a bit hypocritical to get sniffy about fur if you eat meat or wear leather or wool.

Or, for that matter, if you use medication or medical expertise of any kind. Animal testing of medication is the most controversial, perhaps because it is the most recent, human requisitioning of animals lives for our own ends. Because just about every legal drug you use, from your mildest headache tablet to the most effective blood pressure medication, has been tested on an animal, and a live one at that.

Drugs are tested on animals, human tissue is sometimes retained in pathology labs, post mortems are a brutal violation of a dead body – these are among the collateral realities of medical progress that we'd prefer not to dwell upon, if possible. We're all happy to benefit from the knowledge and expertise that medical science gained from these practices, but feel obliged to be outraged when confronted with the gory details in emotive language and provocative photographs.

The term 'vivisection' is a sort of linguistic cluster bomb in the arsenal of animal rights advocates – if it's even close to the target then they don't stand a chance. So John Banville, a writer of the most scrupulous and painstaking precision, knew exactly the stir he'd cause when he lobbed that device into the School of Medicine in Trinity College with a letter to *The Irish Times* ten days ago.

It had come to his attention, he wrote, 'that animal

vivisection is carried out regularly' in the biology department of the College. He had been informed by the National Animal Rights Association (NARA) that 'they test on mice, rats, rabbits, guinea-pigs and those cute little puppies with the big eyes and floppy ears (I just made that last bit up)'. 'They' even test on 'sheep, pigs and horses when they can' – presumably when Igor can shepherd them unnoticed down Grafton Street and along College Green.

A NARA spokeswoman had assured him, he said, 'that a scientist from the college had spoken to NARA protesters on the street and admitted that the only reason they still use animals is because it's cheaper and more convenient'. And laughed an evil laugh, I bet, before shuffling back into the bowels of the college for more unspeakable experiments on cuddly creatures.

Ever since, villagers with torches have been metaphorically circling the college as a debate about vivisection kicked off in online discussion forums and on letters pages. Given that he undertakes meticulous research for his novels, Banville's admission that he rejected an offer to discuss the matter with a college scientist is quite extraordinary. 'My position on the matter is not open to discussion,' he wrote. Now why is a mind as brilliant, inquiring and capacious as Banville's firmly closed to an argument that might just sway it?

I guess unyielding certainty is always more satisfying than exploring complexities that could unsettle your convictions, but maybe we're at cross-purposes here. If you believe that animal lives are just as important as ours, there is absolutely no argument for employing animals to test human medicines – the idea is just as repulsive as using children to test veterinary drugs. If you believe, though, that human life is paramount, then you must admit that there are certain circumstances in which it is preferable to test drugs on animals rather than on humans. It really is that simple.

I'd hate to think of animals suffering unnecessarily to make face creams and make-up, and I make a point of buying products that haven't been tested on animals. But if there's a convincing case for using animals to test human drugs, I'd like to hear it at least. So I rang the Medical School in Trinity and spoke to one of the professors there.

For a start, she said, the implication that medical students are slicing up living creatures with impunity is false. Most of the research is conducted on rats and mice that are bred in strictly controlled circumstances with the best of veterinary care and husbandry. The researchers are licensed and experienced, and every experiment on a living animal has to be individually cleared in advance with the Department of Health and Children, and must follow the most stringent codes. The animals are anaesthetised and treated afterwards with painkillers.

There are ongoing efforts to find alternatives to animal experimentation but, for the moment, some drugs and procedures can only be tested on living creatures. You can't test the effect of blood-pressure medication, for example, on dead tissue.

The mystery scientist who spoke to the NARA protesters admitted, according to Banville, 'that the only reason they still use animals is because it's cheaper and more convenient'. Cheaper and more convenient than what? Testing on impoverished humans who don't have a whole lot more choice than the rats and mice? Testing on human tissue if, given the recent furore over organ retention, you can get anyone to donate it any more? Or not testing at all?

If you buy the animal rights lobby line that there are acceptable alternatives to animal testing, then you must conclude that these researchers are torturing helpless creatures just for the hell of it. I will readily admit I like wearing my silver fox-fur coat because it feels so good. I really doubt, though, that our most eminent scientific brains actively choose to experiment on animals for that same reason.

January 2009

Nothing to stop the dead speaking ill of the living

DOES IT BOTHER you to think about who might turn up at your funeral? Do you care what they might say about you, and where they'd sit in the church? Would you spin in your grave at the thought of fair-weather friends filling the front pews wreathed in black and stricken with ostentatious grief? Would it kill you to imagine sworn enemies gathering to network and gossip and make snide remarks about the modest turnout? Do you mind if people send flowers or would you prefer charity donations, would you like mourners to call to your home, or have tea and sandwiches with your relatives after you'd been buried?

Tony Gregory cared and, knowing he was about to die, he put quite a bit of thought into the matter of his funeral. For a man who claimed to see no logic in the notion of an afterlife, he showed an uncommon desire to control proceedings after death. But then, as a politician himself, he'd been to enough send-offs to predict how things would go if he didn't take charge.

There'd be eulogies and orations and soliloquies and recitations and lone pipers and marching bands and wreaths in the shape of starry ploughs, there'd be a two-page *VIP* photo spread of celebrities comforting politicians, and they might even make him wear a tie.

He couldn't know he was going to die in the very week that Beverly Flynn helped ratchet public respect for politicians down a notch or two, though he'd have been hard-pressed to pick a time when Irish politics could not benefit from a light dusting of the inner-city grit of Gregory's ornery integrity. They'd have been out in their droves to ally themselves to one of the few politicians to live out a lengthy career without a whiff of corruption or venality. That was a no-brainer, and Gregory was having none of it.

And yet there was an unseemly amount of bitterness evident in the tone of a funeral service that belittled and embarrassed former colleagues who turned up to pay their respects. You had to wonder if somebody could have done with clearing a little brush from around his heart before he died, because old slights and injustices still rankled to the end.

At Gregory's own instruction, for example, there was assigned seating for just three dignitaries – the President, the Taoiseach, and the Lord Mayor of Dublin. If the Taoiseach chose to send his aide-de-camp then protocol, Gregory had decreed, was to be breached and the representative seated in the body of the church. He was overruled on that one, and the aide-de-camp was seated in the front row for the removal, while the Taoiseach himself turned up for the funeral, so further awkwardness was avoided in that regard at least.

But there was still plenty of awkwardness to go round. Bertie Ahern, whom Gregory accused in his final *Hot Press* interview of seriously dirty tricks back in 1981, hobbled into the church on his crutches to find himself a seat in the throng. And for those politicians lucky enough to find a seat to squirm in, there was further discomfort in store. When Fr Peter McVerry remarked that, unlike Gregory, most of them would be quickly forgotten, his homily was interrupted by sustained and pointed applause. The first six rows of seats were firmly marked 'canvassers only', and so-called friends who had never 'so much as put a leaflet in a letterbox' during his lifetime were left in no doubt what he thought of them, during a very barbed address by Gregory's long time friend, Councillor Maureen O'Sullivan.

She told the congregation that most of them would not be welcome at the graveside, nor would there be refreshments afterwards for any but his closest friends, relatives and most stalwart supporters.

This was all in keeping with Gregory's wishes, which were characteristically unorthodox to the last. Because it is rarely that we ever see the wishes and enmities and grudges of the deceased, who is after all dead and gone and beyond satisfaction or revenge, shape a funeral service to such a palpable degree. Maybe existing funerary custom and practice, where the most hypocritical displays of grief and the most unwelcome of mourners go unchallenged, is disingenuous. Perhaps your final send-off is the best possible place to settle old scores. It is firmly *verboten* for the living to speak ill of the dead, but there's nothing at all to stop the dead pouring great scorn on the living, and Tony Gregory made gleeful use of that loophole. Even a few weeks before he died he was denied speaking time to address the Dáil on education cuts, so he must have relished the chance of a clear run to express himself, at last, without the Ceann Comhairle's interruption, and we can hardly fault him for taking it.

But once you're dead then you have no active say in how you are remembered – that's up to your friends and family. And that's why it is not customary to dwell on grievances and cranky quirks because that, usually, is not how the bereaved wish to recall a deceased loved one. At Gregory's funeral Councillor O'Sullivan took care to distinguish between the politician's unsmiling public face, and the humorous, gregarious, vivacious storyteller known only to his friends. What a shame that funeral did nothing to reconcile the two for the thousands who liked and admired Gregory without ever having the chance to meet him at all.

Tony Gregory never wore a tie to the Dáil because, he said, few in his constituency ever wore a tie to work. I always felt that this stance undermined the honour his constituents had bestowed upon him. They might not have had white collar jobs, but that didn't mean those fiercely proud inner-city Dubs wouldn't have scrubbed up in their absolute Sunday best, out of respect for their State's hard-won sovereignty, if they ever had the chance to walk through the doors of Dáil Éireann.

Nor would a true, working-class Dub ever like to think that a mourner who attended his funeral was sent home with his belly stuck to his back for want of a cup of tea and a ham sandwich. Ironically, in doing precise service to his wishes, Gregory's friends did a disservice to the man himself.

In that final interview Gregory spoke movingly of how, despite his doubts, he felt his mother's spirit to be watching over him, and of his belief that intense love, such as that of a parent for a child, can live on after death. It is for such hopeful, reflective, unruly humanity that Gregory deserves to be remembered. It's a pity those who organised his funeral took the view that less edifying emotions, like spite and rancour, should survive him too.

July 2009

Holding a funeral for three dozen glass slides

OVER THE NEXT few days, parents whose babies died in the Rotunda Hospital in Dublin will be contacted and invited to make the most distressing return visit imaginable. After they lost their longed-for babies, most will have consented to post mortems and to the retention of some organs, whole or in the form of microscopic slides, so as to help establish why those babies died.

Those grieving people have all had funerals for their babies and, unlike previous generations of parents who lost babies in stillbirths or late miscarriages, they have graves to visit. In so far as it is possible when a baby dies, they have had closure. They have names and perhaps photographs, locks of hair, hand and foot prints by which to remember those babies, so often inexplicably perfect, some of whom may never have drawn a breath.

But now they are to be offered mementoes of a different nature. Now that the new independent audit of hospital procedures has found that some whole or partial organs were retained for periods longer than covered by the original consents, they'll be asked if they want to come and collect those sad little relics themselves.

This is, quite simply, a trauma which should never have been landed at the doors of these bereaved people. The so-called 'organ retention scandal' is a chapter of history that had no capacity to hurt anybody until it was uncovered in the full glare of gory, gloating media exposure. At its height, one newspaper carried a headline declaring 'I buried my baby in 36 parts', a reference to a family's decision to re-open a grave and hold a funeral for three dozen glass slides. How did this awful drama help anybody, bar those trying to flog newspapers with ever more sensational headlines, and all those cynical ambulance-chasing lawyers with euro signs flashing in their eyes?

The practice of removing and retaining organs for further study is one that doctors have engaged in as long as doctors have existed. It is perhaps the single most significant reason why we have the miraculous, life-saving medical advances we all enjoy today. They didn't take those organs for personal gain or perverse cruelty. They took them to learn from them, so as to prevent other lives being lost, other families suffering, in the future.

At times, as we now know, they were unforgivably cavalier in the way they treated these human parts once they'd served their purpose. But to doctors, that's all they were: spare parts, parts that had failed, parts that had thwarted life. They cannot afford to be sentimental about dead tissue, because if they were, then doctors, and perhaps those working with ill babies most of all, wouldn't be able to get out of bed in the morning. Call it arrogant, insensitive, high-handed, God-complex stuff – but don't call it a scandal.

At the peak of the hysteria over organ retention a few

years back, one pathologist in a children's hospital told me he'd
had death threats. Another, a good doctor genuinely wounded
by the cries of butchery and disgrace, talked of all the diseased
kidneys and livers and lungs and hearts he'd removed from ill
children in transplant operations. Not once, he said, did any
parent ask for their return so they could bury them. Yet
another doctor, in a maternity hospital, pointed out to me that
women who'd miscarried frequently came back five or even
ten years later pregnant again. They'd expect an up-to-date
analysis of the previous problem so as to prevent a recurrence,
not a decade-old file on a long gone sample. Once it was
available, they didn't ask why.

We are a largely Christian people, but all faiths share the
same basic belief: that human remains are just that, all that
remains when the human essence is gone, the empty shell of
a departed spirit. We afford remains dignity, of course, but
because of what they represent, not for what they are. All those
people who buried their babies without organs had paid their
proper respects, observed the correct and comforting rituals of
ceremonies and burials, prayers and farewells. It is simply unconscionable for a hysterical handful to force those families to
make that trip to a baby's grave and re-open it a second time.

The only people to profit from the organs retention
practice were patients. Some hospitals sold pituitary glands to
pharmaceutical companies for trifling sums in triple figures,
but again, the principle beneficiaries were babies affected by
growth disorders who were treated with the resulting drugs.
All the rest of us, every single parent of a healthy child, every
son or daughter or spouse or sibling of a recovered patient,
we've all had cause to celebrate the medical breakthroughs –
in treatments, vaccinations, surgical procedures – developed
because organs were retained and studied.

Two of my children needed life-saving surgery shortly
after birth. The particular operation is a relatively new one, 30
years ago they might well have died. Even a few years earlier,
I was told, it had involved risky and invasive surgery that left

a five-inch scar. By the time my babies' turns came, though, it had been perfected so thoroughly that the keyhole operations took less than 20 minutes and left scars that have almost vanished. I am enormously grateful for that, not just to the surgeons but to the parents who weren't as lucky but, most of all, to all those babies whose remains, once studied, supplied that gift of life-saving knowledge.

I cannot imagine how distressed such bereaved parents will be this morning, and how many must be dreading that call from the hospital to tell them their infants' organs are ready for collection, and I pity them the wrenching choice between re-opening a grave or else asking the hospital to make the disposal. But I have very selfish reasons for not being able to consider this a scandal.

July 2009

'I Must Not Upset Gays; I must not ...'

GAY PEOPLE SHOULD be allowed to marry and adopt children. People should not be judged on how they look and dress. Children brought up by gay couples do at least as well, if not much better, than the children of heterosexual households. The Pride parade is intended as a celebration, not a provocation. And Miss Panti, aka Rory O'Neill, is to be addressed as 'she'.

I did consider devoting this week's column to simply writing the above paragraph out one hundred times, like Bart Simpson at the blackboard. Because these, in a rather more temperate nutshell, are the gist of the points made in the hundreds of letters, emails, phone calls and internet postings prompted by the column I wrote here last week. I'll ignore, just for the moment, the many nasty comments about my children and my competence as a parent, and the threats to lobby Rupert Murdoch for my immediate sacking, which would be serious if they weren't so funny.

Some, though, did make strong and considered arguments against the opinions I'd expressed, and their conclusions are summarised above. But let's not lose sight of the fact that they are opinions. If they were statements of fact, then I'd deserve to be made write them out dozens of times so as to drill them into my skull, but they're not. They are points of view, they are opinions, no more or no less valid than mine. This is still a relatively free country so you are at liberty to agree or disagree with them, as you wish. And so am I.

The main source of irritation in last week's column seemed to be my view that marriage is an institution of a particular nature designed for a particular purpose. Some people were annoyed that I said gays were now demanding that it be reinvented to suit them, and claimed they were merely asking that it be opened to include them.

I do not see how that is possible. Marriage is primarily intended for the protection of children who may result from a union of a man and women, which is the only sort of union capable of producing offspring. The child of an unmarried couple in this country still has no legal status with regard to the male parent – no right to maintenance, to access, to support. Despite the existence of modern scientific procedures that can conclusively establish paternity, an unmarried father is still perfectly free to deny and abandon his child without any fear of legal or social consequences and every year, thousands do so. Civil marriage guarantees the civil and legal status of any child born of the union of a male and a female spouse.

Possibly the silliest argument against this interpretation is the one that goes, 'Oh, so does that mean that married couples who don't have children should have their marriage licences revoked then? Does it mean they're not really married?' This nonsense deliberately confuses the objective of protecting offspring with the obligation to produce them. Legal marriage between a man and woman recognises the potential that children may result and seeks to secure their status in advance since, as already pointed out, it's too late to guarantee it after the event. Whether or not the couple produce children is irrelevant once the potential has ever been present. That potential does not exist in a same-sex couple. And, as a 67-year-old woman recently gave birth in Britain, it is clear that a married couple in their 60s are still more likely to produce a child that equally shares their genes than a gay couple in their 20s. And that's not a matter of opinion, that's a fact.

The Civil Partnership Bill offers same-sex couples the right to form unions that are identical to marriage in all respects other than those relating to children. I have absolutely no doubt that there are many happy same-sex couples raising secure, contented children. They're not all gay, either: many, for instance, will be mothers and grandmothers living together to raise a child where an unmarried father has done a runner which, under our current legal structure, he can do with impunity.

Gays argue that because such stable homes exist they should have equal rights to adopt, or rather, to be considered as adoptive parents. There is, I will concede, a strong argument there – single people can adopt, so it makes little sense to prevent the legal partner of a gay parent adopting that parent's child, once there's no credible objection from the other natural parent. But where the State has a duty to place an orphaned, or reluctantly relinquished, newborn in the optimum circumstances for a secure, balanced and socially typical upbringing, then I believe that a married heterosexual couple should be the first choice. That's my opinion; you don't have to like it.

Boiled down to a single sentence, though, the one line that my many critics of the past week would have me write on that blackboard is 'I must not upset a gay person'. I must not disagree with their opinions, I must not dissent from their agenda, I must not express any view that deviates from the party line, and I must not say that men in cutaway green wedding dresses look a bit daft. For a community which expects and demands so much tolerance, there's a vocal, militant and markedly misogynistic gay element that is extremely reluctant to show tolerance for any opinions that don't accord precisely with their own. And no democratic society can afford to indulge groups who seek to punish and silence those who dare disagree with them.

I've been accused, by people who clearly didn't bother to read last week's column, of saying I believe that homosexuality is a lifestyle choice. I didn't, and I don't. I did, however, say that if gays choose to celebrate their identity by parading through the streets in clothing that is overtly sexual and designedly provocative, they've only themselves to blame if people draw that conclusion. I have no time for the Ali G school of debate: if I am a little impatient with a grown man who puts on a frock and a wig to make a serious political point and then takes offence if he's not addressed as a female, it's not 'cos he's gay. It's because I think he's silly. But again, that's merely my opinion.

Whether we like it or not, the way you present yourself to the world is crucial to how you and your message are received. That may be an unsophisticated, superficial and hastily judgemental approach, but it is the prevailing approach none the less. I am sure that the day the Minister for Finance feels free to go into Dáil Éireann to present his Budget clad in a tutu and a biker jacket will be a great and liberating day for all of us. We've just not evolved that far yet. So if you are seriously arguing that you should have the right to be considered as a mature, responsible adult competent to provide a balanced, regular, appropriate upbringing to a stranger's vulnerable child, it's probably best, for the moment, not to do so while wearing fancy dress and a fright wig. That's not a fact, or an opinion – it's just my advice.

If any gay people felt their status or dignity undermined by anything I wrote last week, that wasn't my intention. If anything, in fact, any social grouping with a truly strong, confident and proud identity should welcome robust comment and criticism and see it as part of their lot. The Civil Partnership Bill marks a step forward for the gay community that would have been unthinkable in this country even five years ago, and their leaders ought to concern themselves with securing and building on it, and engaging in sensible and mature debate on the issues that inevitably arise. And leave the name calling and the silly costumes in the playground where they belong.

November 2009

The superglue strategy

A FEW YEARS ago, the Parisian authorities decided to introduce wheel clamping in the French capital. The Parisian people, however, decided they weren't so keen on this odious practice of institutionalised extortion. Neither are we, of course, and we gripe and grumble and ring radio stations to complain about the predatory and heavy-handed tactics of the clampers. But the French did something a little more proactive.

Almost overnight they organised a campaign of very civil disobedience. They armed themselves with little tubes of superglue and, whenever they came upon a clamped car, squirted the glue into the lock. This meant that the clampers couldn't just unlock the devices and had to hack them off. The citizens' wildfire enthusiasm for the campaign meant that the cost of replacing the expensive clamps completely outweighed the profit from the scheme. The private clampers, hoping to make a killing on the city's chaotic parking habits, were forced to think again.

Now, pay attention, class, because that's what a real modern-day revolution looks like. We might fancy that we've got a rebellious spirit to equal the French, given our history, but the truth is that the unjust exercise of power and authority has very little to fear from us. The reason, I suspect, is that we never really embraced one of the central principles of revolution that the French hold dear. We're big on liberty, and even getting used to the notion of equality, but the *fraternité* bit has never been a strong point here. We're great at pulling together in times of practical crises or strife, like disease or flood, but much slower to grasp the concept of national effort for slightly more abstract causes.

Witness, for example, the stream of traffic heading north for cheap booze and Christmas fare last Tuesday morning. There were five-mile tailbacks of southern-registered cars into Newry, and aerial shots of the M50 at 11 o'clock that day looked, perhaps appropriately, like mass evacuation scenes. This had been portentously billed as a Day of Action for the public sector, its chance to register legitimate resistance to Government plans to squeeze it further in the upcoming budget. This was how the unions had hoped to generate some solidarity among equally pinched private sector workers facing further punishment next month, or already jobless as a result of recession and political incompetence. As well as a threat to government, this was also a pitch to the hearts and minds of small businessfolk, retailers and manufacturers and food processers themselves struggling to stay afloat, on the need to maintain public sector employment, investment and services for all our sakes. Oh, and to use your tax revenue to do so.

Yet somehow all those thousands of people who went North to spend their money, and to contribute to Her Majesty's revenue coffers, were able to detach their expectations of the State from their obligations to it. They simply did not make a compelling connection between their retail choices and the resulting impact on the income-generating private sector, upon whom they depend for their pay and pensions. They clearly saw no conflict in the idea of spending their money in another jurisdiction while simultaneously protesting about the state of the economy here.

Those shoppers might argue that there was a legitimate spirit of protest behind that shopping convoy to Newry. And that might have washed, if only there was some sign that it was an orchestrated exodus, designed to make a point about the difficulties of living on low income, and not a bottleneck of unilateral acts of selfishness. Nobody in that line of cars truly expected to spend half the day sitting in traffic, every one of them thought they were being clever by hitting the road early in the morning to steal a march on other shoppers. Somebody else could man the picket lines, demanding fair play for the hospital porters and lowly paid civil servants, but they had better things to do. The inevitable result of this spectacle was greater cynicism, resentment and division between the very people who really ought to be pulling together right now.

And yet it is impossible not to contrast that attitude with the public response to the floods last week. The efforts of ordinary people for friends and neighbours and even strangers affected by the deluge have been remarkable. Dry clothes, money, furniture, labour, transport, shelter have been supplied in abundance this past week. Farmers from across the country have responded with enormous generosity to calls for animal feed and bedding in affected areas, even though all fodder stocks are low after the terrible summer, and nobody can be sure this equally terrible winter won't get worse for everybody yet. And it's not as if they're donating in the hope that, should the floods hit the east coast later on, the farmers in the west will return the favour, because they'll have no fodder to give. This is unalloyed decency and generosity and compassion, and proves we really do have it in us to get through the worst of times.

Barack Obama's adviser Rahm Emmanuel has a useful piece of wisdom for these circumstances: 'Never waste a good crisis.' By reverting to the jaded and divisive old mechanism of strikes and stoppages and marches, we're wasting a good crisis that offers an opportunity to review the notion of 'community' on a national rather than local context. 'Fraternity' certainly means helping to sandbag your neighbour's house when the floodwaters are rising. But it also means helping to shore up a compatriot's business when he's in danger of being swept away by the economic storms.

Instead of throwing petulant little tantrums right now, true 'social partnership' would focus on trying to harness last week's spirit of solidarity to national economic advantage. You wouldn't dream of going shopping to Newry if overflowing sewage was lapping against your front wall, even if the schools were closed and the beer in the Buttercrane Centre was half the price. But the country is drowning in debt, we're still bailing out our banks, and lower-paid workers with big mortgages are being sucked into a vortex of default and despair – sadly, these are not just figures of speech any more.

The people of the West didn't wait for political leadership to tell them how best to respond to protect themselves and their livelihoods – it was just plain common sense to roll up your sleeves, get your hands dirty and make whatever sacrifices were required to play your part. The same applies on a national economic scale. We can pretty much forget about our political or union or religious leaders' capacity or authority to direct us through this crisis for the moment, but that's no reason to give up and go under.

The example of the Parisians with their superglue strategy is worth bearing in mind. If a lone motorist glues his wheel clamp, he's in trouble. If thousands do it, the clampers are the ones with the problem. So if one small mortgage holder goes to his bank and offers them half, they'll laugh at him – if a hundred thousand do it on the same day, it wouldn't be nearly so funny. It worked for the big boys, after all. Whether it takes some such form of extreme civilian action like a mass rebellion on mortgage repayments, or just small acts of sacrifice like shopping local, it can't hurt, as the French motorists discovered, to stick together.